Digital Transformation in Norwegian Enterprises

Patrick Mikalef • Elena Parmiggiani

Editors

Digital Transformation in Norwegian Enterprises

 Springer

Editors
Patrick Mikalef (iD)
Department of Computer Science
Norwegian University of Science and
Technology
Trondheim, Norway

Elena Parmiggiani (iD)
Department of Computer Science
Norwegian University of Science and
Technology
Trondheim, Norway

This work was supported by the faculty of Information Technology and Electrical Engineering of the Norwegian University of Science and Technology, and the Department of Technology Management of SINTEF Digital.

ISBN 978-3-031-05278-1   ISBN 978-3-031-05276-7   (eBook)
https://doi.org/10.1007/978-3-031-05276-7

This Springer imprint is published by the registered company Springer Nature Switzerland AG
The registered company address is: Gewerbestrasse 11, 6330 Cham, Switzerland

Preface

The world today is witnessing a new kind of transformation, one in which digital technologies are playing an increasingly central role. The digital revolution has created major disruptions at many different levels, and now more than ever organizations are trying to find ways to harness the power of novel digital technologies. This ongoing process of harnessing the potential of emerging technologies to radically transform operations has been termed digital transformation.

Over the past two decades digital transformation has become a central research area, with studies delving into what the notion entails, what the value for organizations is, as well as how to optimize this process of transformation in order to reap the benefits of novel digital technologies. Studies to date have identified important enablers and inhibitors of digital transformation that concern technological, organizational, and environmental aspects and have isolated key success factors that improve assimilation into organizational operations. The current body of knowledge has also looked into how organizations can strategically plan for digital transformation, as well as outlines ways in which high-level strategies are implemented in practice.

Nevertheless, despite a breadth and depth of knowledge, one point that is recurringly noted in both research and practice is that digital transformation is inherently contextual. What this means is that aspects of the context in which digital transformation is exercised have a very strong influence on the forms it takes. In the past, contextual factors such as the size-class of an organization, the industry in which it operates, past experience with digital technologies, support from top management, as well as competitive pressures have been found to affect not only the degree to which organizations digitally transform operations, but also the speed at which they initiate such a transformation.

One of the most important contextual elements in shaping digital transformation, however, concerns the country in which an organization is based. The reason behind such differences is multifaceted and has to do with the economic and political stability, the culture around digital technologies and the level of technological infrastructure, the level of education around digital technologies, as well as on the local competitive pressures and main industries that are present in the focal country.

Norway is no exception to such country-specific contextual factors, with a unique set of characteristics that differentiate it from other countries. Among these are some very advanced industries such as oil and gas, hydropower, and fish farming, as well as a large public sector which has a heavy influence also in the private sector. In addition, Norway boasts a very high level of education in high-tech skills, and an ability to attract foreign highly skilled workers. It therefore presents an interesting case of understanding how digital transformation unfolds under these conditions, what challenges characterize different types of organizations, and how they manage to deal with them.

In this book, we have sought to understand digital transformation in the Norwegian context. We draw on a vast body of literature to synthesize what we already know about digital transformation before exploring the Norwegian context in more detail. We then provide a series of cases from the private and public sector. Through these cases, we illustrate the process of digital transformation for some selected cases and highlight a number of key findings. In sequence, we provide some theoretical and practical recommendations based on these cases. We close with a brief overview of some emerging technologies and comment on how they are likely to change different sectors.

The rest of this edited volume is structured as follows:

Chapter 1 introduces the concept of digital transformation and presents an overview through a synthesized conceptual model of the current state of research. It serves as a high-level outline of the current discourse of work and presents some key findings as well as open research areas that still occupy information systems research. The chapter also helps put in context the rest of the cases presented further in this book by presenting an overview of perspective around digital transformation. By providing such a synthesis, Chap. 1 places different elements of digital transformation into perspective which are discussed in detail in Chap. 2 for the case of Norway.

Chapter 2 provides a historical overview of the main events that have underpinned digital transformation in Norway. It presents some key facts about how digital transformation is perceived in the Norwegian context, as well as some contextual factors that influence initiatives within private and public organizations. The goal of this chapter is to provide a more nuanced view of the contextual aspects that characterize the Norwegian ecosystem.

In the following chapters, we will try to dig deeper into this by presenting seven empirical case studies, four in the private sector and three in the public sector.

Digital Transformation in Private Enterprises

The first part of the book presents salient examples of digital transformation processes in private organizations from the energy, utility, and telecommunication sectors.

Chapter 3 begins with a historical reconstruction of digital transformation in the oil and gas domain. As Norwegian hydrocarbon resources are located offshore, the energy industry operating in Norway has a long-established experience in leveraging ICT to enable remote collaboration across offshore and onshore sites. The authors Hepsø and Parmiggiani illustrate how capabilities involving technology, new competence, work processes, and governance have been gradually developed around the digital infrastructure to make remote operations of unmanned offshore facilities possible. The authors use the conceptual lens of infrastructuring—that is, the active work of developing and upgrading infrastructures—to show that the digital transformation has been a sociotechnical and political process of mobilizing organizational and technical capabilities. These capabilities have been bundled in innovative and pragmatic ways and connected to the interests of different stakeholders. After this historical reconstruction, we look at a present case of developing digital applications to make work processes more effective and sustainable at an oil and gas service vendor.

Chapter 4 investigates digital transformation in the telephony and Internet sector. The authors Øverby and Audestad shed light on Norway's pioneer role and involvement in the adoption and development of Internet and cellular mobile telephony since the dawn of ICT in the 1970s with ARPANET. They draw on a historical reconstruction of the mutual evolution of these technologies and telecommunication market structures and regulations in Norway until today. In highlighting the transition from national monopoly to competition, the chapter provides a vivid illustration of the driving-seat role that the Norwegian government has historically had in not only funding but regulating digital transformation in the country.

Chapter 5 looks at another important development in the energy sector, the adoption of Machine Learning (ML) to improve energy management and trading. The authors Xing, Gundersen, and Sizov study a power generation company based in central Norway and provide an in-depth analysis of ML applications in three areas: hydropower trading, wind power trading, and predictive maintenance in wind farms and hydroelectric plants. One important (and open) implication of this study is the consequences that ML applications have for the automation of work processes in organizations. On the one hand, the gains in terms of efficiency are very important in today's uncertain and evolving energy market. On the other hand, however, while some scholars point to a new era of meta-human systems in which humans and machines learn together to create original capabilities, Xing and colleagues also point out that employees working with ML-infused tasks will be forced to work with increasingly more challenging tasks. What these new work configurations will mean for work and organizing in a Norwegian context remains to be explored.

Chapter 6 examines the changing work practices of Aker Solutions' yard at Stord in Vestland county. The authors Kamsvåg, Thun, and Klemets investigate the introduction of a mobile application to support more efficient work processes, reduce costs, increase organizational flexibility, and thereby ease the coming transition to "green" market segments. Along with other determinants, the authors point to the role of training and follow-up procedures as crucial beyond the implementation and test phases. Moreover, they also remind us of the importance of taking background infrastructure, such as Internet connection or paper-based procedures, into serious consideration when developing digital transformation capabilities. Through data collected from 500 respondents working at the yard at Stord, the authors identify both organizational and infrastructural challenges with regard to this specific implementation. The chapter concludes with an analysis of the challenges Norwegian enterprises face when they try to reap the benefits of digital transformation and provide some useful implications for companies in the manufacturing and engineering sectors.

Digital Transformation in Public Enterprises

The second part of the book focuses on ongoing approaches to digital transformation in the Norwegian public sector. Our journey will take us through three very different domains: welfare, municipalities, and healthcare. As discussed earlier, the public sector has been an important driver of digital transformation in Norway. A very substantial portion of the Norwegian public sector is represented by welfare and Norway's Labor and Welfare Organization (NAV) administers approximately one third of the yearly national budget.[1]

Chapter 7 presents a longitudinal study of NAV's IT department and illustrates how the organization approached digital transformation through an organic process in which technical infrastructure, working methods, and organizational chart better supported one another. One important decision in this process, the author Bernhardt shows, was the shift from outsourcing to insourcing the development of IT products. In particular, the organization sought to abandon silo-based systems and data sources by adopting a service platform to facilitate the provision of more efficient citizen-oriented services. An important lesson learned from Bernhardt's account is that digital transformation—at least in mature and relatively complex organizations is hardly about adopting new digital tools, but rather involves a careful management of the interplay between organizational aspects (work processes, organizational charts) and systems.

Chapter 8 moves to another significant arena that is currently exploring approaches to enhance digital service performance. The municipality sector faces tighter constraints in terms of capacity and financial resources compared to welfare and is obviously characterized by significant variations and decentralization. Data-driven innovation can therefore be a means to overcome such constraints, for example in the context of Smart Cities. The authors Bokolo, Petersen, and Helfert illustrate how Enterprise Architecture can be leveraged as a governance tool to achieve seamless urban mobility services. The authors find that such an approach can help urban planners and developers to take more efficient decisions and hence reduce the gap between IT and business strategies.

---

[1] https://www.nav.no/en/home/about-nav/what-is-nav

Chapter 9 addresses the healthcare domain, which is traditionally a fertile terrain for experimenting novel technologies. Medical practice, and particularly the work of surgeons, has transformed in the last years through the introduction of intelligent robots and tools that can facilitate less invasive surgery or augmenting medical images. The authors Trocin, Skogås, Langø, and Kiss present and discuss the case of the Operating Room of the Future, a research infrastructure integrated with a university clinic where operating rooms are augmented with intelligent technologies such as ML, Artificial Intelligence (AI), and interactive dashboards to support the analysis of medical images. As Trocin and co-authors observe, this constitutes a valuable snapshot in the ongoing transition in healthcare from completely human-based to human-AI "hybrids" decision-making processes.

Critical Reflection and Closing Thoughts

Chapter 10 provides a synopsis of the main findings from the case studies presented earlier, as well as on the different perspectives that characterize research and practice. These perspectives are consolidated in a framework for digital transformation based on which suggestions for future researchers and practitioners are posited. Specifically, the framework identifies four main phases of digital transformation and highlights some key points that need to be considered when engaging in projects. It is also used to derive future avenues for research, underscoring the importance further studies in certain areas of digital transformation.

Chapter 11 delves into the practical implications of the case studies and presents some key lessons learned. Based on an overview of the different cases, the chapter presents emerging themes across five layers: unit or project, organization, organization ecosystem, ethical and environmental sustainability, and society. It then further identifies two emerging trends: the co-evolution of organizational forms and new technologies and the fact that digital transformation increasingly happens on the organizational ecosystem level. The consequences of these are then discussed, as well as the need to actively engage with sustainability policies. The chapter concludes with a discussion of the long-term effects of digital transformation initiatives with attention to their ripple effects over time.

Chapter 12 concludes this book by taking a future-oriented perspective and identifying some key emerging technologies that are likely to change the nature of digital transformation in the coming years. It focuses on three broad classes of technologies and for each presents some disruptions that these technologies are likely to have in specific industries.

Trondheim, Norway

Patrick Mikalef
Elena Parmiggiani

Contents

List of Contributors

Jan A. Audestad Department of Information Security and Communication Technology, NTNU Norwegian University of Science and Technology, Trondheim, Norway

Hulda Brastad Bernhardt Directorate of Labor and Welfare, Oslo, Norway

Anthony Bokolo Department of Computer Science, Norwegian University of Science and Technology, Trondheim, Norway

Odd Erik Gundersen Norwegian Open AI Lab, Norwegian University of Science and Technology, Trondheim, Norway
TrønderEnergi Kraft AS, Trondheim, Norway

Markus Helfert Department of Computer Science, Norwegian University of Science and Technology, Trondheim, Norway

Vidar Hepsø Department of Geoscience and Petroleum, Norwegian University of Science and Technology, Trondheim, Norway

Pål Furu Kamsvåg Department of Technology Management, SINTEF Digital, Trondheim, Norway

Gabriel Hanssen Kiss Department of Computer Science, Norwegian University of Science and Technology, Trondheim, Norway

Joakim Klemets Department of Health Research, SINTEF Digital, Trondheim, Norway
Department of Computer Science, Norwegian University of Science and Technology, Trondheim, Norway

Thomas Langø Department of Health Research, SINTEF Digital, Trondheim, Norway

Patrick Mikalef Department of Computer Science, Norwegian University of Science and Technology, Trondheim, Norway
Department of Technology Management, SINTEF Digital, Trondheim, Norway

Harald Øverby Department of Information Security and Communication Technology, NTNU Norwegian University of Science and Technology, Trondheim, Norway

Elena Parmiggiani Department of Computer Science, Norwegian University of Science and Technology, Trondheim, Norway

Sobah Abbas Petersen Department of Computer Science, Norwegian University of Science and Technology, Trondheim, Norway

Gleb Sizov Norwegian Open AI Lab, Norwegian University of Science and Technology, Trondheim, Norway
TrønderEnergi Kraft AS, Trondheim, Norway

Jan Gunnar Skogås Operating Room of the Future, St. Olav Hospital, Trondheim, Norway

Sylvi Thun Department of Technology Management, SINTEF Digital, Trondheim, Norway

Cristina Trocin Department of Computer Science, Norwegian University of Science and Technology, Trondheim, Norway

Liyuan Xing Norwegian Open AI Lab, Norwegian University of Science and Technology, Trondheim, Norway
TrønderEnergi Kraft AS, Trondheim, Norway

An Introduction to Digital Transformation

Patrick Mikalef ⓘ **and Elena Parmiggiani** ⓘ

Abstract Digital transformation has been one of the most studied phenomena in information systems (IS) and organizational science literature. With novel digital technologies emerging at a growing pace, it is important to understand what we have learned in over three decades of research and what we still need to understand in order to harness the full potential of such digital tools. In this chapter, we present a brief overview of digital transformation and develop a conceptual framework which we use as a basis of discussing the extant literature. The conceptual framework is also used as a means of positioning the empirical chapters presented in the rest of this edited volume. Finally, we discuss the role of context in digital transformation and identify some differences that span industry, domain, size class, and country of operation.

1 Introduction

Digitization, digitalization, and digital transformation are terms that often appear in the top of priorities for contemporary managers. While often used synonymously, these notions have very different meanings and entail a radically different approach. Digitization describes the process of moving from analog to digital, while digitalization is defined as "the way many domains of social life are restructured around digital communication and media infrastructures" [1]. Finally, digital transformation has been defined as "a process that aims to improve an entity by triggering significant

P. Mikalef
Department of Computer Science, Norwegian University of Science and Technology, Trondheim, Norway

Department of Technology Management, SINTEF Digital, Trondheim, Norway
e-mail: patrick.mikalef@sintef.no

E. Parmiggiani (✉)
Department of Computer Science, Norwegian University of Science and Technology, Trondheim, Norway
e-mail: parmiggi@ntnu.no

P. Mikalef, E. Parmiggiani (eds.), *Digital Transformation in Norwegian Enterprises*,
https://doi.org/10.1007/978-3-031-05276-7_1

changes to its properties through combinations of information, computing, communication, and connectivity technologies" [2]. Although largely acknowledged that these three terms often follow a sequential order of maturity, most contemporary organizations are now in the process of digitally transforming their operations. Doing so, however, presents a number of caveats, and technology is often only a part of the complex puzzle that must be solved to remain competitive in the digital world.

While there has been a significant amount of research conducted over the past decade in the domain of digital transformation, there is still a lot to learn about this shift. This is largely because digital transformation is subject to a vast array of contingencies and takes place in a fluid and constantly changing environment which requires a holistic understanding of the entire ecosystem in which it unfolds. Among the vast empirical research conducted examining the phenomenon of digital transformation, researchers have examined changes in organizational strategies [3], process [4], structures and decision-making organizing [5], culture [6], as well as industry shifts [7]. Nevertheless, digital transformation is not a phenomenon that prompts effects at these different levels, without at the same time being influenced by them simultaneously. Therefore, there is a complex interplay between the forces that affect digital transformation and its effect on them.

For this article, we ground our understanding of digital transformation on the abovementioned definition of Vial (2019). This definition regards digital transformation as a process that encompasses significant changes through the introduction of information and communications technologies (ICTs). Extending the work of Vial (2019), we develop a conceptual model which incorporates theoretical insight from the literature on digital business strategy [8], organizational change management [9], and IT capabilities [10]. The conceptual model serves as a basis for positioning the cases presented in the remainder of the book, as well as for developing a comprehensive understanding of digital transformation as studied in the extant literature. We want to highlight here that the conceptual model presented in this article serves the purpose of creating a comprehensive understanding of what the concept entails, without having emerged from a systematic process of reviewing all relevant literature. Rather, it builds on prominent research streams that have appeared over the years, as well as on the authors' own perspectives.

The next section introduces the conceptual model of digital transformation and presents some key themes that have occupied academic and practical interest over the past decades. In sequence, we briefly touch upon the implications that research has had on practice and conclude with a brief description of the subsequent chapters and the different domains they cover.

2 A Conceptual Model for Digital Transformation

Building on the extant literature on digital transformation, and grounded on the synthesis of recent prominent literature reviews [2, 9], we develop a consolidated perspective of digital transformation as depicted in Fig. 1. The conceptual model makes the distinction between digitalization, which only involves the improvement of organizational activities by leveraging digital technologies, and digital transformation which entails a deeper, core change of the entire business model of an organization with ripple effects on entire industries. Thus, digital transformation requires a broader view of antecedents that spark or condition changes within organizations, as well the outcomes that such changes have on the broader context of operating. By applying this understanding in our conceptual model of digital transformation, we define four key points of interest which are described in more detailed in the sub-sections below. These are by no means exhaustive, and there are obviously complex causal and feedback associations between the key elements that jointly comprise digital transformation. For the sake of simplicity and to provide a concise and understandable overview of digital transformation, this article presents some of the key findings within the four main areas: antecedents, leveraging digital technologies, value generation, and performance.

2.1 *Antecedents*

Antecedents of digital transformation include elements that trigger and shape digital transformation [11]. Such antecedents either have a direct relationship in shaping the actions organizations must undertake to transform their business strategies and operations or act as moderating conditions which influence the way digital transformation is enacted.

Emerging digital technologies are obviously one of the key drivers of prompting changes and disruptions in how organizations operate. Over the past decade, the pace at which such new digital technologies are maturing and reaching production has accelerated, with technologies such as augmented/virtual reality, 3D printing, IoT, cloud computing, blockchain, drones, digital twins, and machine learning, to name a few, creating massive disruptions in entire industries [12]. A prominent example has been the proliferation of cloud computing services which has enabled organizations to deploy digital solutions throughout their value chains, which were previously unable to do so due to the high cost of setting up and maintaining scalable local infrastructure.

Nevertheless, emerging digital technologies alone are insufficient to produce digital transformation effects, as they are heavily dependent on the organizational context in which they are introduced. The history of an organization and the structures, culture, skills, and leadership commitment play an important role not only toward what types of digital technologies will be embraced but also at what

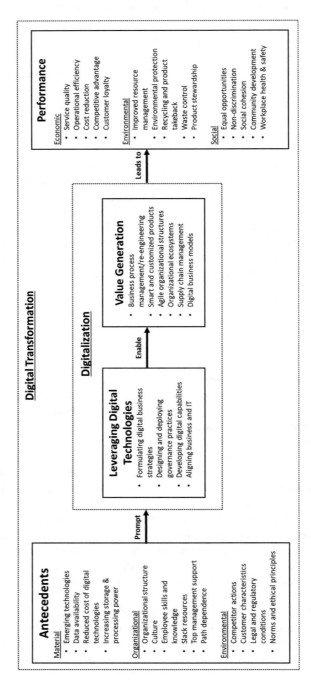

Fig. 1 Conceptual framework of digital transformation

speed and to what breadth within organizational activities [13]. As with any organizational change, rigidity, path dependence, and resistance to change can significantly impact efforts toward digitally transforming operations. These effects can
manifest themselves at different levels within an organization and at different stages
of deploying digital technologies [14]. Hence, there are numerous tensions that
manifest during the process of digital transformation which can either enable or
impede diffusion [14, 15].

Similarly, there are forces from the external environment that can prompt or
restrict the digital transformation process of organizations. For example, changes in
customer behavior or their expectations can necessitate strategic responses from
organizations in order to address the new requirements [16]. On the other hand, such
prompts may be a result of competitive actions which then spark a snowball effect in
entire industries. Some examples of this are the use of touchscreens on mobile
devices or the use of digital distribution channels for audio and video content
which sparked a major disruption through streaming services [17]. Yet, changes in
how digital transformation is deployed can also be a result in new laws and
regulation or even based on acceptable social norms and ethical practices.

2.2   Leveraging Digital Technologies

The process of leveraging digital technologies consists of different levels of planning
and deploying novel solutions. Studies within the digital transformation literature
have shown that the process of doing so includes elements such as developing
strategies of how such transformations will take place, therefore linking digital
transformation to the overall strategy of organizations [3]. In addition, there is a
requirement to convert strategies into deployable practices with concrete rules,
process, structures, and a timeline of activities in order to be able to orchestrate
and manage all relevant resources [18].

In this stream of research, there have been studies that have examined digital
transformation from a number of different standpoints, such as identifying how
digital transformation strategies should be designed and implemented [3], to understanding resource structuring and capability building to leverage different types of
novel digital technologies [19]. Nevertheless, there has been significant heterogene-
ity in findings around how to digitally transform based on the varying emerging
technologies that are prevalent at different points in time. The focus has thus shifted
from integrated large-scale information systems, such as enterprise resource planning (ERP) and customer relationship management (CRM) systems, to distributed,
decentralized, and cross-organizational technologies that facilitate real-time information exchange and knowledge management. During the past 5 years, the focus has
shifted on leveraging data analytics technologies that utilize big data, as well as on
sophisticated forms of analytics which fall under the umbrella term AI [20, 21]. Such
technologies create novel forms of transformations for organizations that can

generate more accurate insight into complex processes, as well as automate many previously manual tasks.

2.3 Value Generation

The forms and scale of value generation from digital transformation have shifted as different emerging technologies mature. While previously digital technologies were used to enhance prior tasks and processes, they are now creating opportunities for organizations that were previously impossible to conceive. For example, the introduction of AI in the pharmaceutical domain in conjunction with the advancing knowledge on genomes has given rise to the novel approach of pharmacogenomics. Furthermore, the scale, speed, and accuracy that can be achieved by leveraging various digital technologies vastly outperform manual ways of executing different tasks. An example of this is the use of recommender systems to provide personalized recommendations to millions of consumers, such as those implemented by Amazon [22]. Nevertheless, the use of digital technologies and leveraging them in the organizational sphere do not only concern marketing and end products. Many digital technologies are now commonly used in organizations in order to improve collaboration and communication and enhance knowledge capturing and sharing, as well as in improving information linkages with external parties such as supplies and other business partners [23].

Value generation by leveraging different digital technologies has been studied extensively from different streams of research. These include the IT capabilities stream of research which seeks to understand how digital technologies along with complementary resources can be converted into hard-to-replicate organizational capabilities that can confer value [24]. In an attempt to understand what digital technologies enable organizations to do, another prominent stream has adopted an affordance perspective, which seeks to examine the way in which novel technological tools can afford individuals and organizations to perform certain actions [25]. Studies that adopt the affordance perspective seek to understand not only what digital technologies can enable organizations to do with the different types of functions offered but also how the process of leveraging unfolds [26]. From a strategy point of view, several studies have examined digital transformation through the lens of how it can support or drive business strategies [27]. The main argument in such studies is that digital transformation should be seen through the lens of the strategic direction organizations want to pursue. Thus, any use of digital technologies must be driven by the strategic orientation of the organization at hand [28].

2.4 Performance

One of the central areas of inquiry within the IS domain has been to gauge the degree to which digital transformation results in tangible performance outcomes for organizations. Most studies have emphasized on economic-related measures of performance such as financial performance or the degree to which digital transformation results in a competitive advantage for firms [17]. This trend has been driven by the fact that investments in novel and often costly digital technologies must justify a financial return [29]. In addition, such economic measures of performance are the predominant way of assessing the impact of digital technologies within the IS domain, which follow studies that are grounded in disciplines such as economics, organizational science, and strategic management. Furthermore, other types of performance metrics such as environmental and social have until recently not been considered as primary to organizational operations. Nevertheless, with the focus on responsible and sustainable business models that promote inclusiveness and social cohesion, studies on digital transformation have begun to examine the effects that such transitions have on these types of outcomes [30]. Several articles have also begun to examine how novel digital technologies can support specific strategies that fall under such paradigms and what the performance effects are using new types of metrics [31, 32]. Yet, while there are an increasing number of studies that take a broader view of performance measures to determine the impact of digital transformation, there are still several research streams that have yet to be integrated or adopted in the IS domain. We discuss these and other opportunities for research and practice in the concluding sections.

3 Context-Driven Digital Transformations

Much of what we briefly described in the previous section highlights the contextual nature of digital transformations. From the drivers that either enable or inhibit organizations to commence their journey of digitally transforming operations, to the contingency elements that underpin the activities of leveraging such digital technologies, to the types of effects that are realized, much of what has been found in the literature on digital transformation underscores the important role of context [33]. Nevertheless, context and contingency elements can come in many "shapes and sizes" and oftentimes involve more than one important element that has an important bearing on the entire process.

For instance, there is a large divide in the literature regarding digital transformation in the private and public sector. These studies have documented that there are significant forces that influence not only the types and outcomes of digital transformation but also the speed of adoption, pace of deployment, and forms of work within the different types of organizations [34, 35]. Similarly, large differences have been identified when comparing among firms that belong to different industries

[36, 37]. The organizational processes that are digitally transformed in various industries are largely dependent on how important they are for the organization at hand. For example, robotic process automation has been central for many firms in the manufacturing or assembly industries since it vastly improves efficiency and cost reduction. On the other hand, being able to maintain good customer relationships, improving profit margins from customers, and identifying untapped market segments have been at the core of retail companies. Therefore, it is interesting to try to draw a mental image of how novel technologies might reshape different industries in a number of varying ways.

Finally, an important contextual dimension when examining digital transformation has to do with the country or region in which such transformation takes place. Several studies have documented that cultural, socioeconomic, and political elements can have a profound effect on what organizations do with new digital technologies, as well the ways in which they leverage them. Country-specific studies have elucidated such practices and shed some light on how organizations engage in the process of digital transformation. As a country with many unique characteristics in terms of socioeconomic and political history, Norway presents an interesting context to study digital transformation. In the next chapter, we present a historical overview of digital transformation in Norway and identify some of these important contextual elements.

References

1. Brennen, J. S., & Kreiss, D. (2016). Digitalization. *The International Encyclopedia of Communication Theory and Philosophy*, 1–11.
2. Vial, G. (2019). Understanding digital transformation: A review and a research agenda. *The Journal of Strategic Information Systems*.
3. Hess, T., Matt, C., Benlian, A., & Wiesböck, F. (2016). Options for formulating a digital transformation strategy. *MIS Quarterly Executive, 15*(2).
4. Baiyere, A., Salmela, H., & Tapanainen, T. (2020). Digital transformation and the new logics of business process management. *European Journal of Information Systems, 29*(3), 238–259.
5. Bilgeri, D., Wortmann, F., & Fleisch, E. (2017). *How digital transformation affects large manufacturing companies' organization*.
6. Vey, K., Fandel-Meyer, T., Zipp, J. S., & Schneider, C. (2017). Learning & development in times of digital transformation: Facilitating a culture of change and innovation. *International Journal of Advanced Corporate Learning, 10*(1).
7. Lanamäki, A., Väyrynen, K., Laari-Salmela, S., & Kinnula, M. (2020). Examining relational digital transformation through the unfolding of local practices of the Finnish taxi industry. *The Journal of Strategic Information Systems, 29*(3), 101622.
8. Bharadwaj, A., El Sawy, O. A., Pavlou, P. A., & Venkatraman, N. V. (2013). Digital business strategy: Toward a next generation of insights. *MIS Quarterly, 37*(2), 471–482.
9. Hanelt, A., Bohnsack, R., Marz, D., & Antunes Marante, C. (2021). A systematic review of the literature on digital transformation: Insights and implications for strategy and organizational change. *Journal of Management Studies, 58*(5), 1159–1197.
10. Bharadwaj, A. (2000). A resource-based perspective on information technology capability and firm performance: An empirical investigation. *MIS Quarterly, 24*(1), 169–196.

11. Matt, C., Hess, T., & Benlian, A. (2015). Digital transformation strategies. *Business & Information Systems Engineering, 57*(5), 339–343.
12. Skog, D. A., Wimelius, H., & Sandberg, J. (2018). Digital disruption. *Business & Information Systems Engineering, 60*(5), 431–437.
13. Morakanyane, R., Grace, A. A., & O'Reilly, P. (2017). Conceptualizing digital transformation in business organizations: A systematic review of literature. *Bled eConference, 21*.
14. Mikalef, P., van de Wetering, R., & Krogstie, J. (2021). Building dynamic capabilities by leveraging big data analytics: The role of organizational inertia. *Information & Management, 58*(6), 103412.
15. Mikalef, P., van de Wetering, R., & Krogstie, J. (2018). Big Data enabled organizational transformation: The effect of inertia in adoption and diffusion. In *Business Information Systems (BIS)*.
16. Westerman, G., Bonnet, D., & McAfee, A. (2014). The nine elements of digital transformation. *MIT Sloan Management Review, 55*(3), 1–6.
17. Verhoef, P. C., et al. (2021). Digital transformation: A multidisciplinary reflection and research agenda. *Journal of Business Research, 122*, 889–901.
18. Meyerhoff Nielsen, M. (2019). Governance lessons from Denmark's digital transformation. In *Proceedings of the 20th Annual International Conference on Digital Government Research* (pp. 456–461).
19. Mikalef, P., & Gupta, M. (2021). Artificial Intelligence Capability: Conceptualization, measurement calibration, and empirical study on its impact on organizational creativity and firm performance. *Information & Management*. https://doi.org/10.1016/j.im.2021.103434
20. Collins, C., Dennehy, D., Conboy, K., & Mikalef, P. (2021). Artificial intelligence in information systems research: A systematic literature review and research agenda. *International Journal of Information Management, 60*, 102383.
21. Enholm, I. M., Papagiannidis, E., Mikalef, P., & Krogstie, J. (2021). Artificial intelligence and business value: A literature review. *Information Systems Frontiers*, 1–26.
22. Smith, B., & Linden, G. (2017). Two decades of recommender systems at Amazon.com. *IEEE Internet Computing, 21*(3), 12–18.
23. Mikalef, P., Pateli, A., & van de Wetering, R. (2021). IT architecture flexibility and IT governance decentralisation as drivers of IT-enabled dynamic capabilities and competitive performance: The moderating effect of the external environment. *European Journal of Information Systems, 30*(5), 512–540.
24. Kim, G., Shin, B., Kim, K. K., & Lee, H. G. (2011). IT capabilities, process-oriented dynamic capabilities, and firm financial performance. *Journal of the Association for Information Systems, 12*(7), 487.
25. Stendal, K., Thapa, D., & Lanamäki, A. (2016). Analyzing the concept of affordances in information systems. In *2016 49th Hawaii international conference on system sciences (HICSS)* (pp. 5270–5277). IEEE.
26. Wang, H., Wang, J., & Tang, Q. (2018). A review of application of affordance theory in information systems. *Journal of Service Science and Management, 11*(01), 56.
27. Drnevich, P. L., & Croson, D. C. (2013). Information technology and business-level strategy: Toward an integrated theoretical perspective. *Mis Quarterly, 37*(2), 483–509.
28. Steininger, D. M., Mikalef, P., Pateli, A., de Guinea, A. O., & Ortiz-De, A. (2021). Dynamic capabilities in information systems research: A critical review, synthesis of current knowledge, and recommendations for future research. *Journal of the Association for Information Systems*.
29. Ebert, C., & Duarte, C. H. C. (2018). Digital transformation. *IEEE Software, 35*(4), 16–21.
30. El Hilali, W., El Manouar, A., & Idrissi, M. A. J. (2020). Reaching sustainability during a digital transformation: A PLS approach. *International Journal of Innovation Science*.
31. Kristoffersen, E., Blomsma, F., Mikalef, P., & Li, J. (2020). The smart circular economy: A digital-enabled circular strategies framework for manufacturing companies. *Journal of Business Research, 120*, 241–261.

32. Parmiggiani, E., & Monteiro, E. (2016). *A measure of 'environmental happiness': Infrastructuring environmental risk in oil and gas offshore operations.*
33. Zhu, K., Dong, S., Xu, S. X., & Kraemer, K. L. (2006). Innovation diffusion in global contexts: Determinants of post-adoption digital transformation of European companies. *European Journal of Information Systems, 15*(6), 601–616.
34. Pittaway, J. J., & Montazemi, A. R. (2020). Know-how to lead digital transformation: The case of local governments. *Government Information Quarterly, 37*(4), 101474.
35. vom Brocke, J., & Schmiedel, T. (2015). *BPM-driving innovation in a digital world.* Springer.
36. Liere-Netheler, K., Packmohr, S., & Vogelsang, K. (2018). Drivers of digital transformation in manufacturing.
37. Meyer, M., Helmholz, P., & Robra-Bissantz, S. (2018). Digital transformation in retail: Can customer value services enhance the experience? *Bled eConference, 23.*

The Case of Norway and Digital Transformation over the Years

Elena Parmiggiani (ID) **and Patrick Mikalef** (ID)

Abstract Norway is generally characterized by a pervasive presence of digital services. It is currently undergoing a digital transformation across different domains, from daily life to public and private enterprises. In this introductory chapter, we first unpack the main drivers of digital transformation in Norway so far and its enabling conditions based on three illustrative examples: the development of Altinn, a digital platform supporting digital communication between citizens and public and private organizations; the evolution of BankID, Norway's electronic identification system; and the current push for open data sharing leveraging experiences in the energy industry. We identify key common enabling conditions: a trust-based cooperation across social partners and across public and private sectors, the public sector's driving role, cross-organization consolidations and consortia, and application-oriented initiatives. In the second part of the chapter, we summarize the content of the subsequent chapters in this book shedding light on different facets of digital transformation in Norway.

1 Introduction

Norway regularly tops digitalization rankings in Europe together with the other Nordic countries [1]. While reality is obviously more convoluted than what official rankings tell, among the reasons why Norway scores so high are the facts that Norwegians are considered to be early adopters of digital technologies and have

E. Parmiggiani (✉)
Department of Computer Science, Norwegian University of Science and Technology, Trondheim, Norway
e-mail: parmiggi@ntnu.no

P. Mikalef
Department of Computer Science, Norwegian University of Science and Technology, Trondheim, Norway

Department of Technology Management, SINTEF Digital, Trondheim, Norway
e-mail: patrick.mikalef@sintef.no

© The Author(s) 2022
P. Mikalef, E. Parmiggiani (eds.), *Digital Transformation in Norwegian Enterprises*,
https://doi.org/10.1007/978-3-031-05276-7_2

very high digital skills and that the Internet and mobile infrastructure provide very good coverage and connectivity [2]. There are indeed several examples that corroborate the results of these rankings. If we were to take a picture of everyday life in Norway, we would observe that almost every citizen in Norway adopts online banking; pays their bill online; interacts with public agencies through digital channels such as platforms, chatbots, and video-based meetings; performs their tax return electronically; and exchanges money seamlessly via mobile payment apps. A look at the private sector and the industry would provide a similar picture: companies invest significantly in digital platforms for collaboration, virtualization, and data sharing and analysis. While Norway seems to struggle to improve its performance in terms of digital public service delivery [3], we observe that, for example, the healthcare sector has been an early attractor of significant investments toward a shared digital infrastructure (including data exchange standards[1] and platforms) to share electronic patient records. This has sometimes raised heated discussions in the media about whether some of the larger projects meet actual user needs [5].

From this perspective, the Norwegian road to achieving digitalization has so far been uneven but, overall, quite successful. As we observe in the previous chapter, digitalization implies the restructuring of work and private life around digital infrastructure. The experiences in the public and private sector that we present in this book make it clear that today's picture is path-dependent, that is, it is the result of specific social, political, and technical elements that make Norway a special case of a digital transformation process involving deep core changes of entire business models. It is therefore worth it to reflect on what are relevant characteristics of the Norwegian case and what lessons can be drawn. As a result, we ask: *How did digital transformation unfold in Norway, and what were the enabling conditions?*

The answer to this question is complex and multifaceted. The purpose of this chapter is to draw the contour of an initial answer in Sect. 2. The following chapters will then continue the conversation by looking at different facets based on in-depth case studies from public and private organizations. For now, we start by pointing to some concrete examples which we believe are illustrative of the Norwegian approach to digital transformation and some of its key enabling conditions.

2   Digital Transformation, the Norwegian Way

To trace the Norwegian experience with digital transformation, it might be interesting to start by asking when digital transformation started in Norway. Research in science and technology studies and related fields has vividly demonstrated that digital transformation is associated with the possibility of quantifying the qualities

---

[1] A notable example was the early-stage adoption of the EDI (electronic data interchange) standard in the 1980s to share patient journals [4].

of human and natural phenomena, such as territories into borders, people into statistics, and perceptions of hot/cold into measurable temperature [6, 7]. This translation of quality into quantity is a key antecedent of what we today call data-driven decision-making [6]. This has been done, for example, for taxation [8] and census [9] purposes. This perspective would then invite us to set a tentative start date to digital transformation in Norway in 1967, when Folketrygdloven ("The National Insurance Scheme") first took effect [10]. The aim of the law was—and still is—to provide a compulsory insurance scheme for all people living in Norway so that they would receive financial support from the State in case of reach of pension age, illness, unemployment, maternity/paternity leave, accidents, rehabilitation, and so on. Such a systematic and centralized structure is dependent on having a sufficient and updated overview over citizens' data across different areas, for example, labor, welfare, healthcare, employment, taxation, and so on. Arguably, and not specific to Norway alone, this has been a key driver behind the Norwegian State's investments in better and more integrated digital systems to share citizen data across silos. Part of the reason for this is that Norway has a relatively small population while being one of the richest countries in the world. As a result, the State's investments in information and communications technologies (ICT) have been significant over the years.

Furthermore, part of the roots of digital transformation in Norway are tightly interwoven with the Scandinavian or Nordic model generally characterized by a strong welfare state, a trust-based system between authorities and citizens, and a three-party collaboration approach involving the State, business organizations, and workers' organizations (particularly unions). The development of the early-days computing applications, also in private organizations, happened indeed in this particular context in the 1960s, 1970s, and 1980s under the umbrella of what came to be known as participatory design (PD). The aim of PD was to raise the voices and include the knowledge of less powerful stakeholders in the design of IT systems that were oriented toward actual work practices [11]. While PD has spread across several European countries, several important projects took place in Norway, Sweden, and Denmark directly involving trade unions, who had the opportunity to influence power relations in the workplace through the design of IT (ibid). While it is debatable to which extent the PD-oriented tradition is still alive in Scandinavia in the 2020s, it has left an underlying heritage in today's digital transformation in Scandinavia and Norway.

Let us now look closer at three concrete examples.

A first example comes from the public sector and is represented by a public communication platform, Altinn.[2] Currently, Altinn is a platform that supports digital communication with the public administration for citizens and companies which includes a common solution for authentication and login. Altinn was not born as platform, however, but as a government portal for the mandatory reporting of company's financial statements [12]. Started in 2003, the architectural solution provided by Altinn solved a very specific bureaucratic problem: already in 2005, it

---

[2]https://www.altinn.no/

made it possible for the Norwegian Tax Administration to generate a citizen's or organization's tax statement by integrating data across the national population registry and the national registry of business, banks, and insurance companies. A turning point was the adoption in 2006 of ID-porten, a public authentication gateway developed by the then Agency for Public Management and eGovernment that provided a standardized login and a flexible solution for different commercial electronic IDs to be used (ibid). This facilitated the integration of services and user communication *across public and private actors* to a degree that is almost unprecedented [13].

At a first glance, the Altinn platform is a fascinating piece of technology consisting of a modular platform ecosystem[3] enabled by shared infrastructure and standards. However, its success is context-dependent and goes beyond technological aspects. The cross-silo integration it offers is possible because the Norwegian State is allowed to access citizen's financial information with high granularity. In a democratic regime, this can only happen under the auspices of a *trust-based* (tillitsbasert, in Norwegian) system among State, citizens, and organizations [11, 15]. In terms of digital transformation, this implies that citizens and companies tend to be willing to share their data because they trust that the data will be used responsibly through efficient control mechanisms. Such mechanisms allow authorities to collect data and use them for specific, limited purposes.

This example also clearly illustrates that *the public sector is a driver of digital transformation in Norway*, as opposed to a simple adopter. While large investments have certainly played an important role, the trust-based relationship between citizens and authorities permeates and affects digital transformation efforts. The troubled genesis of the Smittestopp contact tracing app launched by the Norwegian Public Health Agency at the outset of the covid-19 pandemic in the first half of 2020 further strengthens this observation. In the Smittestopp case, privacy concerns were raised among the population and in the media as the app gathered location-based data in addition to a Bluetooth connection. The Data Protection Agency forbade this form for user data collection, and the app was ultimately withdrawn, redesigned, and re-deployed later that year, however with a low adoption rate [16].

A second example of the peculiar nature of digital transformation in Norway comes from the private sector and is the trajectory of BankID. BankID is a public key infrastructure (PKI) solution that is today the de facto standard solution for electronic identification (eID), authentication, and electronic signing in Norway [17]. In the late 1990s and early 2000s, the spread of Internet services motivated efforts from Norwegian banks to develop their own eID and authentication systems to access online banking services. The Norwegian banks had already "a history of cooperating to develop shared infrastructure whilst competing at the service level" (ibid p. 227) through BBS (Bankenes BetalingsSentral AS; later merged with its Danish counterpart into Nets AS[4]), a company started in 1972 owned by a consortium of Norwegian banks with the aim of developing common information services, standards for

---

[3]For a definition of platform ecosystem, see, e.g., the work of Constantinides et al. [14].
[4]https://www.nets.eu/

invoice and accounting, and other information technologies. After several rounds of negotiations and discussions, the banks agreed on a shared standard architecture for identification and signing to be delivered by BBS. BankID was launched by SpareBank 1 in 2004 (ibid).

Such a standardized infrastructure as BankID is often described as remarkable in other countries. It is however important to underline that it would not have been possible without the Norwegian banks' ability to join forces toward the pragmatic goal of improving electronic services. Somewhat reminiscent of the Altinn case, the BBS/BankID solution sheds light on the *strong collaboration and consolidation efforts that have occurred in Norway across public and private organizations.* While such efforts were also motivated by the urgent need to compete against stronger, international players, their *ripple effects* beyond economic competition generated significant technological innovations. Examples abound. One worth mentioning is Vipps,[5] a widespread mobile app that provides a very simple interface and is currently almost the de facto standard for exchanging sums of money between people or between people and companies and which integrates BankID (and the BankAxept payment circuit) to enable electronic identification and payment in online and physical stores.

Contrary to other digital transformation trends that are common across all Nordic countries, this aspect is quite specific to Norway. The Norwegian industrial sector has traditionally had few or no very large ICT companies, differently from, for example, Eriksson and Spotify in Sweden or Nokia in Finland. Whereas big companies would have substantial resources to drive digital transformation, in the Norwegian context, *digital transformation has been largely oriented toward specific applications* and characterized by *concerted cross-organizational and cross-sector efforts* [18].

Finally, a third example of the Norwegian way to digital transformation spans across the public and the private sector and relates to initiatives for open data sharing.

The petroleum sector is Norway's largest industry measured in national income and investments and export revenues and has, as such, contributed significantly to the national welfare state. Diskos[6] (the Norwegian national data repository for petroleum data) is a national data portal established in 1995 and controlled by the Norwegian Petroleum Directorate and a consortium of oil and gas companies operating in Norway. All these companies operating on the Norwegian continental shelf must share the data resulting from their exploration and production operations on the Norwegian continental shelf. While Diskos has the clear goal of promoting transparent reporting to authorities, sharing and trading of data between licensees, and providing access to public data, it is also a unique and successful case of State-mandated data sharing of sensitive business data. Diskos has recently been open for

---

[5] https://vipps.no/
[6] https://www.npd.no/en/diskos/

additional players, such as universities in Norway and abroad to access the data for research purposes.

For someone familiar with the competitive nature of the oil and gas business in other countries, such as the USA, the UK, or South America, a shared and open (upon membership) solution like Diskos is almost unimaginable. Yet, it is revelatory of a significant trend in the Norwegian way to digital transformation, that is, Norwegian governments' constant efforts to *mandate data sharing across industries and sectors*, today with the aim of promoting a data-centric economy under the banner of "data as a resource" [19]. This too is the result of the concerted and application-driven nature of digital transformation in Norway. Another important aspect worth mentioning is the conscious and pragmatic choice of building on and *taking stocks of the enormous experience in digital data management developed through five decades of oil and gas activities* toward promoting the so-called Green Shift and lower CO_2 emissions. At the time of writing, the Norwegian government has appointed an expert group with the aim of proposing a set of guidelines for sharing and (re)use of industrial data [20]. The emphasis on digital data and their sharing across industrial domains are indeed at the center of national strategies, where the Norwegian government, for example, writes that "The growth of the data economy is expected to be an important driver of economic growth... Increased access to and better utilization of data within the industry can contribute to start-up companies, growing companies and the established companies developing new business models, products and services" [19].

3   Conclusions

To conclude, although in broad strokes, we painted a picture pointing to some of the most important tenets of the journey to digital transformation in Norway: trust-based cooperation across social partners and across public and private sectors, the public sector's driving role, cross-organization consolidations and consortia, and application-oriented initiatives. It is important to remark that despite promising statistics, this journey has been—and still is—a bumpy ride happening at different rhythms in different contexts. It also contains several unresolved challenges, such as a better inclusion of local districts, particularly in northern Norway, spectacular failures of digitalization projects, and uneven digitalization in the public sector, where data silos still affect service efficiency. Our summary nevertheless indicates that it was none of those tenets alone, but their combination and interaction over the years that have resulted in the picture of digital transformation in Norway as it looks today. In the following chapters, we will try to dig deeper into this by presenting seven empirical case studies, four in the private sector and three in the public sector.

Acknowledgments We are deeply grateful to our colleagues Eric Monteiro and John Krogstie who provided invaluable input to the content of this chapter by sharing their precious experience and knowledge with us. We would also like to thank Alexander Kempton for providing feedback and suggestions.

References

1. Ministry of Local Government and Modernisation. *Norge fortsatt blant de ledende landene i Europa på digitalisering [Norway still among the leading countries in Europe in terms of digitalization]*. Accessed February 22, 2022, from https://www.regjeringen.no/no/aktuelt/norge-fortsatt-blant-de-ledende-landene-i-europa-pa-digitalisering/id2886756/
2. DESI report. *Norway #2 on digitalization in Europe.* Accessed February 22, 2022, from https://www.norway.no/en/missions/eu/about-the-mission/news-events-statements/news2/desi-report-norway-2-on-digitalization-in-europe/
3. Krogstie, J., & Gulliksen, J. (2021). Norge og Sverige leder digitaliseringskappløpet: Men ikke i offentlig sektor [Norway and Sweden lead the digitalization race. But not in the public sector]. *Norges Tekniske Vitenskapsakademi.*
4. Hanseth, O., & Monteiro, E. (1997). Inscribing behaviour in information infrastructure standards. *Accounting, Management and Information Technologies, 7*, 183–211. https://doi.org/10.1016/S0959-8022(97)00008-8
5. Ekroll, H. C. (2020). *Akson: Dette er diskusjonen om hvordan det nye milliardsystemet for kommunene bør lages.* https://www.aftenposten.no/norge/i/PR33n7/dette-er-diskusjonen-om-hvordan-det-nye-milliardsystemet-for-kommunene
6. Monteiro, E., Østerlie, T., Parmiggiani, E., & Mikalsen, M. (2018). Quantifying quality: Towards a post-humanist perspective on sensemaking. In U. Schultze, M. Aanestad, M. Mähring, C. Østerlund, & K. Riemer (Eds.), *Living with monsters? Social implications of algorithmic phenomena, hybrid agency, and the performativity of technology* (pp. 48–63). Springer International Publishing.
7. Crosby, A. W. (1997). *The measure of reality: Quantification in Western Europe, 1250-1600.* Cambridge University Press.
8. Scott, J. C. (1998). *Seeing like a state: How certain schemes to improve the human condition have failed.* Yale University Press.
9. Porter, T. M. (1996). *Trust in numbers: The pursuit of objectivity in science and public life.* Princeton University Press.
10. Krogstie, J. (2021). Personal communication.
11. Kensing, F., & Greenbaum, J. (2013). Heritage: Having a say. In J. Simonsen & T. Robertson (Eds.), *Routledge International Handbook of Participatory Design* (pp. 21–36).
12. Bygstad, B., & D'Silva, F. (2018). *The sovereign digital platform – a strategic option for societal development.* Platformization workshop – working papers. 7.
13. Norwegian Ministry of Local Government and Modernisation. (2016). Meld. St. 27 (2015–2016). Report to the Storting (white paper) – Digital agenda for Norway in brief. ICT for a simpler everyday life and increased productivity. Norwegian Ministry of Local Government and Modernisation.
14. Constantinides, P., Henfridsson, O., & Parker, G. G. (2018). Introduction—Platforms and infrastructures in the digital age. *Information Systems Research., 29*, 381–400. https://doi.org/10.1287/isre.2018.0794
15. Dahlen, Ø. P., & Skirbekk, H. (2021). How trust was maintained in Scandinavia through the first crisis of modernity. *Corporate Communications: An International Journal, 26*, 23–39. https://doi.org/10.1108/CCIJ-01-2020-0036
16. Trædal, T. J. (2021). *Smittestopp-appen fanger opp lite smitte. FHI tror folk glemmer appen, men mener den er ekstra viktig nå [The Smittestopp app detects too few infections. FHI believes*

people forget about the app, but they think it is extra important now]. https://www.aftenposten. no/norge/i/9KxKPM/under-1-av-20-smittetilfeller-deles-i-smittestopp-appen

17. Eaton, B., Hallingby, H., Nesse, P.-J., & Hanseth, O. (2014). Achieving payoffs from an industry cloud ecosystem at BankID. *MIS Quarterly Executive, 13.*
18. Monteiro, E. (2021). Personal communication.
19. Norwegian Ministry of Local Government and Modernisation. (2021). Meld. St. 22 (2020–2021). Report to the Storting (white paper). Data som ressurs – Datadrevet økonomi og innovasjon [Data as a resource – Data-driven economy and innovation]. Norwegian Ministry of Local Government and Modernisation.
20. Ministry of Local Government and Modernisation. *Oppretter ekspertgruppe for deling av industridata [Appoints expert group on the sharing of industry data].* Accessed February 22, 2022, from https://www.regjeringen.no/no/aktuelt/oppretter-ekspertgruppe-for-deling-av-industridata/id2879480/

Part I
Private Enterprises

From Integrated to Remote Operations: Digital Transformation in the Energy Industry as Infrastructuring

Vidar Hepsø and Elena Parmiggiani

Abstract The energy industry in Norway has a long tradition in using information technology to enable integrated operations, namely, remote collaboration between personnel at offshore installations and experts at onshore office environments. Currently, the industry is undergoing a digital transformation in which remote operations of unmanned offshore assets are the emerging standard. To ensure trustworthy and reliable operations, offshore remote sensing capabilities must be established through not only technical means but also a broader transformation involving new competence, work processes, and governance principles. In this chapter, we reconstruct this transformation and ask: *What are the emerging capabilities that develop around the remote operation digital infrastructure?* We unpack how the new digital infrastructure is a continuation of the practices and systems that have been established over time. We use historical reconstruction with vignettes from the development of a new generation of remotely operated offshore installations in oil and gas and wind facilities to describe the ongoing digital transformation as a process of infrastructuring in which the infrastructure gets increasingly entangled with internal and external systems, stakeholders, and agendas. In doing so, we shed light on how the established local and situated solutions evolve and are compensated for through the technical and organizational principles of the emerging information infrastructure.

V. Hepsø
Department of Geoscience and Petroleum, Norwegian University of Science and Technology, Trondheim, Norway
e-mail: vidar.hepso@ntnu.no

E. Parmiggiani (✉)
Department of Computer Science, NTNU, Trondheim, Norway
e-mail: parmiggi@ntnu.no

P. Mikalef, E. Parmiggiani (eds.), *Digital Transformation in Norwegian Enterprises*,
https://doi.org/10.1007/978-3-031-05276-7_3

21

1 Introduction

Offshore operations in the energy industry are undergoing a digital transformation. When most major oil companies and globally operating service companies addressed their future way of doing business in the mid-2000s, they described it as oil exploration and operation enabled by information and communications technology. So-called integrated operations (IO) then relied on instrumented and automated oil and gas fields that integrated people and technology to remotely monitor, model, and control all processes in a safe and environmentally friendly way to maximize their value [1]. In Norway, the Norwegian Oil and Gas Association (Norsk olje og gass) defined IO as a bundling of a company's resources to configure sustainable capabilities: integration of people across geographical, organizational, and disciplinary boundaries, integration of processes in terms of business integration and vendor collaboration, and, finally, integration in relation to technology: data, sensors, protocols, fiber optics, standardization, and others [2].

IO encompassed both processes, methods, improved information and communications technology (ICT), and high-bandwidth fiber-optic networks that allowed real-time data sharing between remote locations. The effect was that experts from different disciplines could collaborate more closely, which facilitated a more rapid response and decision-making [1]. In Norway, IO and the knowledge associated with this development were created in the borderland between universities, companies, national legislative/governing bodies, and various global actors. Technologies for collaboration within the oil and gas industry that came with IO challenged traditional geographical, disciplinary, and organizational boundaries.

The industry thus moved over many years from being isolated islands of operations to becoming more open ecosystems. The Norwegian Oil and Gas Association [2] stressed the opening of existing boundaries, when they argued that IO would be implemented over two generations with increasing integration, across geography, across disciplines, and across organizational boundaries. The first-generation (G1) processes would integrate processes and people onshore and offshore using ICT solutions and facilities that improve onshore's ability to support offshore operationally. The second-generation (G2) processes would help operators utilize vendors' core competencies and service more efficiently [2]. As oil companies are now entering G2, we observe that by utilizing digital services and vendor products, operators are increasingly able to update reservoir models, update their drilling targets and well trajectories as wells are drilled, manage well completions remotely, and optimize production from reservoir to export.

In this chapter, we describe the transition from traditional, bounded operation to first G1 (IO) and then G2 (remote operations) as an ongoing process of infrastructuring [3]. We ask: *What are the emerging technical and organizational capabilities that develop around the remote operation digital infrastructure?* We identify and discuss the increasing degree of entanglement of the infrastructuring process over time (cf. [4, 5]). In doing so, we unpack how the new digital infrastructure is a continuation of the established practices and systems that came with

IO. The transition toward trustworthy and reliable remote operations depends on establishing *remote sensing* capabilities that encompass not only new technologies but a broader digital transformation involving new competence, work processes, and governance principles.

This chapter is structured as follows. We start by defining integrated and remote operations as an infrastructuring process. Then we define this development from the late 1970s up to the present, as three distinct phases, and present what happened over these 30–40 years to challenge the notion of digitalization as a transformation process. To cover this period with distinct phases, we must paint with a broad brush. We have focused on operation and maintenance, and we are not able to portray all the features that characterize this development in other interesting oil and gas domains like drilling, production, and reservoir management. Still, we hope the reader will appreciate our attempt to draw some long lines related to the infrastructuring of ICT in the oil and gas business in Norway.

2 From Integrated to Remote Operations as Infrastructuring

The movement from integrated to remote operations is still ongoing. We thus look at this phenomenon as an example of the evolution of emergent infrastructures over time [4]. An information infrastructure perspective on IO and remote operations treats both as open-ended sociotechnical systems ([6]: 576, emphasis in original):

> As a working definition, [information infrastructures] are characterised by openness to number and types of users (no fixed notion of 'user'), *interconnections* of numerous modules/systems (i.e. multiplicity of purposes, agendas, strategies), dynamically *evolving* portfolios of (an ecosystem of) systems and shaped by an *installed base* of existing systems and practices (thus restricting the scope of design, as traditionally conceived). [Information infrastructures] are also typically stretched across space and time: they are shaped and used across many different locales and endure over long periods (decades rather than years).

Collaborative practices are achieved through collections of—rather than singular—artifacts from this perspective. Infrastructuring, the active process of developing information infrastructures, allows us to better capture the efforts required to integrate human and material components, the continuous work required to maintain it [3], as well as the elements of continuity in such complex systems [7]. As an analytical tool, infrastructuring overcomes the blurred boundaries between phases of design, implementation, use, and maintenance in infrastructure evolution [8] and thus highlights the ongoing, provisional, and contingent work that goes into working infrastructures of IO and remote operations. Sardo et al. [5] demonstrate how infrastructuring work during normal periods aimed at maintaining stability in the oil and gas branch is a source of valuable innovation and change at the intersection of different interlocked infrastructures. Governing stability and change in such settings is thus an endeavor orchestrated by actor constellations—or *action nodes*—that control the infrastructural interlinks and keep the industry stable while innovating it (ibid). In the context of IO, Parmiggiani et al. [4] illustrate this process in the case of real-time subsea environmental monitoring during offshore operations. The authors show how this infrastructuring process unfolded through increasing degrees of entanglement of the emergent infrastructure with different stakeholders, agendas, and other infrastructures. One fundamental instance of such an entanglement is represented by onshore support centers which enable companies to move work tasks from offshore platforms to land and which were central in the transformation from bounded to integrated operations, as we will show later [9, 10]. Hepsø and Monteiro [9] conceptualize these as *centers of calculation* (see [11]), namely, venues in which knowledge production builds upon the accumulation of resources through circulatory movements to other places over time. To enable such control centers, several artifacts and practices have become entangled: fiber-optic networks to shore, proper standards for communication and sharing of data, collaboration tools, and new work practices and competence. All these elements were necessary to enable real-time data and information to move from the local setting on an oil installation to a central location where experts could work with the data and mitigate the needed action. This was a sociotechnical bundling and development of capabilities that made it possible for local and bounded distinct readings/data to be transferred to any place in a larger ecosystem.

Another example is the aforementioned case of real-time subsea environmental monitoring during offshore operations. This is a compelling illustration of the entanglement of remote sensing capabilities for trustworthy and reliable operations. Monteiro and Parmiggiani [12] discuss how the objects of interest in remote work are digital representations that are unhinged from their physical counterpart (see also [13]). Technologies such as the Internet of Things (IoT) have been the vehicle of this decoupling as they can synthetize human sensing abilities to an increasingly effective degree [12]. Such *remote sensing* is not simply a matter of new technologies but depends on establishing sociotechnical capabilities to make sense of the digital representations as well as gradually tying these representations to organizational and political concerns (ibid).

We are influenced by this phased development and describe a similar journey from integrated to remote operations through three phases: bounded, integrated, and remote operations. These phases bear similarities to the three generations developed by the Norwegian Oil and Gas Association [2], but they are not completely the same since at the time (2005) they were considered scenarios. We present the technical, organizational, competence, and governance capabilities that were developed in this process. How these infrastructuring capabilities developed over time is crucial to understand the transition from integrated to remote operation but also to see how remote operations is not a replacement of, but a continuation of, IO.

3 Three Phases of Development

3.1 Generation 0: Bounded Operations (1980–2000)

In the early part of this period, the oil industry in Norway is under development, and it matures substantially. It is important to develop competence and prove to be a good and reliable producer of oil and gas. Being heavily dependent on US competence in the early days, the industry is developing a unique Norwegian style both when it comes to petroleum and work environment legislation, working culture, petroleum engineering, and design. We have called this the phase of bounded operations.

The Norwegian Oil and Gas Association ([2]: 9–12) described this phase as follows: "The day to day control and optimisation process normally is managed by one or two operators located in the central control room (CCR) offshore. From this room the operators optimise wells and process trains in accordance with the production & injection plan, monitor critical systems and equipment and handle alarms, emergencies and shutdowns. In some cases, they manage dozens of wells and facilities that daily produce several hundred thousand barrels of oil equivalents. The decisions they make to optimise production are most often based on their own judgment and knowledge of the operation at hand. The CCR operators are supported by field operators that they guide through VHF and UHF radios. The field operators manually measure readings of critical instruments and valves, regulate manual controls, carry out first line, preventive maintenance, prepare and start up equipment after shutdowns, manage work orders, plan maintenance work and participate in the safety team. Support from onshore functions is limited and normally only available 5 days a week from 8 a.m. to 4 p.m., meaning that decisions of key importance to production as well as safety are made without support from the engineers that have developed the plans which the operators are implementing."

The ICT infrastructure is thus *bounded*, with poor integration of IT systems, high cost for data storage, and poor capabilities for data transfer (low-bandwidth satellite) onshore-offshore. The main collaboration tools are e-mail, telex/fax, and telephone but hardly any real-time collaboration. IT is an expense, and IT expenditure must be kept as low as possible since it is difficult to document the business value. Most installations are fully manned (in the hundreds) with functions needed both to plan and execute the work offshore, and the level of instrumentation and sensors in the facility are simple or non-existing. Human operators in the field are used to compensate for this lack of instrumentation and readings to have an overview of the process and safety conditions out in the offshore facility. The operators conduct a "check-and-report" task in the plant, where they are on regular rounds using their senses to look for aberrancies, in the form of leakages, strange sounds, etc. If there is a situation out in the facility, the control room sends out an operator to verify the situation. The crew knows the facility in and out and tend to spend their time on the same installation, often the same shift with colleagues they know and trust, over many years. The offshore world is stable and divided in siloed disciplines.

The Norwegian Oil and Gas Association writes: "...most operative decisions are made offshore, in isolation or with limited support from experts onshore. Plans are relatively rigid and primarily changed at fixed intervals. The organisational structure is traditional, meaning that personnel onshore and offshore belong to several different units with different goals and Key Performance Indicators (KPIs). Plans are made, and problems solved in a fragmented manner. Basic as well as advanced education aims to develop disciplinary specialists, not professionals with a good understanding of value chains and work processes. IT systems are specialised, and it is difficult and time-consuming to gather the data necessary to optimise processes" ([2]: 09).

There is no real-time support organization onshore that can provide immediate help offshore for diagnosis and troubleshooting, and offshore and onshore seem to be very remote. In the late 1980s and early 1990s, the first condition-based monitoring of equipment concepts is implemented, vibration analysis is one example, and sand management is another [14, 15]. Reliability analyses like bathtub curves and mean time between failures (MTBFs) exist as concept and theories. The understanding of plant degradation mechanisms improved, as did the reliability and availability of this kind of equipment. These methods and models exist, but in disciplinary islands, when incorporated in software, it is difficult for such models to travel across the offshore and onshore boundaries.

3.2   Generation 1: Integrated Operations (2000–2015)

After the turn of the millennium, the Norwegian Oil and Gas Association, the Norwegian Petroleum Directorate [16], and the Petroleum Safety Authority Norway (PSA) increasingly saw IO as an opportunity for the Norwegian society [17–20], a potential to brand new integrated technologies and work processes in a sophisticated Norwegian style based on the tradition we have related to democratic industry collaboration. The initial growth period was over, the industry was maturing, and the focus was to continue the growth in a situation where the expected production output of the business would drop (due to less expected new discoveries) in the years to come. IO is in these years becoming the "Zeitgeist" of the industry, that is, the new management and regulatory mindset.

It is hard to give an exact year for the start of the era of IO in Norway. Around the end of the twentieth century, many new elements aligned. First was the coming of the fiber-optic infrastructure onshore-offshore, the increasing integration between telecom and information technology leading to new types of applications like videoconferencing and software collaboration tools, and the coming of enterprise resource planning systems like SAP. Important was also the ability to store and then access large amounts of historical data and information at low cost. At the same time, the first onshore support centers were set up. There was also a concurrent development in sensor development that enabled eased readings of petroleum-related phenomena either in the reservoir, well, or the process facility. Finally, standardization of ICT tools was also linked to new industry data formats and standards, like the XML standards for drilling data (WITSML), production data (PRODML), and process data (OPC). Norwegian petroleum authorities took a role in the development of standards for daily and monthly reporting systems between the authorities and the oil companies: drilling reports, production reports, resource reporting, and environmental reporting.

The Internet was now becoming a more mature platform for new services. Methods that had existed as standalone tools or concepts could now be incorporated into a *real-time* infrastructure. For example, condition-based equipment monitoring of equipment concepts was implemented and integrated with real-time data. Similar implementations were now possible to improve sand detection and management [14]. Methods and models could now be verified and improved with real-time data. This new situation led to an increase in new models and software incorporating phenomena that had not been possible to represent in the past. A compelling example of this was the integration of real-time subsea environmental monitoring modules with offshore facilities starting in the mid-2000s. These new modules made it possible to gradually shift from ex-post mitigation of environmental damage to preventive approaches to halt possible, future emissions based on real-time data [21].

As these cases illustrate, the models developed as part of these new approaches are not just integrated with real-time data and moved out of their local and bounded settings, but they had to become *accessible in onshore control centers*, too. To really integrate these new capabilities into the existing operations and maintenance work processes, it took time to develop the appropriate work processes and data governance mechanisms. As a result, in this period, the work processes and operational model of the business thus changed substantially. The Norwegian Oil and Gas Association described this in the following way: "The primary control of the process will still be with the operators in the CCR offshore. The engineers in the onshore support centre will have access to real-time information about the operations offshore and the competence and tools necessary to monitor and control the process, simulate the process and advice the CCR of how to get most out of the plant. The combined problem-solving capability will be improved since specialists will be able to give proactive advice regarding optimal operation and can support the offshore operators actively when problems arise. The operators in the CCR will still be supported by field operators. They will be equipped with first generation wireless mobile computers and video and audio equipment that allow them to access information online concerning the controls and equipment they are dealing with and discuss problems and solutions with onshore experts in real time" ([2]: 16).

The operators still conduct a "check-and-report" task in the plant, where they are on regular rounds using their senses to look for aberrancies, in the form of leakages, strange sounds, etc. However, the CCR now has additional tools, like CCTV and more instrumented systems with sensors that can track aberrancies and operational perturbations. This means that the situation more often can be confirmed without sending out the operator. Onshore collaboration centers start to monitor important pieces of rotating equipment like pumps and gas turbines. The engineers working with rotating machinery are moved onshore.

The first onshore operation centers came alive around the turn of the millennium. These centers of calculation [11] were an important precondition to understand the unbounded space that opened with the development of IO and later with remote operations. The technological capabilities were also realized in so-called collaboration rooms that facilitated for cooperation by utilizing videoconferencing, sharing of large data sets, and remote control and monitoring [10, 22]. With IO collaboration centers onshore, parts of the company buildings onshore were redeveloped with such new collaboration facilities. The offshore installations office facilities of old installations were modified to house video collaboration spaces, and all new installations were developed with offshore collaboration facilities (see [23, 24]). These new spaces and the coming of real-time data opened bounded offshore sites. This is a process that we will later show has expanded with remote operations, where boundaries are even more obscure and where all control functions ultimately can be operated from anywhere given the proper barriers and cybersecurity mitigation. Functions and people that had been offshore were now moved onshore with more centrally organized planning of activities and execution of scheduled activities offshore. A mechanical or automation engineer that in the past followed up one asset now followed up several assets with increasing new data streams and tools available for operational support.

The first years were dominated by strong technology optimism [25, 26]. In an official Norwegian Report to the Parliament (Storting), it is explicitly stated that most initiatives related to IO have addressed technology development and technology implementation [17]. An increased focus on issues related to safety, new work processes, and integration of information in the whole oil and gas value chain is heralded: "[Integrated operations] means that established functions and work tasks can change and be moved between those that do the different tasks and where they are executed. These changes must be done in a reasonable way with employee involvement" ([17]: 35 translated from Norwegian). Around 2005, there is a considerable shift in relation to the impact of technology associated with IO. Instead of focusing on personnel flexibility, involvement in the change process is stressed.

The active and positive participation from all involved parties were from now on increasingly seen as instrumental to be able to succeed with IO [16, 20]. From now on, the change processes associated with the passage to new operational concepts are addressed via increased focus on human and organizational factors, change management, employee participation, and measures to improve HSE and organizational culture [20].

In conjunction with this were a maturation of the *management mindset around IO* and an increasing awareness on their value potential [19]. Future strategic possibilities were described [20], the need for improved skills [27] and the consequences of implementing IO [28]. Those that participated in this infrastructuring discourse were not only the oil companies that originally had articulated the claims of IO but also unions; the oil industry association; the authorities/regulator, universities, and research institutions like SINTEF and IFE; contractor companies like Aker Kværner and FMC; and software and sensor development companies. IO thus became an arena where a multitude of actors met, often with different agendas and objectives.

The number of workshops and conferences that attracted industrial companies and research and government institutions took up speed in the same period.

In this period, *petroleum engineering and design* also underwent substantial changes. A change in installation type had preceded this from the mid-1990s onward. Giant concrete installations were taken over by new floating/anchored concepts, and subsea installations became the new standard partly due to moving into deeper waters on the Norwegian continental shelf. Since most oil companies started to move traditional functions onshore, this reduced the need for office space and offshore accommodation. The manning levels of these new installations moved from the hundred(s) to below 50. Offshore installations were now designed and built with IO in mind. One example is Statoil's (now Equinor) Kristin platform where the disciplinary coffee areas had been integrated into one area, where the whole offshore office environment was an open space area, and where the platform management sat in a collaboration room with live feed of video to the onshore collaboration center/room [23, 24]. Other examples were the Ormen Lange and Snøhvit gas fields that were built as remotely operated subsea systems, with a 180–200 km pipeline to the beach where the gas production was monitored from the onshore control room. However, except for Snøhvit, Ormen Lange and a few other simple installations IO lost remote operation along the way. The coming of the Åsgard subsea booster station in 2015 was a hallmark in remote operations. The decision was taken to control the booster station from the local control room at Åsgard. The booster station, with subsea gas turbines, the size of a soccer field was by then the most complicated subsea factory ever built.

3.3   Generation 2: Remote Operations (2016–)

It took many years to mature the remote operation mindset. We have argued earlier that there was an overoptimistic belief in IO at the turn of the millennium. Remote control was heralded with great technological enthusiasm and was later taken out of the colloquial use of IO that was around collaboration across boundaries, not around remote operations. This notion of IO took precedence. Around 2010, more people that previously had worked with IO started to work with autonomy questions in oil and gas ([29]: 9). "Autonomy becomes relevant when human risk is too high, or humans are unfit or not cost-effective decision makers. Such situations are typically characterised by the need to collect and assess data and make decisions in fractions of a second or dealing with latency imposed by distance. In these situations, autonomous technology enables humans to set overall goals and delegate operational decision-making and execution of decisions to autonomous systems."

It took time before autonomy and artificial intelligence began to take momentum, and we come back to this. When Rosendahl and Hepsø [1] co-edited the book on *Integrated Operations* in 2012–2013, remote control had not proven to be as important as heralded. There were many reasons for this: mistrust in the reliability of the remote operations technology, lack of good operational models and concepts for remote operations, fear of loss of safety, loss of jobs, and others. Still, the sociotechnical complexity of operational and technical aspects of remote operations was the most important. Facilities had to be built differently, with less maintenance hours so that maintenance campaigns were possible, moving either to unmanned or periodic manning model [30]. There were challenges with the existing project development/engineering methods; they were not configured to build larger unmanned remotely operated installations, since the mindset was tuned to existing conceptions and practices. Over time, this changed. One of these changes addressed that remote operation had to leverage some important lessons from IO that had a high focus on new ways of working enabled by new ICT [30]. Edwards et al. describe the road to low manning, remote operation as a configuration of complexity of the installation systems, instrumentation needed to remotely control, and a low number of maintenance hours. All these together form a path to an operational model based on remote operations.

Over time, the focus changed from the technical concept of remote control, which included the technical capabilities that need to be in place to make remote control possible, to remote operations that is a socio-technical configuration. This is where the operational concept is the key and where the technical, organizational, and competence capabilities are included in the concept. The implementation of IO on the Norwegian continental shelf was relatively successful; severe challenges were faced regarding the development of new work practices and the management of change [1].

Still, much of the implementation of onshore-offshore collaboration became natural with better collaboration tools, videoconferencing, and integrated information infrastructures making IO invisible, a key feature of infrastructures. IO is now taken for granted.

The new understanding of remote operations developing in this phase is linked to the coming of digitalization, which becomes the new "Zeitgeist" and also becomes a key feature of the management mindset. Emerging paradigms are now the Internet of Things (IoT) and Industry 4.0 approaches to automation and manufacturing. As Gartner group defined it [31], "digitalization is the use of digital technologies to change a business model and provide new revenue and value-producing opportunities; it is the process of moving to a digital business"—as opposed to digitization, namely, the conversion of the analogue into a digital format.

The convergence of ICT tools and infrastructure that started with IO took up speed. One visible development is the change from bounded proprietary and expensive videoconferencing rooms and solutions to integrated and standard desktop video on each employees PC. Coupled to this was also the coming of social media used internally on the company intranets. Cheap storage and transfer of data became colloquial in the era of IO, but now oil companies and vendors start developing digital platforms with APIs to ease the communication and sharing of data across boundaries. This is addressed as a big data challenge. Traditional oil and gas vendors and software companies develop their own digital platforms and services to gain new market shares. Digital twins and analytics services are built on top of existing services, for example, a condition-based monitoring service is built on top of the equipment delivery. The emerging big data domain with machine learning and artificial intelligence provides the possibilities for these new services. Cloud-based infrastructures are important for eased access and sharing of data, and internal/external cloud services begin to take over both for admin systems and more business-critical software tools. This emerging cloud infrastructure with storage and communication solutions, VPN, and remote access of systems proves critical during the COVID-19 pandemic. From March 2020, most companies in Norway started working remotely, only keeping the business-critical operations and oil and gas installations to be operated as usual, while all support was conducted from the homes of the employees. It surprised many how well this virtual cloud-based operational model with MS Teams worked; it kept most of the businesses going.

As of 2021, there exists a larger ecosystem around a remotely operated asset that can consist of different types of centralized or unbounded centers. The IOGP recommended practice for remote operation [32] describes the following sociotechnical configurations in this infrastructure. First is the remote collaborative center which is the collaboration center we recognize from IO. They can sometimes be distributed over several locations (i.e., multiple interconnected collaborative centers). Typically, they can have less access controls than a control room; however, this depends on operational or security risks. Over time, these collaborative centers have taken over remote monitoring or monitoring and diagnostics of production, operations, and equipment conditions remotely using data generated and exported from the production site outside the control room. Remote at vendor premises, the second configuration, also came with IO and refers to any remote location belonging to a vendor (or subcontractor) and in their private premises. Contracts define the physical access and security restrictions at the vendor premises. Connection across boundaries to the operators usually involves communications links via public networks. This sociotechnical configuration normally performs monitoring but can also conduct remote operation of equipment given the right access and cyber physical safety. Remote access from anywhere is the final configuration defined by IOGP and refers to any external location, in a private or public area (e.g., a home, hotel, or airport), where people can sit distributed outside company/vendor premises and can access control functions.

In this new situation, the control room can exist in various sociotechnical realizations based on instrumentation level, installation reliability, maintenance load, manning, and operational principles. It can also operate several installations from the same location regardless of geography. IOGP argues that this location can be far away from the actual production site but is within the premises managed by the company. The primary purpose is to remotely control and operate the production site (s), but it may also include dedicated remote engineering or maintenance rooms. Since these connections allow interaction with safety critical equipment, physical access controls are typically strictly enforced. Remote control refers to remote actions such as control commands (adjusting plant or equipment operational parameters, set point changes, alarm acknowledgement, manual start/stop commands, etc.), set point changes, and operations monitoring on detailed graphical displays (e.g., process conditions, equipment status, alarms, errors). Safety functions can also be performed from the remote control room (such as executing manual shutdowns, operating critical action panels, etc.) [32]. Remote control requires read and write access to the system to enable operator interaction with the process and equipment on the production site. There are different preventive controls and recovery preparedness principles/measures in manned or unmanned situations and if there are people on site, or not.

The main control room is located outside the production site boundary and in a safe zone. A remotely operated but manned installation can have a local offshore control room, but during normal operations, the command and control of the installation are conducted from an onshore control room. Examples of this on the Norwegian continental shelf are the Martin Linge (Equinor) and Ivar Aasen (AkerBP) installations. Such an installation typically has a lean organization close to the emergency preparedness role requirements, and the crew are always on the installation in shift rotation. Compared to traditional oil and gas platforms described earlier, the biggest difference is that the onshore control room is always in control.

The concept of "check-and-report" is changing. If the installation is manned, they still conduct traditional "check-and-report" tasks in the plant. However, when the installations are manned only part of the time, for example, during maintenance campaigns every 2 of 6 weeks, the control room is dependent on using CCTV or the instrumentation of the offshore systems and equipment to follow up aberrancies and situations offshore. Moving sensor platforms in the shape of drones and robots are now introduced. On the subsea systems, resident subsea drones are deployed on fit for purpose garages and charging stations and used for inspection and check-and-report tasks. Crawling and flying drones are tested out on the topside installations to perform the same type of tasks. The remote sensor capabilities (CCTV coverage, remote actuation capabilities of equipment, and sensor systems) are more advanced since the installation is operated most of the time without any crew. The visit intervals are dependent upon the maintenance load and instrumentation level of the installation, often scheduled in maintenance campaigns. Ad hoc visits by helicopter can happen as last resorts. Maintenance campaigns typically range from manned for 2 out of 6 weeks to as little as one or two scheduled short campaigns in a year. A new installation type subsea-on-a-stick saw its light [33]. The idea of this design is to keep the simplicity and high reliability of subsea systems and make it more accessible on an installation above water.

Competence requirements also change. Even though situated offshore, competence is important; it is increasingly difficult to develop this competence on installations where there are no humans or onboard just for shorter periods of time. At the same time, the ability to read and diagnose offshore aberrancies and abstract this into digital knowledge becomes more important. More of the input in a remote operation situation is gathered indirectly through sensor readings, calculated values, models, and simulations. Using models for prediction and analytics had started with IO, where predictive and analytical capabilities were implemented and integrated with real-time data because of the new ICT infrastructure that developed. Methods and models could be verified and improved with real-time data, and models and software could travel across boundaries. Competence for understanding, working with, and governing data grew in this period. Now, machine learning and AI are increasingly used to improve the predictive analytics of models. Models were integrated with real-time data and moved out of their local and bounded settings already with IO. Now however, new and larger centralized centers can streamline both the ICT tool development, work processes, data governance, and competence development to scale up the operation and maintenance services. This development coincides with a more centralized organization model where support and competence centers provide services to lean organized local assets. The work processes and data curation/governance are better integrated into the existing operations and maintenance work processes, thanks to better integrated ICT tools and a more mature digital cultural practice.

3.4   Way Forward (2021–): The Boundaries of Infrastructuring

In 2021, is everything becoming boundaryless with digitalization and have all boundaries gone? Not quite, the final bounded frontier are industrial automation and control systems (IACS), the main control and automation systems of the control room. It includes the hardware and software that can affect or influence the safe, secure, and reliable operation of an oil and gas facility. This bounded area is called the operational technology (OT) domain. OT has existed as a digitally bounded island since the 1970s. Most new facilities include connections to enterprise networks to enable data export for plant monitoring and other types of administrative systems whether these are collaboration systems, portals, etc. that are more open to the external world. Still, these domains are strictly separated. The latter is the administrative domain defined as IT, and the colloquial understanding of digitalization has until recently been mostly connected to the "IT world." Typically, the separation between OT and IT is implemented using firewalls that create a zone and conduit model to achieve appropriate network segmentation and restrict any direct connections between the OT and IT systems. An intermediate network or demilitarized zone (DMZ) network between OT and IT networks is typically used to prevent direct connections between enterprise network and control system networks. This makes it possible for office network-based systems and users to view data from control systems in a secure manner. The DMZ acts as a protection gateway between the safe zone and the enterprise network.

With the increased reliance on digital technologies, it is important to ensure that the design of the systems addresses the risks from safety hazards as well as cybersecurity threats. The dominant model for enterprise reference architecture for both OT is the Purdue Enterprise Reference Architecture (commonly known as the Purdue model) for control systems and network segregation. It shows the interconnections and interdependencies of all the main components of a typical OT architecture. When this architecture was developed in the 1990s, the big concern was keeping computing and networks deterministic so that they wouldn't fault. Network segmentation was a means for keeping traffic in a control network at deterministic levels. Purdue has set the standard for why and how control system networks needed to be segmented and what expectations each layer had for responsiveness. Once the Purdue model became the industry standard, many companies started using these network models to facilitate new I/O for safety systems, and it has over time become a standard for addressing ICT security as well.

Purdue provides a model for enterprise control, which end users, integrators, and vendors can share in integrating applications at key layers in the enterprise. Still, as we have shown in this chapter, the industry has moved from a stable bounded order informed by the Purdue model to a situation below where the network architecture is opening, providing new possibilities and configurations but also new risks. This is a similar movement from bounded operation and integrated operations to a more open-ended future with remote operations that introduces new possibilities but also challenges.

The first trend is the movement from confined bounded applications using horizontal integration to increased vertical integration between OT and IT by more and more hybrid types of integration. While the traditional OT systems were built from scratch using vendor-specific proprietary standards with almost esoteric and specialized proprietary OT competence, the new systems are more based on higher compliance with international standards, like OPC UA, and are gaining more off-the-shelf qualities. The development of the applications becomes standardized and uses standards often associated with admin IT systems, like Windows servers and TCP-IP. During this travel, OT was characterized by good bounded connectivity and poor connectivity to other systems. We are entering a situation with the emerging Industry of Things technologies where every piece of equipment and machinery can be connected to each other. In the old bounded days, risks could be decomposed and made controllable either by technology/boundary management or by competence (few people knew the OT systems to be able to hack them). When OT systems use standard protocols and technologies that have known weaknesses, new risks emerge in a potentially large ecosystem. New types of connectivity also create new vulnerabilities (USB sticks, phishing, laptops, and smartphones).

4 Discussion: Balancing Entanglement and Modularization

In our presentation of the infrastructuring process that characterizes the movement from integrated to remote operations and onward, we have stressed that it is due to many concurrent capabilities that developed in parallel and became bundled. It would be easy to focus solely on telecommunication and ICT that developed over this period. However, we have demonstrated that the development was more the consequence of a mobilization of many organizational and technical capabilities that were configured in innovative ways over time by entangling different infrastructures, stakeholders, and interests.

We have shown that this process was a distributed and collective one. First, a diverse set of stakeholders influenced the infrastructuring process, but none were in complete control (cf: [5]). In addition, the "Zeitgeist," which is the management mindset, and the operational models also shifted over time. The oil industry business got increasingly centralized along the way, and new organizational institutions and control/collaboration centers developed [9]. The nature of work and the human operator's ability to assess physical phenomena "around check-and-report" also evolved, thanks to the improvement of remote sensing capabilities. Change in competence was substantial and so were the methods to address risk and understand the emerging situation. Over the years, we also saw a substantial development of petroleum engineering and change in design.

In Table 1, we outline the capabilities that concurred in each phase of this infrastructuring process. It is important to observe that while each phase succeeds in solving some problems that affected the previous one, it also unearths new, previously unexplored questions (cf. [21]).

One analytical implication of our study is a reframing of the role of control centers. Much literature has given prominent importance to control room-based work and technology configurations to perform remote monitoring (see, e.g., [34]). We however show that so-called control rooms (such as operation centers) are not bounded locales, but centers of calculations [11]. This conceptual shift is important because it emphasizes that control rooms are only the visible part of a broader sociotechnical process where knowledge circulates, transforms, is aligned, and accumulates over time.

More in general, our study runs counter the rhetoric of modularization as key enabler of digital innovation. The literature on digital transformation often heralds the importance of the modularization of digital services and the associated capabilities [35, 36]. The story of innovation that we have told in this chapter challenges this view. Although we have seen that technological optimism tends to resurface in the energy sector, the transition toward remote operations is much more than a story about exploiting the properties of modularization allowed by digital technologies. Rather, it is one where heterogeneous factors have become bundled over time and aligned with different actors and agendas over time. Infrastructuring is a useful lens to understand the process of aligning the new capacities with the existing tools, work practices, and the corporate and societal institutional arrangements that started with IO first and continued with remote operations. This evolution is not characterized by clear-cut boundaries or modules. Although a degree of modularization is obviously present, at the same time, the gradual yet increasing entanglement of the infrastructure with internal and external systems, stakeholders, and agendas played a key role. Paying attention to how the modularization is balanced by entanglement over time is important on the analytical level to better understand the success of some innovation processes. This observation subscribes to the literature in information systems stating that digitalization is hardly complete transformation, but a process that build on the existing sociotechnical configurations. For example, the experience

Table 1 Types of capabilities developed as part of each phase in the evolution of offshore operations

Capability	Bounded operation (1980–2000)	Integrated operation (2000–2015)	Remote operations (2016–)
Operational model	Local self-contained units and practices (IO generation 0). Assets have resources to manage on their own	Emerging ICT infrastructure enables integration across spatial and disciplinary boundaries. IO enable centralization of limited personnel resources; local assets lose control of resources	Tighter integration across boundaries and operations becomes possible from anywhere. Tight centralization with support and competence centers and lean and small local assets
Zeitgeist	Build and develop the oil industry in Norway	Develop a distinct Norwegian IO O&G approach that could be exported	Digitalization, development of digital platforms, and services that are scalable
Management mindset on ICT	ICT necessity but a cost with no substantial business value	Move from viewing IO as technology optimism to becoming a factor in change management; create a value potential competitive edge and new operating model	Digitalization becomes a transformative force and a precondition for the business and future operations. "Data is the new oil"
Work practices/ human involvement in tracking oil and equipment phenomena as "check-and-report"	Human sensors (operators) in the field supervising the technology with a bounded and simple control room Work is sequential, slow pace with few possibilities for sharing data and developing real time communication, tied to the local	Human sensors in the field but with more smart instrumentation and hand-held ICT. Increased use of onshore resources and collaboration centers Videoconferencing, digital field workers Collaboration centers Real-time information and collaboration across boundaries	Partly or fully remotely operated. High degree of instrumentation replaces humans in unmanned periods. Dependent on new sensing capabilities via fixed or movable sensor platforms (drones) operated from a remote control room/function Increasingly digital check-and-report. Loss of the local or re-representation of the local in technical terms (real-time feeds, digital twin)
Competence	Bounded in space in separate disciplines and sites (onshore/offshore) often within the company	Opens up to become more multidisciplinary across domains and competence. New	Multidisciplinary in character, more need for understanding models and inferences of the machines

(continued)

Table 1 (continued)

Capability	Bounded operation (1980–2000)	Integrated operation (2000–2015)	Remote operations (2016–)
		digital skills for collaboration needed	with increased ML/AI and man-machine teaming. Loss of local context
ICT development and standardization	Bounded IT infrastructure, poor integration Telex, fax, telephone, low-bandwidth satellite communication	Fiber-optic networks, standardization of data transfer, fusion of ICT technologies (XML, PRODML, OPC)	IoT, AI, integration between OT and IT systems, Industry 4.0, platforms, big data, digital twins. Development of cloud-based digital platforms and APIs for sharing data
Petroleum engineering/design	Traditional design where process complexity and system design defined operational concept and model. ICT treated as a simple sub-delivery in the project with little understanding of potential value	ICT is becoming an important element in petroleum engineering when building new fields, is focused on integration, and could enable new ways of working and influence operational concept and design of technical systems	Operating model and digitalization/ICT infrastructure become the basis for petroleum engineering and what is needed in the facility Simplification of design and higher degree of automation
Models and centers of calculation	Theories and models formalized in software (i.e., sand management, condition-based monitoring, model predictive control) but bounded. Few models, dependent upon local settings and practices. Lack of computable standards and access across distance	Domain-specific models become accessible across distance and improved with real-time data. Enabled standardization and movement from the local to the central location and distributed collaboration with some predictability	Models become the premise for operations in most domains and for scalability. Models and predictive capabilities integrated in real-life phenomenon with real-time data across time and space

with IO was a crucial precondition to the rather quick uptake of digitalization in remote operations. Our story thus illustrates that the installed base of the infrastructure [6] matters significantly and its role in directing subsequent innovation should not be underestimated in theories of digitalization.

Finally, our analysis challenges views of firm-centric innovation in favor of a data economy-based innovation. The infrastructuring process that we have described encompasses constellations of stakeholders (such as energy companies, service organizations, regulatory agencies, and other interest groups) that operate at the interlinks of the infrastructures that get entangled with one another (see also [5]). As a result, it involves the energy sector as a whole, as opposed to one or few innovative firms. This trend seems to become more apparent as we enter a phase in which sector-wide IT architecture (e.g., Purdue) and data collection (e.g., IoT) standards dominate. A compelling example of this transition from firm- to data economy-centric innovation is the development of oil and gas software, which used to be dominated by large companies like Schlumberger. It is interesting to see how this company has developed along these same three phases we describe. Schlumberger started in a bounded space where the business model was dependent upon selling domain-specific software to the oil and gas clients. All proprietary software development was done inhouse. From 2007 to 2008 onward, they developed their Ocean platform, where users that had Petrel licenses could develop apps that worked inside the Schlumberger software portfolio. Opening the application program interfaces (APIs) of Petrel made it possible to build on their existing platform, develop a proprietary customer ecosystem, and keep the existing revenue model plus introduce a new with the Ocean App Store.[1] Schlumberger opened the ecosystem to a certain extent for collaboration in software development with major customers and sub-vendors. This opening of boundaries is similar to what we saw with IO. However, recently, their revenue and software development model are changing. Schlumberger now supports the development of a vendor-neutral environment for the development of an open data platform and ecosystem. The OSDU initiative[2] was initiated by their major competitor Halliburton Landmark. This is an open ecosystem where neither Landmark nor Schlumberger has architectural control of the software development. Nobody could have foreseen that Schlumberger would join this open ecosystem 5 years ago.

5 Conclusions

The main contribution of this chapter was to (1) understand the emergence of capabilities for remote operations as an historical process where (2) capabilities become bundled as the infrastructure entangles with other infrastructures and interest groups.

A corollary of our analysis relates to the importance of historical reconstructions: we believe that studies of digital transformation should rely on a longitudinal perspective on the factors that led to the current innovations in the industry. To do this, methods such as researching document archives or retrieving digital traces should not be underestimated.

---

[1] https://www.ocean.slb.com/en

[2] The Open Group Open Subsurface Data Universe (OSDU) Forum delivers an open-source, standards-based, technology-agnostic data platform for the energy industry that stimulates innovation, industrializes data management, and reduces time to market for new solutions. See also https://osduforum.org/about-us/who-we-are/osdu-mission-vision/

To conclude, we are aware that our analysis was limited to a Scandinavian context. Other aspects might emerge from the study of digital transformation in the energy industry in other parts of the world, such as the United States or South-East Asia. However, we believe that our main contribution is still applicable, although with different observations in relation to, for example, the role of regulatory agencies.

References

1. Rosendahl, T., & Hepsø, V. (2012). *Integrated operations in the oil and gas industry: Sustainability and capability development*. IGI Global.
2. Norsk olje og gass. (2005). *Digital infrastructure offshore*. Accessed September 21, 2009, from http://www.olf.no/io/digitalinfrastruktur/?29220.pdf
3. Karasti, H., Pipek, V., & Bowker, G. C. (2018). An afterword to 'Infrastructuring and Collaborative Design'. *Computer Supported Cooperative Work (CSCW), 27*(2), 267–289.
4. Parmiggiani, E., Monteiro, E., & Hepsø, V. (2015). The digital coral: Infrastructuring environmental monitoring. *Computer Supported Cooperative Work (CSCW), 2*, 423–460.
5. Sardo, S., Parmiggiani, E., & Hoholm, T. (2021). Not in transition: Inter-infrastructural governance and the politics of repair in the Norwegian oil and gas offshore industry. *Energy Research & Social Science, 75*, 102047.
6. Monteiro, E., Pollock, N., Hanseth, O., & Williams, R. (2013). From artefacts to infrastructures. *Computer Supported Cooperative Work Journal, 22*(4–6), 575–607.
7. Pipek, V., & Wulf, V. (2009). Infrastructuring: Toward an integrated perspective on the design and use of information technology. *Journal of the Association for Information Systems, 10*(5), 447–473. Article 6.
8. Karasti, H., Baker, K. S., & Millerand, F. (2010). Infrastructure time: Long-term matters in collaborative development. *Computer Supported Cooperative Work (CSCW) Journal, 19*(3–4), 377–415.
9. Hepsø, V., & Monteiro, E. (2021). *From integrated operations to remote operations: Sociotechnical challenge for the oil and gas business*. Presented at IEA 2021.
10. Rolland, K. H., Hepsø, V., & Monteiro, E. (2006). Conceptualizing common information spaces across heterogeneous contexts: Mutable mobiles and side-effects of integration. In P. J. Hinds & D. Martin (Eds.), *CSCW'06. Proceedings of the 2006 20th anniversary conference on Computer supported cooperative work* (pp. 493–500). ACM.
11. Latour, B. (1987). *Science in action*. Harvard University Press.
12. Monteiro, E., & Parmiggiani, E. (2019). Synthetic knowing: The politics of internet of things. *MIS Quarterly, 43*, 167–184.
13. Lusch, R., & Nambisan, S. (2015). Service innovation: A service-dominant logic perspective. *Management Information Systems Quarterly, 39*(1), 155–171.
14. Østerlie, T., Almklov, P. G., & Hepsø, V. (2012). Dual materiality and knowing in petroleum production. *Information and Organization, 22*(2), 85–105.
15. Østerlie, T., & Monteiro, E. (2020). Digital Sand: The becoming of digital representations. *Information and Organization, 30, 1*, 01–15.
16. NPD. (2006). *Integrated operations forum*. Accessed September 21, 2009, from www.npd.no/English/Emner/E-drift/E-driftforum/coverpage.htm
17. NOU. (2005–2006). NOU Official Norwegian Report to the Storting no. 12. Health, safety and environment in the petroleum activities (2005–2006). Accessed April 27, 2021, from https://www.regjeringen.no/contentassets/da47b0ff07c14288821c68c9c7e19d82/no/pdfs/stm200520060012000dddpdfs.pdf

18. Norsk olje og gass. (2005). *Integrated work processes: Future work processes on the Norwegian continental shelf.* Accessed September 21, 2009, from http://www.olf.no/getfile.php/ zKonvertert/www.olf.no/Rapporter/Dokumenter/051101%20Integrerte%20arbeidsprosesser,% 20rapport.pdf
19. Norsk olje og gass. (2006a). *Verdipotensialet for Integrerte Operasjoner på Norsk Sokkel (The value potential for integrated operations on the NCS).* Accessed September 21, 2009, from http://www.olf.no/?31293.pdf
20. Norsk olje og gass. (2006b). *HMS og Integrerte Operasjoner: Forbedringsmuligheter og nødvendige tiltak Norsk olje og gass-report 2006* [HSE and Integrated operations: Opportunities for improvement and necessary measures - Norwegian Oil and gas-report 2006]. Accessed April 27, 2021, from https://www.yumpu.com/no/document/view/19796540/io-og-hmspdf
21. Parmiggiani, E. (2015). *Integration by infrastructuring: The case of subsea environmental monitoring in oil and gas offshore operations* (PhD Thesis). NTNU.
22. Hepsø, V. (2009). 'Common' information spaces in Knowledge Intensive Work: Representation and Negotiation of meaning in computer supported collaboration rooms. In D. Jemielniak, L. Kozminski, & J. Kociatkiewicz (Eds.), *Handbook of research on knowledge-intensive organizations.* Idea Group.
23. Næsje, P., Skarholt, K., Hepsø, V., & Bye, A. S. (2009). Empowering operations and maintenance: Safe operations with the 'one directed team' organizational model at the Kristin asset Safety. In S. Martorell et al. (Eds.), *Reliability and risk analysis: Theory, methods and applications* (pp. 1407–1414). Taylor & Francis Group.
24. Skarholt, K., Næsje, P., Hepsø, V., & Bye, A. S. (2009). Integrated operations and leadership – how virtual cooperation influences leadership practice. In S. Martorell et al. (Eds.), *Safety, reliability and risk analysis: Theory, methods and applications* (pp. 821–828). Taylor & Francis Group.
25. Edwards, T., Mydland, Ø., & Henriquez, A. (2010, March 23–25). *Insights and lessons learned from the application of iE.* Presented at the SPE Intelligent Energy Conference and Exhibition held in Utrecht, The Netherlands. SPE-Number-MS128669.
26. Hepsø, V. (2006). *When are we going to address organizational robustness and collaboration as something else than a residual factor?* Society Petroleum Engineers (SPE) paper no 100712.
27. NPD. (2006). *Mapping the needs for competence for the extensive use of integrated operations in fields on the Norwegian shelf.* Norwegian Petroleum Directorate (NPD). Accessed September 21, 2009, from http://www.npd.no/NR/rdonlyres/3F964DEA-7A44-4E15-B170-E50FF2D03 9F1/10943/XS6416kompetanserapportengendelig030406.doc
28. NPD. (2005). *Utredning om konsekvenser av omfattende innføring av e-drift (integrerte operasjoner) på norsk sokkel for arbeidstakerne i petroleumsnæringen og muligheter for utvikling av nye norske arbeidsplasser, OD (2006)* (Study on the consequences of the comprehensive introduction of e-operation (integrated operations) on the Norwegian continental shelf for employees in the petroleum industry and opportunities for the development of new workplaces in Norway). Accessed September 21, 2009, from http://www.npd.no/NR/rdonlyres/4B68AADC-4 653-456E-BAA9-EEB6B37CCCD3/10938/SluttrapporteDriftogkonsekvenserrevidert121205.pdf
29. NFA (Norwegian Society of Automatic Control). (2013). *Autonomous systems: Opportunities and challenges for the oil & gas industry.* Report. Accessed April 27, 2021, from https://nfea. no/wp-content/uploads/2018/02/Autonomirapport-NFA.pdf
30. Edwards, A. R., & Gordon, B. (2015). Using unmanned principles and Integrated Operations to enable operational efficiency and reduce Capex and OPEX costs. SPE-Number-MS176813.
31. Gartner. (n.d.). *Definition of digitalization.* Accessed May 28, 2021, from https://www.gartner. com/en/information-technology/glossary/digitalization
32. IOGP (International association of oil and gas producers). (2018). *Selection of system and security architectures for remote control, engineering, maintenance, and monitoring.* Report 626, October. https://www.iogp.org/bookstore/product/iogp-report-627-selection-of-system-and-security-architectures-for-remote-control-engineering-maintenance-and-monitoring/

33. NPD. (2016). *Unmanned well-head platforms UWHP*. Summary report. Accessed April 27, 2021, from https://www.npd.no/globalassets/1-npd/publikasjoner/rapporter/unmanned-wellhead-platforms.pdf
34. Mentler, T., Rasim, T., Müßiggang, M., & Herczeg, M. (2018). Ensuring usability of future smart energy control room systems. *Energy Informatics, 1*(1), 26.
35. Henfridsson, O., Nandhakumar, J., Scarbrough, H., & Panourgias, N. (2018). Recombination in the open-ended value landscape of digital innovation. *Information and Organization, 28*(2), 89–100.
36. Yoo, Y., Hendridsson, O., & Lyytinen, K. (2010). The new organizing logic of digital innovation: An agenda for information systems research. *Information Systems Research, 21*, 5.

The Norwegian Mobile Telephony and Internet Markets

Harald Øverby and Jan A. Audestad

Abstract Norway has been a pioneer in the development and adoption of the Internet and mobile telephony technologies. Already from an early stage, Norway was involved in research, development, and testing of initiatives such as the ARPANET project and the Nordic Mobile Telephone (NMT) system. Today, access to the Internet and mobile technologies—including smartphones—is globally widespread. The major objective of this chapter is to describe how the market for the Internet and mobile telephony in Norway has evolved since its inception in the 1970s until today. The historical and current market structure of telecommunications is discussed. Moreover, the chapter investigates the role and significance of mobile virtual network operators (MVNOs). Finally, the chapter examines the regulations imposed by the Norwegian Communications Authority (Nkom) on dominant stakeholders in the Norwegian telecom market.

1 Introduction

The Internet and mobile telecommunications are the two chief enabling technologies underpinning the digital economy. The early version of Internet—put into operation in 1969—evolved from the ARPANET project initiated in 1966 [1]. Advanced Internet protocols were developed in the 1970s. Throughout the 1980s, the Internet was mainly used by the military, research organizations, and universities. However, following the commercialization of the World Wide Web (WWW) in 1993, the Internet was quickly adopted by the public. Today, more than 50% of the world's population has access to the Internet, and almost 100% of the Norwegians has access to the Internet [2].

The first-generation (1G) automatic cellular mobile telecommunications network was launched in the Nordic countries in 1981. It was replaced by the

H. Øverby (✉) · J. A. Audestad
Department of Information Security and Communication Technology, NTNU Norwegian University of Science and Technology, Trondheim, Norway
e-mail: haraldov@ntnu.no

© The Author(s) 2022
P. Mikalef, E. Parmiggiani (eds.), *Digital Transformation in Norwegian Enterprises*,
https://doi.org/10.1007/978-3-031-05276-7_4

second-generation (2G) mobile network (GSM) in 1991, supporting fully digital transmission of voice and data. Data rates were significantly improved with the third-generation (3G) mobile network (UMTS) launched in 2001. Today, many countries have fully deployed the fourth-generation (4G) mobile network (LTE) and are currently in a transition phase to the 5G mobile network.

Norway has been a pioneer in the development and adoption of these technologies. Today, close to 100% of the population in Norway has access to the Internet, mobile telephony, and mobile broadband. Moreover, the Internet is accessed mostly using wireless terminals, such as laptops and smartphones.

This chapter investigates the evolution of the Internet and mobile telephony access in Norway. New market actors, such as virtual operators, are discussed along with historical and current regulations.

The rest of the chapter is organized as follows: Sects. 2 and 3 present a brief overview of Internet technology and cellular mobile technology evolution, respectively. Section 4 presents the adoption of Internet access and mobile telephony in Norway from a historical point of view. Section 5 discusses the telecommunications market structures, including the de-monopolization of this market that took place in 1998. Section 6 presents how the de-monopolization has opened for two new market actors: the resellers and the virtual network operators (VNOs). The regulation of the telecommunications markets is discussed in Sect. 7. Finally, Sect. 8 concludes the chapter.

2 Internet Technology Evolution

The major goal of the ARPANET project was to build and demonstrate a data communication network based on packet switching. It was also the first communication network to implement the TCP/IP protocols—later to become the key protocols of the Internet. The ARPANET project was funded by the US Department of Defense and launched in 1966. Packet switching was a novel technology at that time, challenging the established circuit switching technique used in telephone networks. The two key advantages of packet switching over circuit switching were efficient resource sharing and resilience against node and link failures [3]. Some scientists and engineers doubted packet switching could be implemented due to its complexity.

In 1969, the ARPANET project built an experimental packet switched network connecting a few computer sites. In subsequent years, the ARPANET was refined and expanded to the network shown in Fig. 1. The first international connection in the ARPANET was to Norway via a satellite link in 1973.

Why Norway was the first country outside the USA to be interconnected to ARPANET may seem strange. The reason was the Cold War and the need for monitoring test activities with nuclear weapons, in particular, in the USSR. A seismic array was built in Norway for this purpose, and data from possible test activities was sent to the USA. One and a half years later, ARPANET terminals were

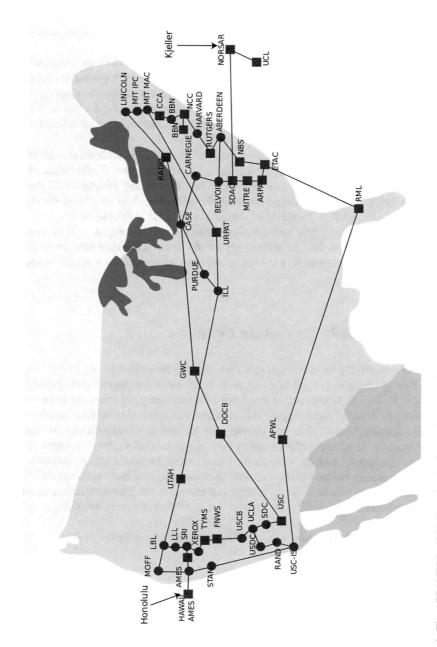

Fig. 1 The ARPANET in 1974. Note that the first node outside the USA was at Kjeller in Norway. The figure is adapted from [4]

established by the Norwegian Defence Research Establishment (FFI) and the Tele-communications Research Establishment (TRE) as the first non-military terminal outside the USA. These terminals were also connected to the American network over satellite links. This brought Norway to the forefront of early packet data research, soon also involving research groups at the University of Oslo.

ARPANET was the predecessor of the Internet in which the key technologies in the current Internet were developed and tested. This includes packet switching, protocol layering, and the TCP/IP protocol suite [1]. Many of the early services of the Internet, such as e-mail and file transfers, were also first developed and tested on the ARPANET. The ARPANET was decommissioned and replaced by NSFNET in 1990 and became the first part of the current Internet.

The early Internet was mainly used at universities and research establishments. The network was hardly known outside these circles until the World Wide Web (WWW) was commercialized and taken into use by several telecommunications carriers in 1993, thereby becoming available to the public. The WWW technology had been invented by Tim Berners-Lee at CERN already in 1989. However—since it was not invented by the telecommunications industry—it took a long time until they discovered the potential the new technology would have for the data communication market, a market the carriers had strived to build up for more than a decade without succeeding.

3   Cellular Mobile Technology Evolution

The development of public cellular mobile technologies started in the 1970s. As of 2021, five generations of mobile systems have been developed and deployed, illustrated in Fig. 2. Observe that there are approximately 10 years between each generation of mobile technology—this denotes the approximate time needed to research, specify, standardize, and develop the technology. Even though 5G tech-nology has been launched and is currently in deployment (2021), the development of the sixth-generation mobile technology has already begun. Each generation of mobile technology builds on the previous generations, and both enhance existing functionalities and add new functionality. For instance, the fifth-generation mobile technology adds functionality to support the evolving Internet of Things (IoT) devices.

Altogether, five generations of mobile systems have been developed:

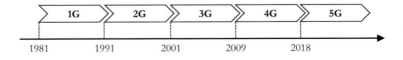

Fig. 2 Overview of the generations of mobile technologies and their year of release

- *First generation (from 1981):* This includes the NMT (Nordic countries), TACS (UK), Radiocom 2000 (France), and C-Netz (Germany) offering only analogue telephony. These systems supported primitive roaming capabilities, though the more advanced methods used in NMT became the basis for the more sophisticated roaming capabilities of GSM.
- *Second generation (1991):* 2G (GSM) offering digital telephony, data communication at speeds up to 10 kilobits per second (kbps), and short message service (SMS) over signaling channels. GSM was designed for automatic international roaming and non-disruptive handover when the mobile terminal moves from the coverage area of one base station to the coverage area of a neighboring base station during conversation.
- *Third generation (2001):* 3G (UMTS) is a dual system offering packet radio services at a data rate of 128 kbps (initially) for Internet services and narrowband GSM services for telephony and SMS. The architecture consists of two separate network architectures for data and telephony but using the same radio interface based on spread spectrum technologies. 3G is an extension of both the Internet and the telephone network.
- *Fourth generation (2009):* 4G (LTE—Long-Term Evolution) is an extension of the Internet offering only packet radio services including voice over IP (VoIP), narrowband data, broadband data, and streaming services over a dynamic mix of narrowband and wideband data channels. Interconnection with the fixed telephone network is via conversion units at the interface between the telephone network and the 4G network.
- *Fifth generation (2018):* 5G is based on 4G but offers new features such as very high data rates, edge computing (cloud computing close to the mobile user, e.g., in the base station, to reduce latency), network slicing (allowing independent providers to operate simultaneously over the same infrastructure offering complex services to the same user), and connection of millions of remote sensors and other devices. 5G will be one of the basic technologies of the Internet of Things.

4   Internet and Mobile Telephony Access Adoption

Figure 3 shows the percentage of the population in the age span from 9 to 79 years having access to the Internet for Norway and the world. Observe that Norway adopted the Internet exceptionally quickly in the years 1998–2008. The Norwegian market for Internet access became saturated in 2012 when 95% of the population had access to the Internet. In 2020, about 98% of the population has access to the Internet in Norway.

Figure 4 shows the number of cellular mobile subscriptions per 100 inhabitants. Observe that the Norwegian market became saturated in 2008. In comparison, the world market passed the world's population in 2019, even though there still exist countries in which mobile cellular subscriptions are not widely adopted. The obvious reasons are that, in the developed world, some people have more than one

Fig. 3 The Norwegian and world Internet access. Data is collected from [2, 5, 6]

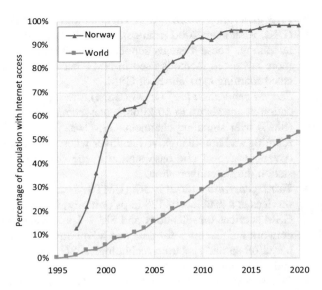

Fig. 4 The Norwegian and world mobile cellular subscriptions per 100 inhabitants. Data is collected from [2]

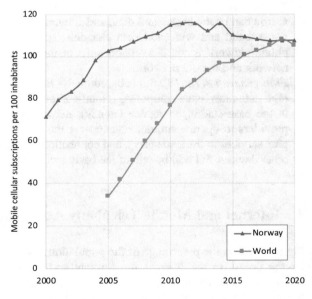

subscription—e.g., one for private and one for work—and that mobile phones are used in autonomous communications equipment in machines and infrastructures. However, access to mobile cellular (voice) technology is more widespread than access to the Internet. Norway is a pioneer in the adoption of the latest generations of mobile technology, including 4G and 5G (see Fig. 5).

The number of fixed telephone subscriptions in Norway has declined since the early 2000s. Today, there are less than seven fixed telephone subscriptions per

Fig. 5 The Norwegian and world mobile broadband subscriptions per 100 inhabitants. Data is collected from [2]

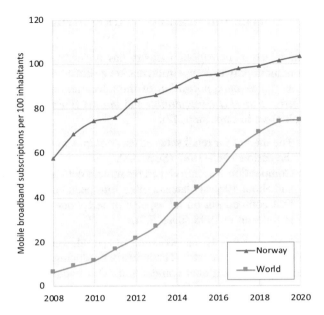

Fig. 6 The Norwegian and world fixed telephone subscriptions per 100 inhabitants. Data is collected from [2]

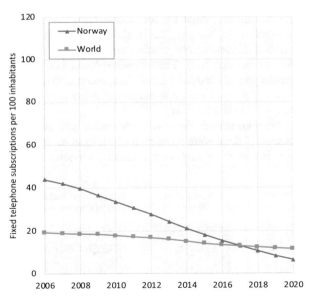

100 inhabitants as shown in Fig. 6. This shows that mobile technologies have been replacing the fixed telephone service for quite a while. The same trend can also be observed on a global scale.

5 Telecommunications Market Structures

The telecommunications industry has undergone an evolution in market structure from monopoly to competition market as illustrated in Fig. 7. This process is referred to as the *de-monopolization* of the telecommunications market. Other often used terms are *market deregulation* and *market liberalization*. The evolution in Europe took place in three steps [7]:

1. The market for retail sales of user equipment was opened for competition during the period 1985–1987 (Sect. 5.1).
2. Competition was introduced for mobile network operation, first in the UK (1982) and about 10 years later in other European countries (1991) (Sect. 5.2).
3. Full competition on all aspects of telephone network operation in Europe was introduced in 1998 (Sect. 5.3).

Note that this is the evolution of the telecommunications industry and not the Internet service industry. The industry producing Internet-based services has always been open for a global competition. This competition has produced a few digital monopolies, such as Facebook, Apple, and Google, and governments are now attempting to regulate these monopolies to foster more competition and innovation on the Internet.

Traditionally, most telecommunications operators in Europe were state-owned monopolies. In Norway, Televerket (Norwegian Telecommunications Administration) had this monopoly position until 1998 when all aspects of telecommunications were de-monopolized. The evolution toward de-monopolization took place simultaneously in EU and associated European countries (the EEA). Since the evolution in Norway followed the same evolution as the rest of Europe, the general evolution in Europe is presented next.

The argument in favor of monopolies was that it would be more expensive for the users if there were more than one telephone operator in the region because of the large investments in telecommunications infrastructures required. Moreover, the

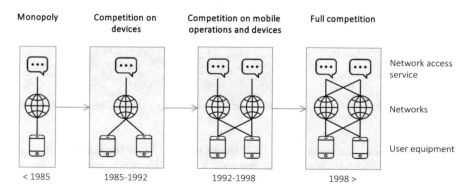

Fig. 7 Evolution of the telecommunications business [7]

technology used prior to the 1980s (electromechanical telephone exchanges interconnected by coaxial cables and radio relays) had an economic lifetime of several decades, often as much as 50 years. Therefore, it was deemed inefficient to allow several telecommunications carriers to build their own communication networks delivering the same set of services. Telecommunications was then regarded as a natural monopoly.

The state monopoly owned the network, offered the few services supported by the network, and sold or rented out telephones, local switchboards, data modems, and other terminal equipment. Consumers usually had one choice concerning network provider, telecommunications service, and type of user equipment. The governments also decided the charges the subscribers had to pay for subscriptions and use of the services.

During the late 1980s, it was questioned whether it would be better to open up for full competition in telecommunications considering the rapid evolution of digital networks and digital switching, the growing need for computer communications, and advances in mobile network technologies. This came at the same time as the internationalization of the industry started in general. Many companies expanded to become international corporations with factories in several countries. This evolution also triggered the governments to consider opening national monopolies for full competition to enhance innovation and making services and industrial products cheaper for the consumers. De-monopolization and the belief in free markets became the *zeitgeist* of the late 1980s. However, the process to transform the monopolistic telephone operators into competitive businesses in a competitive market took a long time because new competition laws and market legislation had first to be put in place and enough time had to be allowed for the monopolies to reconfigure their business models to face a situation where they had to fight for market size and revenues.

5.1 De-monopolization of User Equipment

In the early 1980s, the first public data networks were put into operation, and the first automatic mobile networks were up and running. The number of different types of user equipment had exploded, and the monopolies were too bureaucratic and too inexpert to handle this profusion of new equipment. Responding to this, starting from about 1985, the authorities opened the sale of user equipment for free competition; however, the equipment had to be approved by the telecom operator or a separate regulatory authority before the new device could be connected to the network to ensure that the equipment met international and national performance standards.

The number of independent retailers of various types of user equipment grew rapidly, in particular, for sales of ordinary telephones and mobile phones. An important offspring of the deregulation was that the telecommunications operators no longer owned the telephone apparatus, the data modem, or the local switchboard at the user premises as they did before sale of user equipment was opened up for competition. This equipment was regarded as a technical extension of the network and, as such, an integral part of the network. After the deregulation, the operator's responsibility and ownership of equipment ended at the network interface device (NID) on the wall of the house; this technology is often referred to as "wire-to-the-wall" and, in the optical age, "fiber-to-the-premises." The manufacturers could now build the data modem into, for example, computers, fax machines, and copying machines. This simplified the use of data communications but had little impact on the number of users of data communications until the Internet was incorporated in the portfolio of the telecommunications operators in the mid-1990s.

The first regulatory authorities were established during this period to ensure fair competition and to avoid that the telecommunications monopolies misused their market power to hinder other retailers to establish their independent businesses. The predecessor of the regulatory in Norway (Nkom) was established in 1987. The regulatory authorities also issued licenses for sale of equipment and followed up that the retailers had access to enough technical expertise for installation and maintenance of equipment.

5.2 De-monopolization of Mobile Network Operations

In 1981, the Nordic Mobile Telephone (NMT) had just been put into operation in the Nordic countries. NMT was the first cellular system offering automatic roaming and undisruptive handover of calls when the mobile terminal moved into a new cell. Already in 1982, NMT was about to become the preferred common European land mobile system. British Telecom participated together with the Norwegian Telecommunications Research Establishment (now Telenor Research) preparing the NMT for implementation in the UK. France declared that they also would choose NMT if the UK did so. Germany had decided to build their own system (C-Netz) but promised to build an "NMT highway" through the country to interconnect "NMT countries."

In 1982, Prime Minister Margaret Thatcher and her government decided that there should be full competition on mobile communications in the UK with two independent operators. This implied that the UK had to choose a system other than NMT; otherwise, one of the competitors would have too big advantage. Europe was then left with four incompatible automatic land mobile systems: NMT in Norway, Finland, Sweden, Denmark, Iceland, Spain, the Netherlands, and Switzerland; TACS in the UK and Ireland; C-Netz in Germany; and Radiocom 2000 in France.

This was, in fact, the major incentive for the Netherlands to suggest in 1982 that Europe should develop a new pan-European digital mobile system—the Global System for Mobile Communications (GSM). GSM was originally an abbreviation for the name of the group developing the technology—Groupe Spécial Mobile. In 1992, the GSM system was put into operation, and EU and EFTA decided that each country should have at least two competing land mobile networks. GSM was an ideal place where the de-monopolization of telecommunications could start. In

Norway, this resulted in two operators: NetCom (now Telia Norway) and one subsidiary of Televerket (now Telenor Mobil). Both operators commenced operation in 1992.

GSM was a completely new network where all operators had to build the network infrastructure from scratch. The new infrastructure consists of base stations, telephone exchanges supporting entirely new functions, and entirely new databases for subscription handling and location management. The only advantage the telephone monopolies had was transmission lines that could be used to interconnect the new devices, thereby reducing the need for investments in basic infrastructure; however, by simple regulatory requirements, all mobile operators in the region had equal opportunities to lease such lines from the monopoly operator for the same price as a subsidiary of the monopoly operator.

Televerket, and all other European telecommunications operators, continued as monopolies offering fixed telephone services. Hence, from 1992 onward, consumers could choose between at least two providers of mobile telecommunications services in Europe, while fixed telephone services and data communication were still restricted to the offers of the monopoly operator.

A mobile operator established in one country could now also establish subsidiaries in other countries, thereby increasing the market of potential subscribers and, as a result, enhancing its business prospects and boosting its financial value. Several mobile telecommunications companies then rapidly developed into large international conglomerates.

5.3   De-monopolization of All Telecommunications Operations

In 1998, the EU opened all aspects of telecommunications for full competition. The process toward full deregulation had started already in 1987 by the Green Paper on the Development of the Common Market for Telecommunications Services and Equipment. The earlier monopole operator was referred to as the *incumbent operator*.

Note that in 1998, fixed telephone services were still regarded as the most important business in the telecommunications industry despite that mobile phone and data services were growing rapidly. More than 20% of the Norwegian population owned a mobile phone at that time.

Mobile communications had already been de-monopolized as described above, and the Internet had existed for several years as an independent network not owned by anyone. In 1998, Internet had just started to be included in the business portfolio of the telecommunications operators in Europe but was still regarded as a rather minor addition to their portfolio. Almost unrecognizably, the Internet had started to replace the X.25 data network as carrier for data communication services, in particular in Norway, where Telenor sponsored communication lines for interconnecting universities and research establishments with high-speed Internet connections. Telenor Research was in the forefront of this evolution.

While the network operators could levy differentiated charges on the services offered by the telephone network (local calls, long distance calls, international calls, calls to value added services, and so on), it turned out that this was not possible for Internet services. The revenue basis of the telecommunications industry was about to change.

Both the Internet and the mobile phone have altered the business landscape of telecommunications entirely. Now, about 20 years after de-monopolization, the fixed telephone service is about to be replaced by cellular mobile networks, and the telephone service, fixed or mobile, is itself soon incorporated as one out of numerous data services on the Internet using voice over IP technology. By the end of 2020, only about 7% of the population in Norway had a subscription for fixed telephony. The number of subscriptions is still decreasing by about 13% per year. The fixed telephone service in Norway will disappear entirely in 2024. The service has been replaced by telephony over mobile networks and VoIP over broadband cable networks.

The deregulation process took several years because the telecommunications network was regarded as a public utility that was best served by the old state monopolies (the incumbents). Moreover, it was a long and difficult process to establish the rules and procedures for regulating the market so that new entrants had a fair chance to compete with the incumbents.

After 1998, anyone in the EEA could become a network operator, service provider, or retailer of user equipment. However, the stakeholders in this market were subject to some regulatory restrictions related to the competition between network operators—including virtual network operators—on price, performance, customer care, and quality of service. These regulations included mandatory cooperation between network operators to ensure full connectivity between users of competing networks at reasonable prices and quality of service and non-discrimination of application service providers accessing the network, in particular, preventing network operators from giving advantages to application service providers owned by themselves.

To understand the present situation, it is important to note that the deregulation of 1998 had to do with the telephone network only. The driving force for the de-monopolization was the political idea that a competitive market would be more efficient and offer lower prices than the monopoly. This conclusion may be true for fixed and mobile telephone operation, but the development of Internet services has shown that this is not always true. A concern for policy makers now is that free competition has led to the undesirable situation that several companies in the data or Internet business have had a tremendous increase in market value and revenues during the last few years. Some of these companies have also become ad hoc monopolies in their market segments (e.g., Google, Facebook, and Netflix) by acquisitions of competitors. These companies also benefit from strong network effects, thereby resulting in robust lock-in barriers for users. Moreover, several of these companies are true global companies. They can operate from anywhere in the world, place their equipment in any country, offer services to anyone and anywhere, and relocate their equipment and headquarter at short notice to avoid interference from authorities. This makes these companies hard to regulate and control.

The deregulation of telecommunications has also generated a new form of competition in the global telecommunications industry. Until 1998, the old monopolies existed within a single country, but after 1998, these companies could also start operations in other countries. Making the situation even more complex, two new types of operators have arrived: resellers and virtual network operators.

6 Resellers and Virtual Network Operators

Resellers and virtual network operators (VNOs) are two stakeholders in the telecommunications market that are direct results of the de-monopolization of this business area. The resellers buy bulk traffic capacity and call time from telecommunications carriers and resell it to their customers with profit. Reselling is particularly popular in the mobile market. The reseller does not own any network infrastructure. In the mobile market, they may issue their own SIM. The profit is generated from discounts they obtain by buying large quantities of traffic capacity and by combining telecommunications services with other services or goods, e.g., service packaging, price profiles, and value-added services.

The reseller is the single point of contact for their customers independently of the operators from which the reseller buys traffic capacity. The resellers are in control of their own systems for customer care, billing, marketing, and sales, either owning these facilities themselves or outsourcing them to specialized providers of such services. The mobile market was opened for resellers in Europe in 1992, just after the first GSM network was put into operation. As of February 2020, there are 13 resellers in the Norwegian market, including Chilimobil and Atea [8].

The virtual network operators buy access to the network infrastructure of network operators (NOs) owning their own network. The most common VNOs are the mobile virtual network operator (MVNO). They deliver services to their customers using the radio network infrastructure of mobile network operators (MNOs) owning base stations and other mobile network infrastructure. Lyca Mobile is an example of an MVNO operating in the Norwegian market. The MVNO issues its own SIMs, operates its own Home Subscriber Server (HSS) for subscription and location management, and has at least one Internet gateway router and/or telephone gateway exchange for access to the network of the MNO. The configuration is shown in Fig. 8 for an MVNO offering 4G services. Data packets from the mobile terminal are then routed from the base station via the gateway router (GW) into the Internet, and data packets coming from the Internet are routed to the gateway router before they are routed into the network of the MNO and delivered to the mobile terminal over the base station.

What makes the MVNO different from a reseller is that the MVNO owns some network infrastructure, while the reseller does not. The actual MNO serving the

Fig. 8 Network with
MVNO with access to
network resources owned by
an MNO

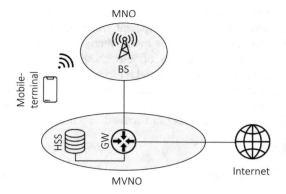

MVNO is not visible for the customers, and the MVNO has roaming agreements with other MNOs independently of the MNO serving the MVNO.

MVNOs are particularly interesting because there are so many of them. The first MVNO (Sense Communications) was established in Denmark in 1997 and in Norway and Sweden in 1999. In 2014, there were 943 MVNOs worldwide.

The number of MNOs in a region is limited by the amount of radio spectrum available, and the dominating mobile operators in EEA are obliged by EU directives to offer services to both resellers and MVNOs to enhance competitions in the mobile market. The effect of competition with MVNOs may not be obvious. Initially, there was strong resistance from mobile network operators (MNOs) to allow mobile virtual network operators (MVNOs) into their networks. They were afraid of increased competition without really appreciating the difference between market share and revenue share. The size and value of mobile operators are measured in terms of market shares and not in terms of revenue shares.

Figure 9 shows the case of two competing network operators (MNO1 and MNO2) and an MVNO leasing infrastructure from MNO1. The MVNO pays a leasing fee to MNO1 for using its infrastructure.

The effect of the MVNO is illustrated by the following simple numerical example, illustrated in Fig. 10: Suppose that the market consists of 3 million subscribers and is equally shared between the two MNOs before the MVNO enters the market. The revenue per user is 1000 money units. Then the revenue for each of the two MNOs will be 1.5 billion money units initially.

At some time after the MVNO entered the market, the two MNOs and the MVNO have 1 million subscribers each generating 1000 money units each; that is, MNO1 and MNO2 have both lost 0.5 million subscribers to the MVNO. Supposing next that the rent the MVNO must pay for using the network of MNO1 is 500 money units per subscriber, then the revenues of MNO1 will be 1 billion from own subscribers plus 0.50 billion from the MVNO; that is, the revenues of MNO1 are 1.5 billion money units. The revenues of MNO2 are 1 billion money units.

Compared to the situation that existed before the MVNO entered the market, the revenues of MNO1 have stayed the same, while the revenues of MNO2 have become

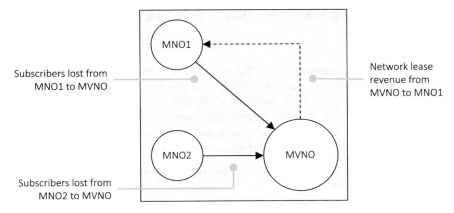

Fig. 9 Competing network operators

Fig. 10 Market shares and revenues for mobile network operators (MNOs) 1 and 2 and mobile virtual network operator (MVNO)

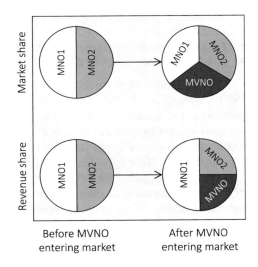

0.5 billion money units smaller. This simple example shows that even if the MVNO is winning many customers from MNO1, housing the MVNO may still be a good business for MNO1 since a large proportion of the revenues of the MVNO is fed back to MNO1 in the form of network leases. Some of these revenues are revenues lost by MNO2 to the MVNO. The result is that MNO2 always loses both market share and revenues.

7   Regulation on the Norwegian Telecommunications Market

The Norwegian Communications Authority (Nkom) is responsible for regulating the Norwegian telecommunications market. Nkom is a member of the Body of European Regulators for Electronic Communications (BEREC), which fosters regulation of digital markets in Europe. Nkom enforces the Electronic Communication Act. The most important task is to ensure fair competition in the mobile market. The purpose of regulating mobile and other telecommunications markets is [9]:

- To avoid market failure such as formation of monopolies
- To foster fair competition
- To secure that the users have correct and adequate information about the market
- To ensure affordable access to the ICT infrastructure, thereby satisfying collective needs of the public
- To protect individuals against unethical business conduct and abuse of personal data
- To promote professional and ethical conduct of market participants
- To stimulate peer-based service innovation and development of new technologies

The regulations apply to fixed and mobile network operators, user access providers, Internet service providers (in particular net neutrality), application service providers, and content providers. The mobile access market is, by far, the most complex market to regulate. In contrast, the regulation of the Internet is mainly to ensure that net neutrality is fulfilled. In Norway, the telecommunications market is regulated by the Norwegian Communications Authority (Nkom).

When Europe opened for full competition of mobile communication in 1992, one of the first companies in each European country to establish itself as a mobile network operator (MNO) was the operator owning the entire telecommunications infrastructure of that country—also called the *incumbent*. Televerket (now Telenor) was the incumbent in Norway. The incumbent had thus an enormous initial market power. To reduce the market power of the incumbent as MNO and allow fair competition, the authorities required that:

1. The MNO had to be commercially separated from the other business areas of the incumbent, including prohibition of cross-subsidizing
2. The conditions for connecting the mobile network to the fixed network infrastructure of the incumbent and lease of infrastructure components (e.g., to interconnect base stations and exchanges) had to be the same for all MNOs, including the incumbent's own MNO

The MNO must have access to exclusive slots in the radio-frequency spectrum. One of the important tasks of Nkom is to allocate and supervise the use of the radio spectrum in Norway. The amount of spectrum allocated for mobile communications is scarce, and there is room for only a few MNOs in the same region. Fair competition for frequency resources is achieved by dividing the spectrum into slots and then auctioning each slot to existing or new operators. This allows only a few MNOs in each country. To increase competition, the market is also opened up for resellers and mobile virtual network operators (MVNOs) as described above. One task of Nkom is to supervise that MVNOs and resellers meet fair competition in the mobile market.

Hence, the mobile market is an oligopoly with just a few MNOs in each country. Some MNOs, including the incumbent, may have market power big enough to take actions that alter competition or establish new market rules. These are referred to as *dominating MNOs*. The main objective of market regulation is then to hinder that dominating MNOs misuse their market power to push competitors out of the market, to hinder new entrants to enter the market, or to unduly exploit the customers by overcharging. In Norway, there are 2 dominating operators and 15 small ones, mostly resellers and MVNOs. The dominating MNOs are Telenor Mobil and Telia Norway with market shares (2020) 49% and 37%, respectively.

Sections 7.1–7.6 provide a list of competition problems that may arise in the mobile market and must be mitigated by market regulations (based on the Annual Report of Nkom, 2020).

7.1 Denial of Interconnection

MNOs are value networks. The value proposition of the value network is to support mediation services within the same user group or between different user groups (multisided markets). MNOs benefit from interconnecting with other national or international MNOs and fixed networks to make their network of relationships between users as big as possible. Full interconnectivity in the international telephone network is also governed by rules set up by the International Telecommunications Union and universally endorsed by the member countries. These requirements apply to both fixed and mobile telephone networks.

However, an MNO with dominating market power may squeeze new entrants out of the market by denying them interconnection or call termination. This means that users of the new entrant cannot call users of the MNO, thereby reducing the value perceived by the users of new entrant dramatically. This conduct is also referred to as *denial of traffic termination*. One of the responsibilities of the Nkom is to supervise that such actions do not take place.

7.2 Excessive Pricing

The terminating MNO is in a kind of monopoly situation since this is the only network in which a particular call can end up (i.e., where the called user lives or are temporarily located). This allows the terminating network to decide the price for connecting the called user, a price the calling network (and the user) must accept. If the price claim is not accepted, the call is rejected by the terminating MNO. The terminating MNO may then be tempted to levy excessive charges. To avoid such behavior, the regulator may set a price cap for call termination, making the prices more predictable for the user. However, lower bilateral termination prices may be negotiated between MNOs to support roaming users.

In Norway (and in the EEA), excessive pricing is avoided by the price cap method; that is, the termination price of all MNOs in the EEA region must be equal to or lower than the price cap set by the national regulator. Outside the EEA, there are several countries in which the termination price is not regulated and can be set independently by the termination MNO.

7.3   Cross-Subsidizing

Cross-subsidizing means to charge excessive prices for one service (the subsidizing service) and to use the additional earnings to reduce the charges for another service (the subsidized service). The major source for cross-subsidizing in the telecommunications market is high termination charges. These earnings may be used to subsidize another service and thereby obtain competitive advantages for that service.

Cross-subsidizing may, to a large extent, be avoided by price-cap regulation of call termination charges as explained above. Cross-subsidizing between fixed and mobile network operation is avoided by requiring that the subsidiaries offering fixed and mobile services are commercially separated.

7.4   Price Discrimination

The terminating MNO may charge lower termination charges for calls from MNOs belonging to the same group (e.g., a subsidiary in another country) and from other MNOs with which the terminating MNO has particular agreements (e.g., bilateral roaming agreements). Such practice may upset competition and should be avoided by regulations.

Price discrimination may also be used for cross-subsidizing by charging low termination charges from own subsidiaries and higher charges from other MNOs.

7.5   Lock-In of Customers

Customers may be locked in by contractually binding the customer for a period of time and to enforce economic penalties if the customer leaves the provider before the end of the contractual period. This may be done by offering cheap mobile phones and services to customers who accepts the contract and mobile phones for market price for those who do not. This is standard competition behavior and is not subject to regulation. Another method is SIM lock where the mobile phone will not accept a SIM from a competing MNO until the lock has been removed. The regulator may set an upper limit for the duration of the SIM lock period or not allow SIM lock at all. In Norway, the operator may apply SIM lock for up to 12 months as part of the subscription.

7.6 Non-price Discrimination

There are also several factors other than price that may twist competition in an undesirable direction. Examples are:

- Dragging out interconnection negotiations, thereby slowing down the market growth of the competitor.
- Deliver insufficient interconnection specifications, also slowing down competition or making interconnection more expensive for the competitor.
- Deliver stripped down functionality, thereby disallowing the competitor access to some interconnection services.
- Reduced quality of technical interfaces (e.g., throttled data rate, slow connection establishment, long latency, and so on).
- Unwarranted requirements (e.g., liabilities in case of network failures).
- Negotiating the interface between MVNOs and MNOs is particularly complicated because it includes both commercial and technical aspects that are much knottier than the interconnection of ordinary MNOs.

8 Conclusions

The Internet and mobile telephony are two enabling technologies for the digital economy. Norway has been a pioneer in the development and adoption of these technologies. This chapter has examined the historical evolution of these technologies and how they impact digital markets. In particular, the transition from national monopolies to competition markets in the telecommunications sector had profound impacts on consumer prices, quality, innovation, and technology development. To ensure fair competition, national regulations are needed.

References

1. Abbate, J. (1999). *Inventing the internet*. MIT Press.
2. ITU Statistics. Accessed August 18, 2021, from https://www.itu.int/en/ITU-D/Statistics/Pages/stat/default.aspx

3. Kurose, J. (2021). *Computer networking: A top-down approach* (8th ed.). Pearson.
4. ARPANET. Accessed August 18, 2021, from https://en.wikipedia.org/wiki/ARPANET
5. Medienorge. Accessed August 18, 2021, from https://www.medienorge.uib.no/statistikk/medium/ikt/347
6. Internet World Stats. Accessed August 18, 2021, from https://www.internetworldstats.com/emarketing.htm
7. Øverby, H., & Audestad, J. A. (2018). *Digital economics: How information and communication technology is shaping markets, businesses, and innovation.* CreateSpace Independent Publishing.
8. Nkom. *Analysis of the market for access and call origination on public mobile telephone networks.* Accessed August 18, 2021, from http://www.nkom.no
9. Øverby, H., & Audestad, J. A. (2021). *Introduction to digital economics: Foundations, business models and case studies* (2nd ed.). Springer.

Digital Transformation in Renewable Energy: Use Cases and Experiences from a Nordic Power Producer

Liyuan Xing, Gleb Sizov, and Odd Erik Gundersen

Abstract The electric power system is changing. The changes include the integration of renewable resources, such as wind farms and solar plants, making the grid smarter so that it can react and adapt to changes and increase customer engagement. These changes of the power system have radical effects, which can only be tackled if it is digitized, so digital transformation of the power system is of paramount concern.

Electrical energy management systems are therefore an integral part of the digitization process. Such systems typically provide the fundamental information and computation capability to perform real-time network analyses, to provide strategies for controlling system energy flows, and to determine the most economical mix of power generation, consumption, and trades. Currently, the maturity of digitization is at different levels for various parts of the electrical power system. Machine learning has been suggested as a tool for making smart grids that can adapt to sudden changes and long-term distributional shifts and recover from errors. The interest in implementing machine learning methods into energy management systems has grown in recent years, and many companies are taking the first steps.

TrønderEnergi is a Norwegian power generation company that does exactly this. It aims at increasing the value of renewable energy and at the same time reducing the cost. In the context of hydropower and wind power, there are several use cases that undergo digital transformation in TrønderEnergi. Examples of such use cases are (1) hydropower trading, (2) wind power trading, and (3) predictive maintenance on wind farms and hydro plants. These use cases as well as the digital transformation processes are introduced in detail in this chapter along with our practical experience. We discuss how machine learning helps to improve the functioning of the existing

L. Xing (✉) · O. E. Gundersen
Norwegian Open AI Lab, Norwegian University of Science and Technology, Trondheim, Norway

TrønderEnergi Kraft AS, Trondheim, Norway
e-mail: liyuan.xing@tronderenergi.no; odderik.gundersen@tronderenergi.no

G. Sizov
TrønderEnergi Kraft AS, Trondheim, Norway
e-mail: gleb.sizov@tronderenergi.no

P. Mikalef, E. Parmiggiani (eds.), *Digital Transformation in Norwegian Enterprises*,
https://doi.org/10.1007/978-3-031-05276-7_5

systems and optimize operations. Inspired by these use cases, we believe digital transformation will continue to make inroads in other applied areas in energy management systems and form the digital electric power ecosystem.

1   Introduction

1.1   Current and Future Electric Power Systems

An electric power system (EPS) is a network of electrical components deployed to supply, transfer, and use electric power [1]. A typical example of an EPS is the electrical grid that provides power to homes and industries within an extended area. The electrical grid can be broadly divided into the generators that supply the power, the transmission system that carries the power from the generating centers to the load centers, and the distribution system that feeds the power to nearby homes and industries.

The structure of future EPSs may be represented in an aggregate form as a three-level super-mini-micro system (see Fig. 1 in [2]). In Norway, the structure is mainly super grid with large hydro and wind renewable energy resources, mini grid with many small hydro plants connected to a distribution network, as well as micro grid with micro hydropower plants, batteries, and electric vehicle charging.

Renewable energy flows through Norway as summarized in [3]. Specifically, Norway is the seventh largest hydropower nation in the world and the largest in Europe. Moreover, developments of both onshore wind and floating offshore wind have come fast. Fosen wind is realizing Europe's largest onshore wind power project in Central Norway. Equinor (Norwegian state-owned multinational energy

Super-Mini-Micro Grid Structure

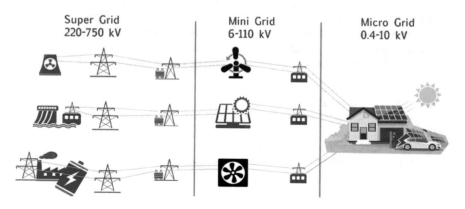

Fig. 1   Three-level super-mini-micro EPS, from [2]

company) is currently the world's leading floating offshore wind developer. In October 2017, the company opened Hywind Scotland, the world's first floating offshore wind farm. Large-scale energy storage could hold one of the keys to the successful scaling of renewable energy production. To this end, the Norwegian company Ruden has developed an "underground electric battery" in existing geological structures.

Globally [4], hydropower accounts for 54% of the renewable power generation capacity, and wind energy is the second largest renewable energy after hydropower which accounts for approximately 24%. As mentioned in [5], Norway has endorsed the EU Renewable Directive and has plans to increase its renewable energy ratio from 58.2% in 2005 to 67.5% by 2020. As of 2020 [6], 1690 hydropower plants account for 88% of the Norwegian electricity production capacity while 53 wind farms account for 10%. However, wind power is currently the dominating for of investment. Due to the latest controversy in wind farms on land in Norway, the general expectation is that the growth in wind power will come from offshore wind farms.

With renewable electricity at the supply side of the upstream for the zero or minimal greenhouse gas emissions and sustainable developments, the same holds true on the downstream where consumers become more sustainable by adapting to variability of the renewable energy sources. Norway is the electric vehicle capital of the world, as reported in [7]. Specifically in 2020, 74% (54% fully electric cars and 20% plug-in hybrids cars) of the new cars that were sold in Norway were electric vehicles. The political goal is for all new car sales in Norway to be zero emission (electric or hydrogen) by 2025. Moreover, customers are increasingly valuing services that use digital technology (e.g., smart homes, office buildings, supermarkets) for energy savings. Intelligent demand will be an increasingly important dispatchable resource. In this way, customers are more engaged in energy supply and demand, as pointed in [8].

Sensors and information technology are increasingly permeating the distribution power system (middle part of Fig. 1) [7]. For example, the regulators in Norway have already required to implement smart meters by 2019-01-01, as cited in [9]. In addition, 7.4% of hydropower came from distributed small-scale hydroelectric power plants (SSH) in the middle grid in 2017 [5]. There is an increasing interdependence of information technology and energy technology, with smarter grids opening pathways to greater functionality (e.g., situational awareness) and active management of more diverse sets of resources providing a range of services that can be monetized in energy markets [8].

Yet the pathway to electric power system evolution is highly sensitive to each local situation and its technical, economic, and political factors. Among many others [8], the three main and fundamental trends, including renewable resources integration, smart grid, and customer engagement as aforementioned, have driven the electric power system evolution in Norway.

1.2 Challenges and Opportunities for Energy Management Systems

Radically evolving power systems and rapidly developing technology bring a unique set of challenges and opportunities for the EMS (as defined in [10]) to monitor, control, and optimize the performance of the generation and transmission systems, adding value through computer-aided tools.

The perpetual task in EPS is balancing energy production and consumption. It means that the amount of electricity fed into the electricity grid must always be equal to the amount of electricity consumed; otherwise, there's a blackout which is a total crash of the power grid. Therefore, multiple parties (high-voltage transmission system operator (TSO), access responsible parties (ARPs), producers of electricity, and large consumers) are involved in managing the balance on the grid. Moreover, several energy markets are designed to incentivize producers to provide accurate power production forecasts and help to balance the power system. Specifically, wind power producers participate in the physical market by nominating production forecasts to spot/day-ahead market (12–36 h ahead), trading on the intraday market (usually 1–8 h ahead), and providing re-planning forecasts (45 min ahead) in the balancing market.

Integration of renewable energy sources is one of the main challenges in EPS right now. Renewable energy sources such as solar and wind power depend on weather conditions, which cannot be controlled or predicted accurately. This makes the balancing task more challenging. This challenge can be addressed from different perspectives. From infrastructure viewpoint, more storage can be integrated so that overproduction or overconsumption can be compensated by charging/discharging the storage. From software viewpoint, algorithms for power production and consumption forecasts, as well as automatic bidding and trading in various markets, can reduce the imbalances.

There is increased energy efficiency in the value chain to save cost and reduce environmental impact in both power generation and consumption. Customer engagement becomes more economically feasible and socially acceptable, as one of the trends [8]. Therefore, the rest of the power sector faces the challenge of keeping up and embracing the need to co-optimize electricity supply and demand dynamically. It includes treating largely inelastic demand as a fixed target during planning, regulation and market design, and meeting the demand by building a dispatchable supply stack with utilities and grid operators.

With the increased complexity and risk of the more intermittent and less predictable renewable energy sources, largely inelastic demand, finer time resolution (moving from 1 h to 15 min) for trading, and settlement in Nordic energy markets [11], it is impossible to rely on manual human actions or conventional energy management systems that cannot adapt to the complex market situations based on vast amount of data.

With increased availability of sensor, market, and operational data, as well as the advanced information technologies, there is an opportunity to automate operations in electric power ecosystem to take actions with less human intervention based on continuous check of the system states in a much more detail manner than it was before. Sophisticated computer tools are now the primary tools in solving difficult autonomous decision-making problems that arise in the areas of power system planning, operation, diagnosis, and design. Among these computer tools, machine learning (ML) has grown predominantly in recent years and has been applied to various areas of power systems.

ML is the study of computer algorithms that improve automatically through experience and using data [12]. ML algorithms build a model based on sample data, known as "training data," to make predictions or decisions without being explicitly programmed to do so. Therefore, they are used in a wide variety of applications where it is difficult or unfeasible to develop conventional algorithms to perform the needed tasks.

1.3   Digitization Maturity Levels

Basically, electric power system is a typical example of industrial internet of things (IIoT) [13], which refers to interconnected sensors, instruments, and other devices networked together with computers' industrial applications for better addressing fluctuations in production, demand, and pricing, adjusting bid and trade in energy markets, dispatching resources, planning predictive maintenance, as well as maximizing economic benefits.

Most electric power companies already have many digital solutions for energy management in place, but the digitization stays at different maturity levels for various applied areas of power system. Measuring and evaluation of the digitization levels in structured way can make digital transformation process easier to implement. The IoT pyramid [14] represents successive stages of digitization and also serves as a reference framework for the maturity assessment. In the pyramid, there are five stages from bottom to top as follows, where implementation of the top ones is more difficult and requires the ones below to be implemented first.

Connectivity: Collect/provide relevant data through vertical and horizontal integration.
Information: Derive data from information and create transparency.
Knowledge: Make knowledge explicit and provide it as per requirements.
Forecast: Detect patterns and use them for forecast.
Autonomy: Autonomous system decisions.

We try to explain and concretize these five stages with (a) traffic lights example from [15] and (b) another example of predictive maintenance for wind turbines in the energy domain.

Connectivity: Data are facts, symbols, and signals about who, what, when, and where. For example, (a) red is a signal of traffic lights; (b) vibration amplitude is an important sensor signal for wind turbines.

Information: Information has meaning by linking who, what, when, and where to describe a situation or event. For example, (a) the south facing traffic light on the corner of Pitt and George Streets has turned red; (b) vibration amplitude from a certain component (e.g., bearing) of a wind turbine.

Knowledge: Knowledge has context and provides insights and understanding of something. For example, (a) the traffic light I am driving toward has turned red; (b) check the frequency range of the vibration to identify the defect in a bearing.

Forecast: Predict what is going to happen in the future. For example, (a) the traffic light is going to be green in a minute; (b) forecasting the remaining useful life of the defected component.

Autonomy: It places knowledge and forecast into a framework that allows them to be applied for making decisions. For example, (a) I had better stop the car now but can drive in a minute! (b) preparing and planning the maintenance in advance to avoid unnecessary downtime.

1.4 Present Situation in TrønderEnergi Norway

TrønderEnergi [16] is a Norwegian national player with Nordic ambitions for the next-generation energy management. As a purebred energy company, we deliver the state-of-the-art renewable energy solutions and services of the future, building upon our 70 years of industry experience on hydropower. The company is trying to lead the way in the evolution of the electric power system that is happening in Norway.

TrønderEnergi is a major player in renewable energy for a better society (zero CO_2 emissions). We produce both hydropower and wind power. In 2020, the company had the proportion of hydro and wind around 80/20 (2.4 TWh/0.6 TWh), with the plan to reach 38/62 (2.4 TWh/3.9 TWh) in 2025 and 30/70 (2.4 TWh/ 5.4 TWh) in 2030. The strategy is to become one of the most profitable hydropower producers in Norway and a leading Nordic player in wind power.

TrønderEnergi is also responsible for power trading and innovation in renewable energy. Through market activities, the company positions itself to use the opportunities in new renewable technologies, new business models, and new market models for the power industry.

TrønderEnergi has contributed to establishing Norway's second largest grid company. It holds the ownership in one of Norway's largest grid companies but also moves toward the downstream business and is taking a position in the continued electrification, through partner-based growth in energy services with Ohmia Retail, Ohmia Charging, and Ohmia Construction.

Different from most energy companies, TrønderEnergi employs an inhouse AI department since 2018, counting more than ten ML engineers. Based on the company's digital platform, their main responsibility is to further provide the innovative, reliable, and robust AI energy services for both TrønderEnergi and third parties. Among the different digital transformation enablers, which are technology, organization, and process, the main driving force in TrønderEnergi is coming from organization.

Depending on the application areas, the maturity levels of digitization are in different stages. The AI team facilitates the digital transformation from its current maturity levels toward forecasting and autonomy, as defined in the IoT pyramid, using optimization and decision-making techniques, not limited to ML. The AI department has been working on many key areas in TrønderEnergi from the upstream of hydropower and wind power production forecasting, planning, trading, and maintenance, through the middle stream of power transmission with grid loss estimation [17], to the downstream of power consumption and flexibility. Among these, we are going to introduce in detail upstream use cases from hydropower and wind power trading and predictive maintenance.

1. **Hydropower trading:** transformation from forecast to autonomy
2. **Wind power trading:** transformation from forecast to autonomy
3. **Predictive maintenance:** on wind farms and hydro plants, transformation from knowledge to forecast

1.5   The Changes in Digital Transformation

Digital transformation is the process of using digital technologies to create new—or modify existing—business processes, culture, and customer experiences to meet changing business and market requirements [18]. This reimagining of business in the digital age is digital transformation. The two distinctive characteristics of digital transformation are (1) (re)defining an organization's value proposition and emergence of a new organizational identity [19, 20] and (2) changing the ways people work, thereby affecting the operations, culture, and experiences [21].

Regarding the first point, by automating wind power trading and predictive maintenance, TrønderEnergi is expected to offer a complete range of wind farm management services. The new integrated service across the value chain is key to optimal long-term profitability of the managed assets. Moreover, it enables the scaling of existing services through automation, providing energy management for more assets with less manual inspections, meaning higher efficiency with fewer people. It enables TrønderEnergi not only to manage its own wind farms but become a service provider for operating wind farms belonging to other companies. It changes the business models and adds more values, making TrønderEnergi a leading Nordic wind farm operator.

Regarding the second point, it correspondingly changes how people work. After automating the tasks in the new value chain, manual tasks become limited to monitoring and interventions for rare events that are not reflected in the data and require deep domain knowledge and skills to be handled. This change reduces the amount of work but maintains the demand for domain experts that develop and supervise automation systems. It also allows for the emergence of new skills. For example, operators need to learn how to interact and interpret data and outputs from ML applications that often lack sufficient ability to explain—sometimes erroneous—predictions generated by black box ML algorithms [21].

2 Digital Transformation

2.1 Use Case Background

2.1.1 Power Markets

The Nordic electricity market consists of several markets that provide different "time windows" for trading physical power: the day-ahead market, the intraday market, and the balancing market [22]. In addition, there is a financial market, where price securing contracts are traded. These different markets with their timelines as well as type of trades and market operators are summarized and drawn in [23]. Power producers, TSOs, power-intensive industries, large consumers, and power companies actively participating in the power markets are defined as power market actors.

In the Nordic countries, most of the trading is done on the day-ahead market (spot market), where a daily competitive auction establishes a price for each hour of the next day, called spot price. It is calculated after all participants' bids have been received before gate closure at 12:00. Participants' bids consist of price and an hourly volume in a certain bidding area. Retailers bid in with expected consumption, while the generators bid in with their production capacity and their associated production costs. The spot price is determined as the intersection between the aggregated curves for demand and supply for each hour—taking the restriction imposed by transmission lines into account. It is crucial for price formation within the other time windows, i.e., the intraday and balancing markets and the financial market for long-term contracts.

The intraday market is primarily a correction market, where actors can trade their imbalance, including adjusting any earlier trading if the forecasts turn out to be wrong. Over the years, lead times for intraday trading have gotten shorter, while traded volumes have gotten larger, caused by increased feed-in from fluctuating energy sources. While day-ahead trades are related to market clearing price principles, where the last accepted bid sets the price for all transactions, the prices in intraday trading are set in a "pay-as-bid" process [24], based on a first-come, first-served principle, where best prices come first—highest buy price and lowest sell price. This means prices are assessed in continuous trading based on each transaction that is completed. Therefore, bid prices are often used in intraday trading. The result is that there are no fixed prices for products on the intraday market. Moreover, the intraday bid can be done up to 1 h before the delivery hour and can trade in multiple products (hours). Both the day-ahead market and the intraday market are operated by

Nord Pool that merges bids on the day-ahead spot market (Elspot) and intraday market (Elbas) and publishes the result on their website.

The balancing market is trading automatic and manual reserves used by the Nordic transmission system operators (TSOs) to maintain power balance during the operation hour. The bidding can be updated up to 45 min before the delivery hour, and bids are called in real time by TSOs if the regulation is needed. The last activated bid in the operating hour will determine the price of the balancing power (regulation price) at this hour. When an upregulation takes place, the most expensive bid that has been activated will determine the regulation price for all the called bids, while downregulation takes the cheapest activated bid for regulation price instead. Moreover, in Norway, Statnett has been using a two-price system to price imbalances from the power producers, so that any deviation in the power production in the opposite direction to the regulation direction will be penalized. However, from November 2021 [25], the two-price system is transitioned to the one-price system which removes the possibility to reduce the imbalance by updating a short-term forecast 45 (replan). The main ways to reduce imbalance and consequently costs are to make the day-ahead forecasts more accurate and trade the imbalance volumes on the intraday market.

Financial power markets operate like other derivative trading markets. Trading in these markets has been drawing a lot of attention for decades and is a broad field, not specific to hydropower and wind power trading. Therefore, our focus will be on the daily bidding in the short-term markets.

2.1.2 Digitization Stages

According to digitization levels defined in Sect. 1.3, all three use cases in TrønderEnergi have already been implemented for the first three levels, as summarized as follows:

Connectivity: related sensors installed and connected to a data acquisition system.
Information: data is aggregated and stored in a centralized data platform SCADA.
Knowledge: data is processed, analyzed, and visualized in reports and dashboards available to operators, technicians, analysts, and managers.

Thereafter, TrønderEnergi inhouse domain experts make use of the knowledge for further forecasting and decision-making. When going toward the top of the IOT pyramid, domain experts' knowledge is used to build forecasting and autonomous decision-making systems.

For trading, the next two levels for the digitization of trading involve:

Forecast: power production is forecasted (wind power) or planned (hydropower) using ML and optimization models.
Autonomy: based on the forecasts, the bids are generated and submitted for trading in physical power market. Interactions with the market are implemented through API calls.

For predictive maintenance [26], every breakdown of a key component can cost millions and pose a safety risk. Predictive maintenance utilizes real-time data to detect anomalies and defects and predict failures. Maintenance is important for efficient operation and to avoid unplanned downtime. If the need for maintenance is detected in advance, it can be used to optimize maintenance scheduling to decide when to stop production, order parts, and organize technicians' work to do the repairs. The next two levels for the digitization of predictive maintenance include:

Forecast: predicting the expected lifetime of key components, such as gearboxes and bushings of wind turbines

Autonomy: using the forecasts to optimize the maintenance scheduling and interact with other related systems, such as power production forecasts

2.2 Hydropower Trading

Hydropower is an extremely flexible and stable energy source. Water can be stored in reservoirs until needed, allowing for quick changes in production and low start and stop costs. Well-regulated reservoirs can provide short-term flexibility within an hour, as well as long-term flexibility over days, weeks, and seasons. Therefore, hydropower planning takes long-term water value into account when optimizing the short-term production used for generating bids. It means deciding whether to use available water right now or wait and sell in future hours to maximize profits, which is different from nonflexible and intermittent power sources like wind and solar.

Hydropower is the main source of electricity in Norway with a long history; there are common third-party optimization and automation tools available that can be used for daily day-ahead and hourly intraday planning and trading. Take SHOP [27], for example; it is a modeling tool for short-term hydro operation planning, where the optimized production for the next day is closely related to the bidding in the day-ahead market. Moreover, work process (consisting of several steps by SHOP) can be standardized in Powel Nimbus [28] for production planning and backed trading. Volue Algo Trader [29] is another example; it allows implementation of trading strategies that automatically submit bids to the intraday market. Nowadays, all the trading operations are executed using digital platforms integrated with the corresponding markets through API calls.

With the support of these tools, domain experts are often involved in generating and updating the bids, which are submitted either manually or automatically. For example, TrønderEnergi has several inhouse operators who check and sometimes adjust bids for the short-term markets, after they are generated by automation tools such as SHOP. It makes the trading process semi-automatic and dependent on the domain experts' experience.

2.2.1 Current State

TrønderEnergi, as a hydropower producer, participates in all four markets mentioned in Sect. 2.1. According to the digitization stages described in Sect. 1.3, hydropower trading operates at the stage of partial autonomy—stage 5; especially day-ahead trading is at the highest stage when compared to intraday and balancing trading.

Day-ahead bid is the expected amount of supply at different prices for hydropower the next day. They are sent to the day-ahead energy market Nord Pool before noon every day. The bid is a matrix of price-quantity pairs for each hour of the following operating day, starting at midnight. The market is cleared once every day, and producers are notified of their obligations. Market commitments become known after the spot price is released; producers have the option of re-optimizing the production schedules in order to cover the load with minimum costs.

The Nordic countries deregulated their power markets in the early 1990s, and the day-ahead bidding methods are relatively mature. There are several existing standard bidding methods [29] for hourly bids. These bid methods are based on:

(a) Expected value—bid the optimal volume price independently, given expected price and inflow.
(b) Marginal cost—long-term water value is transformed into cost by using turbine efficiency; bid the marginal cost giving a price-dependent bid which is equal for each hour.
(c) Multi-scenario deterministic—run a lot of price scenarios and find optimal production and then combine them together.
(d) Stochastic optimization—explicitly optimize the bid given a discrete distribution of price and optionally inflow.

Most of the power generation companies in Nordic, including TrønderEnergi, are using the marginal cost-based bidding methods. In TrønderEnergi, it is done by first running optimization with SHOP [27] and then manual processing in Excel. The manual processing includes adjusting the water value from the long-term model due to its weaknesses and to get a better production scenario with fewer stops.

A challenge for multi-scenario deterministic bidding is the crossing price profiles by multiple separate SHOP runs, so a general stochastic hydropower optimization is formulated with uncertain price and inflow. Extra restrictions are added in the bidding period to ensure a well-behaved multi-scenario approach without any crossing price profiles. This stochastic short-term model SHARM [30] is developed and implemented by SINTEF. To the best of our knowledge, it has not yet been used by any Norwegian hydropower company for the day-ahead bidding because of the crucial details left to be solved for implementing it in practice.

As seen from the previous description, the day-ahead bidding is with many manual inputs and multiple SHOP runs for adjustments by the operators. However, there is still room for improving bidding to maximize profit from day-ahead market and automating the process so that the operators can shift their focus from making bids to choosing among the alternatives suggested by the system.

As for bidding in intraday market and balancing market, the time resolution and bidding horizon become smaller (15 min from 2023 [11]) compared to day-ahead market. It will be impossible to generate optimal bids manually for such short intervals. With 1-h interval, the operators try to trade the imbalance at least once a day, sometimes several times per hour, which is still far away from the allowed time resolution that allows for more frequent bid updates based on more recent and accurate information obtained in stage 2.

Specifically, there are three processes included for hydropower handling post spot to trade the imbalance; they are (a) trading in the intraday market for profit; (b) bidding into the balancing market; and (c) renominating in the balancing market to benefit from the single-price imbalance cost as opposed to the two-price imbalance cost (becomes irrelevant from November 2021 [24]).

In TrønderEnergi for hydropower, so far, all these imbalance processes are performed semi-automatically and involve manual works from the operators. For example, (a) intraday trading itself is performed manually, but cost and volume blocks come from automatic processes; (b) bidding in the balancing market is set up manually once per 24 h, and then bids are updated automatically as production schedule changes (for instance, due to an intraday trade); and (c) sending updated nomination data is done either manually or automatically, following an intraday trade.

Therefore, the next step in digital transformation is more automation in scheduling using the latest available information for better prediction and bidding to enable continuous process for trading in intraday and balancing markets at finer time resolution.

2.2.2 Next Steps

The goal with improving the bidding process in the day-ahead market is not only to increase profit but also to reduce the manual work required by the operators. The intention is to fully automate the bidding process. To improve bids, we need to take more uncertainty about the price and inflow forecasts into consideration. To accomplish this, we are moving from deterministic optimization with SHOP to stochastic optimization with SHARM. In addition, operators do not need to manually adjust the water value to get fewer stops as aforementioned, because SHARM takes the probabilities of different load scenarios into account and calculates bids that give the expected highest profit. One of the key points in this transition is to replace the operators' "gut feeling" adjustment for fewer stops with a quantitative method provided by SHARM.

SHARM is a stochastic version of SHOP; it has functionality to determine the optimal bid volumes using a set of discrete scenarios with probabilities for spot price and inflow. In the current SHARM bid, all prices in the bidding period from price scenarios are used as bid prices, and linear interpolation is used where there is no explicit production point; bid matrix is reduced if there are too many points [31].

It might seem that bids generated by SHARM are ready for use, but the reality is that there are crucial details left to be solved to use it practice. On the input side, the selection of bid prices is crucial, and the price scenarios should have a good coverage of extreme low and high prices; meanwhile, they should not miss prices near water value. On the output side, the bid should preserve the production jumps and must run production from the plants by having the stair bid, not always interpolating linearly.

Different from the stochastic optimization SHARM approach, there is research about hydropower optimization using deep learning [32]. Applying deep reinforcement learning and transformers for hydropower planning and bid generation is still in the early experimental stage.

When compared to bidding for day-ahead market, bidding for intraday market is less mature. There is less hydropower imbalance to trade because hydro is flexible and stable. Still, a small amount of imbalance can come from inaccurate pricing and inflow forecasts, incorrect input constraints, and conditions used in production planning. Simple intraday bidding strategies are developed based on spot prices and bids available in the intraday market. More advanced intraday bidding strategies include regulation price forecasts and different preferred risks. However, unlike spot price forecasts offered by many third providers, accurate regulation price forecasts are harder to come by. Relevant data from both the real world and various markets should be collected to predict the regulation price. Moreover, trading strategies with different risks should be allowed for selection, generating the corresponding bids for automatic submission and trading. Further details will be introduced in Sect. 2.3.1 for wind power trading, where intraday trading is more essential.

If the imbalance is not traded in the intraday market, it still can be handled in the balancing market. However, without submission of either intraday or balancing power bids that use the latest information, the deviation of power production might be in the opposite direction from the regulation direction, which will be penalized by additional cost. For the balancing market, because of the transition from two-price to one-price system, the increased focus is placed on trading forecasted imbalance on the intraday market, instead of balancing market.

2.2.3 End Goal

Even with all the processes mentioned in the previous section implemented, there is still work left for the operators that requires a lot of knowledge and experience, for example, adjusting the water values from the long-term model for generating the day-ahead bids and selecting suitable trading strategy and risk parameters for generating the intraday bids. These adjustments originate from errors in the forecasts, which cannot be eliminated because of the uncertainty in future conditions and events. Therefore, better handling of uncertainty in time series forecasting (e.g., prices, inflows, water values) will further improve the bidding performance and reduce human intervention and eventually result in higher autonomy.

Probabilistic forecasts capture uncertainty by predicting a distribution over a range of values. A prediction interval gives a range of values the random variable could take with relatively high probability. For example, a 95% prediction interval contains a range of values which should include the actual future value with probability 95%. Quantiles are a generalization of prediction intervals without making assumptions about the distribution. Many ML methods can predict quantiles by using quantile loss [33], such as linear quantile regression, neural networks, and gradient boosting.

By modeling uncertainty of price scenarios, inflow, and water values more accurately, the SHARM bids can perform even better, and less manual adjustment from operators will be needed. With explicit modeling of uncertainty for the regulation price, it can be used in bidding strategies with preferred risk by selecting different quantiles. Operators and decision-makers will be able to adjust the corresponding risk when they notice special situations based on the information from other sources. Therefore, better bidding and more autonomy in trading can be achieved with better handling of uncertainty.

2.3   Wind Power Trading

Wind power is a nonflexible and highly variable source of energy. The amount of energy produced mostly depends on the wind conditions that can change rapidly. An unforeseen increase or decrease in production creates an imbalance in the market. In addition, increased production can cause congestion in the electric grid. As mentioned in Sect. 1.2, effective integration of wind power into EPS is one of the main challenges the energy industry has right now.

Wind power is traded in the same physical energy market as other energy sources; see Sect. 2.1.1. These markets incentivize accurate power production forecasts to help balance the market. For wind power, the focus is on short-term forecasts, from 10 min to 36 h ahead. The forecast accuracy improves when more recent information is considered. Therefore, to maximize profits, the forecasts are updated frequently, e.g., every 10 min, and forecast imbalance, the difference between the previous and the most recent forecast, is traded in the intraday market. Effective intraday trading involves short-term forecasting of a regulation price, which is the price of electricity paid for the remaining forecast imbalance, after day-ahead nomination and intraday trading.

Control over wind power production is limited to reducing the amount of energy produced, so-called curtailment, used in case of grid congestion and special weather conditions and during maintenance of wind turbines. Long-term planning for wind production is used to plan maintenance, choosing time periods where electricity prices are low. This is different from hydropower with large integrated storage, where long-term production planning is the essential part of the operation to maximize profits from trading in the energy market.

2.3.1 Current State

Wind power trading in TrønderEnergi is automated, including data gathering, data processing, forecasting, and trading. Human involvement is limited to monitoring and interventions to handle rare events that are not reflected in the data. According to the IoT pyramid described in Sect. 1.3, wind power trading is mostly autonomous— stage 5.

An important part of reaching this stage is integration between systems, from sensors installed in wind turbines to market APIs. Several vendors provide systems for integration and automation of the processes involved. TrønderEnergi adapted these systems for day-to-day operations and now focuses on improving algorithms for forecasting and decision-making, stages 4 and 5.

As already mentioned, forecasting wind power production and prices benefits the most from advances in data engineering and ML. Making the data usable for applying ML models is a major part of automating and improving wind power forecasting. For instance, when preprocessing the data, it is important to account for curtailment, e.g., maintenance when power production is reduced or grid congestion. Technical problems in communication infrastructure or external APIs may result in missing or stale data. Power production can also be reduced because of icing. No matter what happens, the forecasting system should be able to generate forecasts, albeit the accuracy of these forecasts might be reduced. Cleaning the data influenced by external factors is also essential to maintain accuracy.

Wind power forecasting is a time series forecasting problem with covariates that capture weather conditions such as wind speed and direction. In theory, the power curve [34] provided by wind turbine manufacturer that indicates how large the electrical power output will be for the turbine at different wind speeds can be used in combination with the weather forecast. In practice, though, the power curve provides poor forecasts of how much power will be produced. Other factors, such the landscape around individual turbines, their location within the park, and wear of turbine components, must be taken into account. Forecasting models might also partially compensate for errors in weather forecasts.

The challenge of wind power forecasting received a lot of attention. The Global Energy Forecasting Competition (GEFCom) since 2012 [35] attracted hundreds of participants worldwide, who contributed many novel ideas to the energy forecasting field, including wind power forecasting. As summarized in [36], the top 5 teams in wind power forecasting GEFCom2014 employ nonparametric approaches and mostly used machine learning models such as gradient boosting machines (GBM) and quantile regression forests (QRFs), based on large numbers of input variables and features, stacking models in multiple layers. When compared to other tracks (solar, load, and price forecasting), wind power forecasting takes the highest place in probabilistic forecasting maturity. This is largely because wind power forecasting is the closest to meteorological forecasting, where probabilistic forecasting is well-established and commonly accepted.

One of the challenges we had to address in TrønderEnergi is the cold-start problem. For new wind parks, there is little production data available, and the quality of data is inconsistent due to configuring and testing wind turbines. In TrønderEnergi, we implemented a type of transfer learning where models trained on other parks are adapted for new park [37].

Wind production forecasts enable trading of wind power in different markets. Because of different pricing mechanisms, the mechanism for trading in different markets is also different. For day-ahead market, wind production bid contains all the forecasted production at any positive price (price can be negative on rare occasions). The actual price we get for this volume is the spot price determined by Nord Pool by balancing the supply and demand. However, in the intraday market, bid prices need to be provided in addition to the imbalance volume between the day-ahead forecasts and intraday forecasts. To gain insights as to what a good bid price is, it makes sense to use an estimate of the regulation price. As such, predicting hourly regulation price for each Nord Pool system area is a key process for bidding in the intraday market.

Regulation price is related to several factors, including historical and forecasted imbalance volumes, spot prices, spot bid curves, and inflows in each Nord Pool system area. Moreover, future imbalance volumes depend on factors such as wind production and other energy sources, spot flow, and buy volumes. These factors need to be modelled for predicting the imbalance volumes and further the regulation prices.

Based on the regulation price forecast, we can determine a reasonable price for bids in the intraday market. Different strategies can be developed and operationalized using automated trading systems that interact with the market. These systems communicate with the market, continuously sending and receiving information about bids and trades. They usually provide APIs and GUIs for both automatic and manual monitoring and control of the strategies.

When compared to flexible hydropower trading where the main trades are done in day-ahead market and less in intraday market, wind power trading relies more on the intraday market because wind power lacks flexibility and is intermittent with large fluctuations. It means more trades with larger volumes are inevitable for wind power in the intraday market.

All the wind production forecasting services and bidding services are running in the cloud at a regular schedule before the deadline for different markets with the latest available information. In TrønderEnergi, market participation for wind power is automated with human involvement mostly limited to monitoring, handling of exceptional situations, and occasional data entry. According to digitization levels defined in Sect. 1.3, wind power trading in TrønderEnergi is implemented on all five levels. Since 2020, TrønderEnergi offers a complete range of wind farm management services, including wind production forecasts and trading. In 2021, TrønderEnergi is a leading Nordic wind farm operator operating 13 wind farms, including Norway's second largest wind farm—Roan wind.

2.3.2 Next Steps

There is room for improvement for each component in wind power trading including wind production forecasts, regulation price forecasts, and trading strategies. More robust and accurate models can increase autonomy and maximize the profit. Based on the analysis of the results from wind power forecasting, we see that not only ML algorithms need to be improved. Other parts of the system such as automatic methods for filtering out the dirty data need to be improved. The workflow processes of the operators may need to be re-organized to make sure the input data required by the ML algorithms is correct and updated, for example, registering availability of wind turbines. These continued improvements seem iterative and never ending.

Going from point forecasts to probability forecasts has the advantage of taking uncertainty into account. As summarized in GEFCom2014 [36], probabilistic wind power forecasting is a relatively mature field. Extension of probabilistic forecasting to regulation prices and imbalance volumes would allow us to develop different trading strategies that account for different risks.

For both point and probabilistic forecasts, the use of ML methods has grown rapidly in recent years, applied to various areas of power systems. Among ML methods for probabilistic forecasting, quantile regression is the most popular method since no assumption about probability distribution is needed. Moreover, Bayesian optimization [38] is often used to find the optimal model parameters for each predicted percentile.

To increase profitability, existing trading strategies must be analyzed, and new state-of-the-art trading strategies must be developed based on lessons learned from the existing ones and literature. Further activities can be created depending on analytical and empirical back-testing results.

Further work on transfer learning methods would be beneficial for wind power forecasting in different wind parks and imbalance volumes and regulation price forecasting in different Nord Pool bidding areas. Trading strategies might benefit from including regulation prices from different areas.

2.3.3 End Goal

Intraday trading is a key component for trading power produced by renewable energies when quickly changing weather forecasts result in an unplanned shortfall or surplus of power from solar or wind power plants. Different from the nonflexible wind power, hydropower is flexible because of the storage in the reservoirs and can be treated as a kind of control reserves. Therefore, depending on the forecasted regulation prices and marginal cost of hydropower, hydropower can be utilized to compensate for wind imbalances in addition to trading on the intraday market. To reach the end goal of maximizing profit and stability, multiple renewable resources should be integrated, and corresponding trading strategies should be developed.

Changing market dynamics because of the intermittent and distributed power production pose new requirements to energy management software system. For example, software systems should allow manual changes in the system, e.g., modify trading strategies and add new data sources. With the regulatory changes in the market such as transition to one-price system, more trades go into the intraday market than the balancing market. Supporting software systems should be able to adapt to these changes.

Software systems that involve ML should be self-adaptable to handle non-stationary distribution or shifts in data. ML models should be re-trained and selected automatically. For cold-start problem with no or little data for new wind farm or new bidding areas, transfer learning can be used to leverage old data on new assets.

2.4 Predictive Maintenance at Wind Farms and Hydro Plants

Predictive maintenance [39] is the process of constantly monitoring the condition of in-service equipment and estimating when maintenance should be performed, i.e., not too late, but not too early either. This approach promises cost savings over routine or time-based preventive maintenance because tasks are performed only when warranted.

For wind farms, the main equipment that needs to be monitored is wind turbines. Depending on the type of wind turbines, among the key components are gearboxes and bushings. The goal is to predict their expected lifetime based on the various related data gathered from the sensors, for example, raw vibration and vibration trend data, as well as real-time SCADA data for different turbine components.

For hydro plants, the equipment that needs to be monitored is rotating equipment (mostly turbines and generators), in particular, the cases [40] of rotor fault (e.g., short-circuit) detection, condition monitoring of pump drainage, generator bearings, turbine hydraulic system, transformer cooling system, and servomotor forces. The relevant data can be collected from sensors, such as vibration sensors (accelerometers), acoustic emission sensors, microphones, and so on.

2.4.1   Current State

In TrønderEnergi, all the relevant data have been gathered and saved in our centralized data platform. The domain experts have the knowledge of how to use and analyze the data for planning the maintenance. As mentioned in Sect. 2.1.2, predictive maintenance stays mainly in stage 3 according to the IoT pyramid described in Sect. 1.3. The further task is to automate the process by developing corresponding predictive maintenance algorithms that can detect anomalies and failure patterns, provide early warnings and remaining useful life, and identify main causes of failure. This will move us into stage 4. Maintenance scheduling, ordering of new parts, as well as coordination with power production forecast can be automated, which is part of stage 5.

Predictive maintenance differs from preventive maintenance [39] because it relies on the actual condition of equipment, rather than average or expected life statistics, to predict when maintenance will be required. Similarly, condition-based maintenance [40] also relies on the actual condition of equipment; however, the approach that is used to determine the condition of the machines differs significantly.

Condition-based maintenance can be defined as equipment maintenance performed when certain indications imply performance degradation. Predictive maintenance [26] relies on advanced statistical methods and ML to dynamically define when a machine needs to be maintained. It looks at patterns across all sensors and makes one multivariate prediction model. The more the data sources and data available, the better the predictions. For this reason, predictive maintenance models usually get better at predicting future breakdowns over time.

Predictive maintenance can find complex indications for breakdowns which will be nearly impossible for humans to spot. However, the results of predicting future breakdowns span from minutes to month depending on the quality and frequency of data available, as well as the ML methods applied. Both data scientists and domain experts should be involved in the data collection process to ensure that the data gathered is suitable for the model to be built. Then it becomes possible to decide which modeling techniques should be used with the available data and the desired output.

There are multiple modeling techniques for predictive maintenance, and the two most used are regression models to predict remaining useful lifetime (RUL) and classification models to predict failure within a given time window. Both classification and regression use supervised ML methods, which model the relationship between features and the degradation path of the system such as part failure, overheating, etc. In the context of predictive maintenance, we might not predict the failure at the exact moment the machine fails. However, we would rather have some predictions prior to this happening, indicating that something is wrong. It means that we are interested in how well our model correctly predicts the probability of future breakdown. Therefore, traditional supervised learning methods need to be adjusted for prediction purposes. The main change is in the label construction methods—how to choose the labels for the failure cases and the labeling strategies. More details can be found in the section of modeling techniques in [41].

When applying different regression and classification ML models for predictive maintenance, some practical issues need to be addressed as well, such as time-dependent split, handling imbalanced data/sampling methods, cost-sensitive learning, and so on, as listed in [41].

2.4.2 Next Steps

Data imbalance is one of the main challenges when applying ML for predicting failures because failures are relatively rare events, e.g., breakdowns in wind turbines.

Moreover, the time series data is usually imperfect and incomplete due to the malfunctions in the sensors and data recording process [42]. Pure data-driven ML might not be the best choice in this case. More advanced ML methods such as transfer learning [37] and hybrid AI [43] are necessary. In addition, predictions from models and causes must be understood by the domain expert (e.g., the wind turbine technicians), why the model believes something is the cause of the problem, so explainability is also important [44].

Transfer learning [37, 45] is a research problem in ML that focuses on applying knowledge gained while solving one problem (source) to a different but related problem (target). For example, knowledge gained while learning to recognize passenger cars could be applied when trying to recognize trucks. In the context of predictive maintenance for wind turbines, the knowledge gained on synthetic data from high-fidelity wind turbine simulators could be applied to real data collected from the wind turbines.

There are different transfer learning algorithms that transfer knowledge from source to target at different levels: data, features, and model. As reviewed in [46], a very broad categorization would be instance-based approaches (augment the target training data with source data and apply selection and weighting based on similarity/relevance for the target data/problem), feature-based approaches (map features from source and target data into a shared feature space where the data is more similar to each other, and train models on the combined, mapped data), and model-based approaches (transfer knowledge at the model/parameter level, modifying or co-training models between source and target). Specifically, the pre-train-refine model-based approach is most common when applied to neural networks [47], but it can also be applied to gradient tree boosting for wind production forecasting [48].

When judging the suitability and feasibility of the transfer learning algorithms, it is important to address the following research questions: In which situations can a model be trained on similar or synthetic data and then transferred to actual data? How similar (e.g., size, characteristics, distributions) must the data be for transfer learning? What is the inherent uncertainty induced by the differences between actual and synthetic data? How to quantify the uncertainty and provide safe limits of usage resulting from the transfer?

The time series data from the low-quality sensors and recording systems of the running devices (e.g., wind turbines) is often of poor quality; it is noisy and incomplete and might contain errors regarding the physical attributes of the devices [42]. Real-world data rarely provides a perfect description of a relevant system. Some systems are affected by stochasticity beyond what is represented in the training data. This may prevent ML models from being successfully applied, e.g., due to a lack of trust in the results caused by unsafe extrapolations. Therefore, data-driven ML models need to be constrained by using the underlying physics of the physical models, that is, hybrid AI [43].

There are several ways to implement physical constraints in data-driven models, either in the model structure itself by using special loss and activation functions and features, as postprocessing, or by implementing data-driven models in analytical expressions [43]. There are two types of constraints: soft and hard. Soft constraint is encouraged but not forced to comply, while hard constraint is guaranteed to be satisfied. Examples for soft constraints can be constraints that are integrated into loss terms. Examples for hard constraints can be constraints that are applied as additional non-trainable layers with physics input in the top of neural networks or feature transformation and reduction to fewer units through dimensional analysis which preserves the physical equations as a preprocessing layer.

Some ML models such as Bayesian neural networks (BNNs) in theory can integrate the physical constraints through probabilistic modeling. However, the problem is how to use priors at various stages in BNNs to enforce physical constraints. Moreover, these networks are usually computationally expensive.

2.4.3 End Goal

The two approaches transfer learning and hybrid AI can be combined for solving problems in this use case. However, both are evolving research fields, especially hybrid AI. They require specific solutions given the case at hand, allowing us to use our domain knowledge, but without a clear methodology for operationalizing them. TrønderEnergi is in the early stage of investigating different methods, including using synthetic data generated from simulators and real data collected from sensors of the wind turbines. We are collaborating with academic and industry partners working with this approach under the umbrella of Norwegian Research Center for AI Innovation (NorwAI) [49].

3 Conclusion and Future

This chapter introduced the current and future electric power system with special focus on trends in Norway. Along with the radically changing power system evolution and rapidly developing innovative technologies, it brings a unique set of challenges and opportunities for the energy management systems. Digital transformation is imperative for most of the energy companies, including TrønderEnergi, as their digital solutions stay in different maturity levels for various applied areas of the power system. Use cases for hydropower and wind power trading and predictive maintenance on the upstream have been introduced in detail according to the experience that accumulated in TrønderEnergi. Hydro and wind trading use cases have been successfully applied to the daily working process with added values, while predictive maintenance use cases are still in research and development.

3.1 Positive and Negative Consequence of Digital Transformation

The digital transformation has both advantages and disadvantages. The positives include more competitive businesses, more productive employees, and improved customer experience [50]. These are achieved in our use cases. Automation reduces manual work and potential for human errors in the daily operations. At the same time, it provides more interesting and valuable tasks to the operators. Moreover, digitalization also standardizes the process, so that it relies less on the expertise and experience of individual operators.

Away from the daily routine tasks, the employees are forced to work with more challenging tasks. They need to learn new skills. However, every person has a different tolerance for stress factors, especially those who get used to routine work. Thus, it is important to provide workers with the support they need to feel motivated and feel secure in their jobs.

Every participant in the power market is focused on digitalization to increase efficiency and occupy new niches. More conservative participants are left behind. Digital transformation makes the business more competitive. Well-suited transformations allow businesses to be more flexible, efficient, and productive, which all help to increase the return of investment [50].

Effective implementation of new digital transformation takes time and effort. Moreover, technological progress is, for the near future, unending. That means that digital transformation must be an ongoing process. The digital market is fast and furious in its evolution. When new solutions enter the market, companies have to be ready to apply them quickly.

3.2 The Role of ML in Digital Transformation

Two stages as defined in Sect. 1.3 can be enabled by ML and are related to digital transformation:

4. **Forecasting**: ML can be used to make more accurate point and probabilistic forecasts. Higher accuracy often creates value within the existing business model. Moreover, it also brings the possibility for new services and business models. Even more value is created when forecasting is automated and scaled to new assets and clients.

5. **Autonomy**: Automatic decision-making and autonomous control are difficult to achieve with a sufficient level of robustness and explainability. The outputs of traditional black box ML methods can be hard to explain and guarantee their correctness. Therefore, "explainable" and "trustworthy" ML are often required for industry applications. Currently, humans are responsible for making decisions and providing explanations, using outputs from ML systems to support them.

The use of ML can bring scale, scope, speed, and automation to organizations and enable new services and business models. It does require that humans change the way they work, adapt, and learn new skills and jobs.

However, learning is not only for humans but also for machines to have better forecasts in stage 4 and autonomy in stage 5. Classic ML learns from data through trial-and-error learning, which is costly, slow, and context dependent and often lacking data as input and explanation as output. With limited available data, transfer learning can be used to utilize data from other related sources, or simulations can be used to produce infinite amounts of relevant data for training. For control tasks that optimize long-term cumulative reward, reinforcement learning can be used as an alternative to rule-based and reactive controllers. Reinforcement learning is investigated for model predictive control to achieve energy savings in assets such as buildings and industrial facilities, where models are calibrated from data collected from interactions with the environment.

Sometimes, both human and machine need to learn jointly, which is called meta-human systems [51]. Hybrid human/machine learning systems exhibit major differences in scale, scope, and speed of learning. Meta-human systems come with higher-level cognitive skills that affect the speed of organizational learning and shape the scale and scope economies of organizations in new ways for delegating, monitoring, cultivating, and reflecting [51]. This approach has the potential to accelerate digital transformation.

3.3 Cybersecurity and Regulations

In [52], it is reported that over 7 million data records get compromised each day and incidents of cyber fraud and abuse increased by 20% in the first quarter of 2020. Online criminals, hackers, and even just bored mischief-makers lurk in the shadows, waiting to rob you, commit fraud, and steal your identity.

When all data and processes of a company or industry are digitalized, cybersecurity becomes a paramount concern. The increased reliance on the internet means the company has a lot more to lose if something goes sideways [51]. The loss not only includes data loss but also loss of control of devices and assets. This is especially dangerous for critical infrastructure such as power plants, hospitals, and transportation. Given the increased risks, technical cybersecurity measures (e.g., firewalls, antivirus software, biometrics) are not enough. Regulations from the government should facilitate protection of the digital ecosystem.

3.4 Digital Ecosystem

A digital ecosystem is focusing on bringing extra value to customers by optimizing data and workflows from different internal departments, tools, systems, as well as customers, suppliers, and external partners, as defined in [52]. It should remove obstacles from the customer journey and enable every participant in the ecosystem to use state-of-the-art technologies and systems to fulfill their individual needs.

These ecosystems offer customers a unified and easy-to-use system that delivers value through a variety of services, products, and insights. This also allows the platforms to grow exponentially and outpace the normal market by using several mechanics involved [53].

The use cases we have described are just parts of the whole digital ecosystem for the electric power system. More integrations are foreseen, for example, hybrid pumped hydro and battery storage for intermittent wind power [54], smart grid [9], and a range of services to consumers. The five key characteristics of a digital ecosystem are customer-centric, data-driven, automated, global, and dynamic [53]. Starting from the digital transformation on the upstream, there is a long way to go for digital electric power ecosystem to reach its full potential.

References

1. *Electric power system from Wikipedia.* Accessed November 30, 2021, from https://en. wikipedia.org/wiki/Electric_power_system
2. Voropai, N. (2020). Electric power system transformations: a review of main prospects and challenges. *Journal Energies, 13*(21), 5639.
3. *The explorer – Green and sustainable solutions from Norway.* Accessed November 30, 2021, from https://www.theexplorer.no/stories/energy/renewable-energy-flows-through-norway/
4. *The world's most used renewable power sources.* Accessed November 30, 2021, from https://www.power-technology.com/features/featurethe-worlds-most-used-renewable-power-sources-4160168/
5. Idsø, J. (2017). Small scale hydroelectric power plants in Norway – some microeconomic and environmental considerations. *Journal Sustainability, 9,* 1117.
6. *Electricity production in energy facts Norway.* Accessed November 30, 2021, from https://energifaktanorge.no/en/norsk-energiforsyning/kraftproduksjon/#wind-power
7. *Norway – the EV capital of the world.* Accessed November 30, 2021, from https://www.visitnorway.com/plan-your-trip/getting-around/by-car/electric-cars/
8. NERL (National Renewable Energy Laboratory of the U.S. Department of Energy). (2015). *Power systems of the future – A 21st century power partnership thought leadership report.* Technical report, NREL/TP-6A20-62611.
9. Coldevin, G. H., & Sand, K. (2015). *Smart Grid in Norway: Status and Outlook.* Smartgrids, the Norwegian Smartgrid Centre.
10. Energy management system from Wikipedia. Accessed November 30, 2021, from https://en. wikipedia.org/wiki/Energy_management_system
11. Guldbrand, A., Vänskä, V., Kåsa, G., & Gregersen, J. (2016). Nordic finer time resolution. Accessed November 30, 2021.
12. Machine learning from Wikipedia. Accessed November 30, 2021, from https://en.wikipedia.org/wiki/Machine_learning
13. Industrial internet of things from Wikipedia. Accessed November 30, 2021, from https://en. wikipedia.org/wiki/Industrial_internet_of_things
14. ROI Management Consulting AG. *Measurement and evaluation of the digitization maturity levels (IoT Scan) and roadmap.* Accessed November 30, 2021, from https://www.

roi-international.com/management-consulting/competences/increased-efficiency-through-digitisation-industry-40/digitization-maturity-levels/

15. Wagenmaker, G. *DIKW pyramid DIKW hierarchy.* Accessed November 30, 2021, from https://www.goconqr.com/mindmap/15347127/chpt-1-3-dikw-pyramid-dikw-hierarchy

16. TrønderEnergi homepage. Accessed November 30, 2021, from https://tronderenergi.no/om-tronderenergi/english/about

17. Dalal, N., Mølnå, M., Herrem, M., & Røen, M. (2020). Odd Erik Gundersen: Day-ahead forecasting of losses in the distribution network. *Proceedings of the AAAI Conference on Artificial Intelligence, 34*(08), 13148–13155.

18. *What is digital transformation?* Accessed November 30, 2021, from https://www.salesforce.com/products/platform/what-is-digital-transformation/

19. Holmstrom, J. (2021). *From AI to digital transformation: The AI readiness framework.* Business Horizons.

20. Wessel, L., Baiyere, A., Ologeanu-Taddei, R., Cha, J., & Jensen, T. B. (2020). Unpacking the difference between digital transformation and IT-enabled organizational transformation. *Journal of the Association for Information Systems, Association for Information Systems.*

21. Huysman, M. (2020). Information systems research on artificial intelligence and work: A commentary on 'Robo-Apocalypse Cancelled? Reframing the Automation and Future of Work Debate'. *Journal of Information Technology.*

22. *An overview of the Nordic electricity market.* Accessed November 30, 2021, from https://www.nordicenergyregulators.org/about-nordreg/an-overview-of-the-nordic-electricity-market/

23. Khodadadi, A., Herre, L., Shinde, P., Eriksson, R., Söder, L., & Amelin, M. (2020). *Nordic balancing markets: Overview of market rules.* 17th International Conference on the European Energy Market.

24. *What does intraday trading mean?* Accessed November 30, 2021, from https://www.next-kraftwerke.com/knowledge/intraday-trading

25. *Nordic Balancing Model: Single price and single position – implementation in the Nordics, Common market design description.* Accessed November 30, 2021, from https://nordicbalancingmodel.net

26. *Condition-based maintenance vs predictive maintenance.* Accessed November 30, 2021, from https://neurospace.io/blog/2019/08/condition-based-maintenance-vs-predictive-maintenance/

27. SHOP homepage. Accessed November 30, 2021, from https://shop.sintef.energy/about/

28. Powel Nimbus. Accessed November 30, 2021, from https://powel-xpprod.enonic.cloud/se/energy-trading-optimisation/trading/powel-nimbus

29. Volue Algo Trader. Accessed November 30, 2021, from https://powel-xpprod.enonic.cloud/energy-trading-optimisation/trading/powel-algo-trader

30. Aasgård, E. K., Skjelbred, H. I., & Solbakk, F. (2016). *Comparing bidding methods for hydropower.* 5th International Workshop on Hydro Scheduling in Competitive Electricity Markets.

31. Aasgard, E. K., Naversen, C. Ø., Fodstad, M., & Skjelbred, H. I. (2018). Optimizing day-ahead bid curves in hydropower production. *Energy Systems, 9,* 257–275.

32. Matheussen, B. V., Granmo, O-C., & Sharma, J. (2019). Hydropower optimization using deep learning. In: *The 32nd International Conference on Industrial, Engineering & Other Applications of Applied Intelligent Systems.* LNAI 11606, pp. 110–122.

33. Ghenis, M. (2018). *Quantile regression, from linear models to trees to deep learning. Towards data science.*

34. Danish wind industry association homepage. *The power curve of a wind turbine.* Accessed November 30, 2021, from http://drømstørre.dk/wp-content/wind/miller/windpower%20web/en/tour/wres/pwr.htm

35. Honga, T., Pinson, P., & Fan, S. (2014). Global Energy Forecasting Competition 2012. *International Journal of Forecasting, 30,* 357–363.

36. Honga, T., Pinson, P., Fan, S., Zareipour, H., Troccoli, A., & Hyndman, R. J. (2016). Probabilistic energy forecasting: Global Energy Forecasting Competition 2014 and beyond. *International Journal of Forecasting, 32*(3), 896–913.
37. Olivas, E. S., et al. (2009). *Transfer Learning. Handbook of research on machine learning applications.* IGI Publications.
38. Brownlee, J. *How to implement Bayesian optimization from scratch in python.* Accessed June 8, 2021, from https://machinelearningmastery.com/what-is-bayesian-optimization/
39. *Predictive maintenance from Wikipedia.* Accessed November 30, 2021, from https://en.wikipedia.org/wiki/Predictive_maintenance
40. MonitorX homepage. Accessed November 30, 2021, from https://www.sintef.no/projectweb/monitorx/
41. *Azure AI guide for predictive maintenance solutions.* Accessed November 30, 2021, from https://docs.microsoft.com/en-us/azure/architecture/data-science-process/predictive-maintenance-playbook
42. Luo, Y., et al. (2018). *Multivariate time series imputation with generative adversarial networks.* Proceedings of NeurIPS.
43. Karpatne, A., et al. (2017). Theory-guided data science: A new paradigm for scientific discovery from data. *IEEE Transactions on Knowledge and Data Engineering, 29*(10), 2318–2331.
44. European Commission. (2019). Ethics guidelines for trustworthy AI. Accessed November 30, 2021, from https://bit.ly/2IjQYf6
45. *Transfer learning from Wikipedia.* https://en.wikipedia.org/wiki/Transfer_learning
46. Zhuang, F., et al. (2021). A comprehensive survey on transfer learning. In *Proceedings of the IEEE*, Vol 109, Issue 1.
47. Tan, C., et al. (2018). A survey on deep transfer learning. In *International Conference on Artificial Neural Networks* (pp. 270–279).
48. Thorstensen, H., Christian, P., & Iversen, G. (2020). *Automatic wind power forecasting as a service.* Master's thesis in Computer Science, Norwegian University of Science and Technology.
49. Norwegian Research Center for AI Innovation (NorwAI). Accessed November 30, 2021, from https://www.ntnu.edu/norwai
50. Digital Adoption Team. *Digital transformation pros & cons: Your challenges & solutions.* Accessed November 30, 2021, from https://www.digital-adoption.com/digital-transformation-pros-and-cons/
51. Lyytinen, K., Nickerson, J. V., & King, J. L. (2020). Meta-human systems = Human + Machines that learn. *Journal of Information Technology*.
52. Simplilearn. *What is digital security: Overview, types, and applications explained.* https://www.simplilearn.com/what-is-digital-security-article
53. MoreThanDigital. Accessed November 30, 2021, from https://morethandigital.info/en/what-is-a-digital-ecosystem-understanding-the-most-profitable-business-model/
54. Javed, M. S., et al. (2020). Hybrid pumped hydro and battery storage for renewable energy based power supply system. *Applied Energy, 257*, 1.

From Intention to Use to Active Use of a Mobile Application in Norwegian ETO Manufacturing

Pål Furu Kamsvåg ⓘ, Sylvi Thun ⓘ, and Joakim Klemets ⓘ

Abstract The introduction of digital technologies is starting to change the prevailing work practices at Aker Solutions' yard at Stord in Vestland county. However, in order to derive business value and attain real transformative effects of digitalization, the challenges related to implementation must be identified and addressed. In this chapter, we examine the ongoing implementation of the mobile application WeBuild, at Aker Solutions' yard at Stord. The overall goal with the application is to support more efficient work processes, reduce costs, increase organizational flexibility, and thereby ease the coming transition to "green" market segments. We use data from an extensive survey with answers from more than 500 respondents working at the yard at Stord to identify both organizational and infrastructural challenges with regard to this specific implementation. Analyses indicate that training and user involvement, functionality and usability, and technical infrastructure are important determinants which influence the active use of the WeBuild application. In more detail, our findings show that functionality adapted to the needs of the respondents' respective disciplines was the strongest predictor of active use and that poor Internet access in certain parts of the yard makes it challenging to use WeBuild and other digital solutions. Further, we discuss how Aker Solution could overcome some of these challenges and attain business value from WeBuild and other digital solutions and initiatives. WeBuild is one of the many digital initiatives in Aker Solutions. By investigating the implications of this specific implementation along several dimensions, this study sheds light on the many difficulties Norwegian companies are facing when they try to reap the benefits of digital transformation. While Aker Solutions get insights with regard to the

P. F. Kamsvåg (✉) · S. Thun
Department of Technology Management, SINTEF Digital, Trondheim, Norway
e-mail: paal.f.kamsvaag@sintef.no; sylvi.thun@sintef.no

J. Klemets
Department of Health Research, SINTEF Digital, Trondheim, Norway

Department of Computer Science, Norwegian University of Science and Technology, Trondheim, Norway
e-mail: joakim.klemets@sintef.no

P. Mikalef, E. Parmiggiani (eds.), *Digital Transformation in Norwegian Enterprises*,
https://doi.org/10.1007/978-3-031-05276-7_6

91

contextual challenges at this specific yard, one can extract important learning points that are useful in other contexts as well. Norwegian manufacturers must learn from each other to succeed with digital transformation.

1 Introduction

Digital transformation encompasses the significant changes taking place in business and society through the use of digital technologies [1]. Although the term has received a lot of attention lately, there is no clear consensus among researchers and practitioners when discussing the content of the phenomenon. However, the vast majority believe that digital transformation differs from digitization and digitalization. Digitization is usually defined as the technical process of converting analog information into digital form, while digitalization refers to enabling or improving processes by leveraging digital technologies and digitized data [2]. Digital transformation, on the other hand, could be considered as the final step in the pyramid which is dependent on digitization and digitalization as sub-levels. Digital transformation, in a business perspective, is about using digital technology to transform the company's services into something significantly better. Thus, digital transformation can be regarded as a redesign of the business at all levels [3].

In this chapter, we examine the ongoing implementation of the mobile application WeBuild, at Aker Solutions' (Akso) yard at Stord. WeBuild is one of the many digital initiatives in Akso and an important part of the company's digital transformation vision. While it could be argued that WeBuild as a stand-alone project is not enough to be classified as digital transformation, the expected outcomes of adopting the application are definitely an important part of the digital transformation process. The following definition of digital transformation from Vial [4] substantiates our consideration that the WeBuild application could be regarded as part of an overarching digital transformation process: "a process that aims to improve an entity by triggering significant changes to its properties through combinations of information, computing, communication, and connectivity technologies." The overall goal with the WeBuild application is to support more efficient work processes, reduce costs, and increase organizational flexibility and by that ease the transition to "green" market segments for Akso. These outcomes, if they are achieved, could be considered as "significant changes" and thereby fulfill the criteria in Vial's definition. However, what is meant by significant change is subjective and up for discussion. We will not be pursuing this matter any further but conclude that WeBuild is part of the comprehensive process of digitally transforming the yards of Akso.

The opportunities and potential gains from digital technologies in an industrial context are well described in the Industry 4.0 literature, and a more sophisticated human-machine interaction is even the main vision and goal in the human-centric approach of *Operator 4.0* [5, 6]. While the opportunities and visions are thoroughly discussed in this literature, there are hitherto little empirical research about the perceived benefits from the use of digital solutions in an industrial environment.

Furthermore, there is limited research that looks at the factors that influence the active use of digital technologies, such as mobile applications and tablets. We believe there is a strong need for more empirical research about these topics, so that companies and all relevant stakeholders increase their understanding and can develop strategies to overcome the many barriers they encounter with regard to technology adoption. Thus, this chapter contributes to research literature on digital transformation with empirical findings on actual use of digital solutions, its influencing factors and perceived benefits, and not only the intention to use.

We rely on data from an extensive survey with answers from more than 500 respondents working at the yard at Stord. By investigating this implementation along several dimensions, this study sheds light on the opportunities that come with an extensive mobile application in an industrial setting. We further identify and discuss some of the most prominent challenges big companies are facing when they try to reap the benefits of digital technologies. Based on the data material we discuss organizational and infrastructural challenges with regard to the implementation of a mobile application through the lens of *technology acceptance literature*. Further, we discuss how Akso can overcome some of these challenges and attain real business value from this mobile application. Our ambition is to uncover the factors that influence the active use of WeBuild and identify the perceived benefits of using the application. Hence, our two main research questions are as follows:

- *RQ1:* Which factors influence the active use of a mobile application in a Norwegian ETO-manufacturing company?
- *RQ2:* What are the perceived benefits of using a mobile application in a Norwegian ETO-manufacturing company?

2   Theoretical Background

To reap the benefits from digital solutions and succeed with digital transformation, you naturally need active use of the technology that is being implemented. This might sound trivial, but it is a real challenge which is often underestimated. *Technology acceptance* is a subject area that is useful for understanding the underlying factors which affect both acceptance of technology and usage. We use the technology acceptance model (TAM) and the *unified theory of acceptance and use of technology* (UTAUT) as theoretical starting points for our analysis. The insights from these frameworks/models are important to bear in mind regarding digital transformation. That is because real transformative change requires more than just technology; it requires changed practices and behavior from humans. To derive real transformative effects from digital technology, you must understand which factors affect use and acceptance.

2.1   Technology Acceptance

Technology acceptance has been studied for decades within several research fields and has become increasingly emphasized with the emergence of new digital tools and devices. One of the most prominent and widely used models is the technology acceptance model (TAM) developed by Davis [7]. The intention to use technology is, according to TAM, influenced by two main factors (belief constructs): perceived usefulness and perceived ease of use. Perceived usefulness is defined as "the degree to which a person believes that using a particular system would enhance his or her job performance." And perceived ease of use is defined as "the degree to which a person believes that using a particular system would be free from effort" [7].

Over the years, TAM has been rigorously studied and expanded. Mathieson et al. [8] proposed a third construct, *perceived resources*, and defined this construct as "the extent to which an individual believes that he or she has the personal and organizational resources needed to use an information system." This construct emphasizes the perceptions of the environment where implementation takes place and the characteristics of the technology itself, thus contributing to a better understanding of technology acceptance [8].

A major upgrade of TAM came with the *unified theory of acceptance and use of technology* (UTAUT), which was an attempt to synthesize existing technology acceptance models and theories [9]. UTAUT holds that there are four key constructs that could explain user intention and behavior: (1) performance expectancy, the notion that the technology will contribute to increased job performance; (2) effort expectancy, the degree of "ease of use"; (3) social influence, the perception of the individual that he/she should use the technology as a result of the influence from important stakeholders; and (4) facilitating conditions, the extent to which a person experiences that the organization facilitates the use of the technology [9]. The first three constructs are direct determinants of usage intention and behavior, while the fourth is a direct determinant of user behavior. Further, UTAUT includes four intermediate variables, age, gender, experience, and voluntariness of use, that moderate the impact of the four key constructs [9]. In the following, we present previous research findings relevant for UTAUT four constructs.

Performance expectancy is derived from the notion that the technology will contribute to increased job performance. In manufacturing and an industrial environment, digital applications can be used for visualization purposes and increase the perceptibility of operations and performance status. Furthermore, the end users might achieve a better understanding of the overall production processes and increased situational awareness, which makes it easier to make real-time decisions [10, 11].

One study within construction found a positive relationship between the use of mobile applications and the improvement of overall productivity, with perceived benefits such as "more efficient management of checklists and documentation" and "better performance monitoring and evaluation" [12]. Findings from a study conducted in the Norwegian manufacturing context revealed that production managers tend to report higher satisfactions with digital technologies being introduced compared with the operators, suggesting that ICT systems and digital solutions often are not implemented or developed with the operator in mind [13]. The last point is of great importance in this setting as well. It is of course crucial that the technology is adapted to the needs of the users.

In a study investigating different aspects of the UTAUT model in a hospital context, some performance expectancy measures were found to affect intention to use a mobile application [14]. The results showed that the use of the application could speed up the administration process and also that employees could save time by applying the solution. These perceived benefits were associated with the intention to use [14].

Effort expectancy, or the degree of "ease of use," could be defined as to which extent a person believes that using a particular system is effortless [7]. In one study, researchers found that variables relevant to effort expectancy, the "ease of use" and the level of effort a user thinks a specific task will require, had an influence on intention to use. If users experience that the use of an application is easy to use and a satisfaction in using it, the intention to use the application will also increase significantly [14].

Social influence is the perception of the individual that he/she should use the technology because of the influence from important stakeholders. The way companies and organizations convey information about technological changes is critical for implementation success and an example of social influence from important stakeholders. To act as an influencing factor, research has indicated that the communication should be aligned with the inherent culture and tailored to the audience [15]. Ideally, communication should take place in the initial phases of the implementation, or even during the development process or selection decision (purchase of off-the-shelf technology). Cross-communication is crucial early in the planning process to set a joint objective for harmonization, coherence, and collaboration for all relevant stakeholders [16]. Thun et al. [17] found that by communicating user needs, practicing flexible involvement of stakeholders, and transparency of the purpose among others enabled the development and implementation process of digital applications.

Facilitating conditions refers to the extent to which a person experiences that the organization facilitates the use of the technology. Training and IT infrastructure are examples of how an organization can facilitate the use of technology. Research shows that the lack of digital skills, and the consecutive need for training, is one of the most significant barriers to the implementation of new technologies [18]. Training could be considered a strategic investment that strengthens the internal resources of an organization by addressing employees' propensity for use and attitude toward current and future technological changes [15]. Training obviously facilitates learning (the users learn to use a new technology), but it could also affect employee perceptions and attitudes about the new technology [19]. Hence, training is an important tool to overcome resistance to change and to increase implementation effectiveness. According to Escobar-Rodriguez and Bartual-Sopena [20], training should have a clear objective, and the mechanism of how it is supposed to enhance task performance and reduce the perception of risk/threats should be clarified. The experience of easiness to learn the app will also be related to the intention to use a mobile application or not [14]. Further, they found that how fast the speed of the application was affected intention to use.

According to Gartner [21], IT infrastructure refers to the IT components, such as the composite hardware, software, network resources, and services, which constitute the foundation of an enterprise IT environment. The physical systems such as hardware, storage, any kind of routers/switches, and even the building itself are generally regarded as the primary components of an IT infrastructure, though networks and software are also important. In addition to these components, there is usually a need for cybersecurity and skills as well.

In one study, researchers used the UTAUT framework to investigate the factors that influence the intention to use mobile applications for learning at universities (with a considerable focus on physical infrastructure). The findings indicated that factors such as device connectivity, device memory, device compatibility, device performance, network coverage, and network speed all had significant and positive influence on the users' intention to use the mobile application [17]. In particular, network speed and device performance were important factors where the influence was very high and noticeably significant.

While most of the research articles we have cited were conducted in a different context than an industrial environment, the findings are relevant as it exemplifies different findings of the four constructs of UTAUT that to a large degree can be said to be transferable and generic. Furthermore, all the articles investigate which determinants affect the intention to use the technology (mainly mobile applications) from the perspective of the end user. As intention to use has a positive association with actual use, the elaborated findings together with UTAUT present a sound theoretical framework relevant when contributing with knowledge about factors that influence active use of WeBuild and perceived benefits of using this mobile application.

3   Method

3.1   Research Context

3.1.1   Digital Transformation at Aker Solution

Aker Solutions' yard at Stord (abbreviated to Akso) is a well-known supplier within the oil and gas industry in Norway. With its approximately 2800 employees and annual results of several hundreds of millions of euros, the company is considered a major competitor both domestically and in the global market. Akso is considered an engineer-to-order manufacturer (ETO) who both plans and executes engineering, procurement, construction, and installation projects. These projects are usually organized as contracting agreements between customer and supplier, where Akso as a contractor/supplier rely on subcontracting partners for various purposes.

Akso has over the years developed and utilized digital tools in order to support their employees and derive efficiency gains. As a result of the latest advances in fields such as artificial intelligence/machine learning, big data analytics, digital support systems for the employees (from operator level to management), and more, *digitalization* has received even more attention than before. As part of their digital transformation vision, Akso has developed a digitalization program with a roadmap consisting of more than 25 projects which is either unfolding or planned for the future [22]. The overall ambition with this program is to increase efficiency and effectiveness of business operations, provide better technological support for their employees, and improve organizational flexibility.

Akso is currently expanding their product portfolio by entering "green" market segments and is looking for ways to improve their organizational flexibility in that regard. By organizational flexibility, we mean the organization's ability to handle continuous shifts between new growth segments (e.g., offshore wind, recycling, and orders from land-based industry) and traditional product areas within the oil and gas industry. Digital tools are considered as important means to increase the organizational flexibility and tackle the new and even more challenging everyday life at the yard, with more projects of different sizes and varied content which run in parallel.

3.1.2   The WeBuild Case: Purpose and Ambitions

WeBuild is a mobile application that aims to make daily work more efficient for all foremen and operators at Aker Solutions' shipyards in Norway. The overall goal with the application is to support more efficient work processes, reduce costs, increase organizational flexibility, and thereby ease the ongoing transition to "green" market segments for Akso. More specifically, the application is supposed to make it faster and easier to get an overview of who is at work, provide important information to the relevant audience, delegate tasks for managers and foremen, retrieve working drawings, provide the opportunity to report completed work, and reduce the overall time spent on several manual tasks.

WeBuild allows for the distribution of work packages (work orders) with all necessary information and job descriptions. The packages include working drawings, instructions, material lists, and time estimates. Both foremen and operators receive this information on their smartphones (illustrated with the screenshots below):

Traditionally, the work packages have been distributed through team leaders (foremen) and kept in hard copy in folders. This manual and analog procedure have made it time-consuming to do updates and perform revision controls [22]. With WeBuild, the foremen and operators can report progress on the project (s) they work on via their personal smartphone funded by Akso, ensuring that all relevant stakeholders are updated in real time preventing both inertia and inaccuracies. Akso believes this digital solution will lead to less time spent on reporting and status updates by foremen, thus freeing up time for preparation and facilitation of the job of the operator and contributing to better information sharing between shifts. This in turn could make the operators more efficient. Further, when more information is made available among the entire workforce via WeBuild, more decision-making and responsibility can be transferred directly to the operators. As a result, some of the layers of the value chain could potentially be removed and provide significant efficiency gains.

Over time, the application will be expanded with a number of new features, such as 3D models of specific work tasks, an overview of available tools located nearby, and visualizations of the competences among the employees. All the aforementioned opportunities and potential gains from WeBuild make the application a key component of the digital transformation process that is taking place at Akso's yards (and the yard at Stord which is being investigated in this study).

3.1.3 Development and Implementation Strategy

The WeBuild application development was led by the IT department at Akso, although most of the engineering resources were hired consultants. As part of the project, the development approach underwent a major transition as the previous waterfall method was replaced with a more agile and user-centered approach. Hence, a group of operators and foremen (i.e., end users) from a few selected teams were invited to participate in the development process as super-users, inviting them to provide insight and feedback to the system design.

The super-users were involved throughout the development process. In the initial phase, a context study was conducted, in which a multidisciplinary user experience (UX) team carried out observations and interviews at the yard to elicit system functionality requirements. After co-creation sessions with end users and the project team, the final use cases for the WeBuild application were decided. Thereafter, the super-users were also involved in providing feedback on user interface prototypes. Also, before new functionality is released to all end users, a system acceptance test was carried out by the super-users. This involved installing and testing the new version of the application for a few days to uncover inaccuracies (i.e., software bugs).

The implementation strategy selected to ensure that end users would accept and adopt the new application into their daily work also leveraged a lot on the super-users. Although initial plans included various training and dissemination activities to support the implementation process, these were discarded in favor of using available resources to realize application functionality. Therefore, the super-users participating in the development process were to a large extent involved in training and promoting WeBuild to their fellow colleagues [23].

3.2 Research Design

3.2.1 Procedure and Participants

A single case study was chosen as method to understand more about the complex nature of digital transformation in a large ETO manufacturing company located in Norway. Field-based studies can contribute with rich data and deep insights from actual work practices. Case studies enable researchers to generate deeper understanding of the phenomenon within its real-world context as well as new knowledge and theory [24, 25]. The case company was selected from an ongoing 4-year research project that started in 2020 with the aim to develop a competitive organizational flexibility.

To answer among others the research question in this chapter, a large digital survey was conducted January 2021. The survey covered different themes and contained different question types, both validated and new indexes, and the part of the questionnaire covering WeBuild experiences also contained open-ended questions. 526 employees working in the production area of the yard participated, and a response rate at 61% was achieved. The sample consist of 479 males and 47 females. Participants had different work roles, among others construction managers (0.8%), discipline managers (4.9%), foremen (16.7%), qualified operators (59.3%), and apprentices (2.3%). The participants came from eight different departments. Since this chapter tries to highlight influencing factors of technology adoption and, in this case, active use of WeBuild, some of the participants were excluded. The relevant sample size is therefore 189, and approximately 80% of those participants belong to two of the eight departments. The majority of the active WeBuild users work as qualified operators (78%).

All participants received a written information letter about the purpose of the survey, how data would be used and stored. Furthermore, it was highlighted that participation in the study was voluntary and that participants would be anonymous. A signed informed consent form was required before participation. The Norwegian Social Science Data Service has approved the study.

3.2.2 Measures

Participants answering "yes" at the question "Have you used WeBuild?" received a question whether they use WeBuild actively during their workday. *Active WeBuild users* vs. inactive WeBuild users was as a result measured by the yes/no question: Do you actively use WeBuild during your workday? *Training* was measured with a one-item yes/no question: Have you received training in use of the WeBuild-app? *Wireless connectivity* was measured by one item "WeBuild delays my progress due to poor Internet access" at a 5-point Likert scale with (1) = totally disagree to (5) = totally agree. Influence of *functionality* was measured by the one-item question "My department has had the opportunity to influence the functionality of the WeBuild application," with three response categories, yes, no, and I do not know, and "WeBuild has functionality that is well adapted to my discipline's need" is measured at a Likert scale (1) strongly disagree to (5) strongly agree.

Other relevant influencing factors were "WeBuild is easy to use" and "WeBuild is a tool that gives me support in my work," all measured at a Likert scale (1) strongly disagree to (5) strongly agree. *Benefits of WeBuild use* was measured with different items at a Likert scale (1) to a very small extent to (5) to a very large extent. For instance, "To what extend have work packages via WeBuild released more time for your core task? To what extend have work packages via WeBuild ensured more efficient work processes? To what extend have work packages via WeBuild improved team collaborations?" We also had questions measuring experience with WeBuild and its relation to the work process of number of deliverables. For instance, "WeBuild gives me more up-to-date and accurate information compared to information on paper" and "I get to complete more deliverables/tasks using WeBuild than before (without WeBuild)" measured with Likert scale (1) totally disagree to (5) totally agree.

3.3 Statistical Analysis

Independent t-test (two-tailed) was used to assess mean differences in between active WeBuild users and non-active WeBuild users. Hedges' g provides a measure of effect size where there are different sample sizes. Chi-square tests were used to analyze whether there is an association between active WeBuild use and training and active WeBuild use and influence of functionality. Logistic regression analysis was conducted to test the predictor variables' influence on the categorical dependent variable, active WeBuild use. There was no problem with multicollinearity between the tested variables. Tolerance and VIF values were good. Linearity of the logit was also tested, and the assumption was met. All analysis was performed using IBM SPSS Statistics version 27.

4 Results

4.1 Descriptive Statistics

The total amount of people that have tried the WeBuild application were 218 of the 526 participants in the survey. 160 of those 218 reported "Yes," while 58 reported "Yes, but no longer" on the question "Have you used WeBuild?" Those 160 answering "yes" received the question "Do you actively use WeBuild during your workday?" 82 reported "yes" (active group) and 78 "no" (inactive group); however, we had to make some small adjustment in the survey resulting in that the inactive group in some of the analysis has 57 users.

67.1% of active WeBuild users have received training, and 75.4% active WeBuild users have got the chance to influence the functionality of the WeBuild application. 32.9% of inactive WeBuild uses have received training, and 24.6% of the inactive group have got the chance to influence the functionality of the WeBuild application.

4.2 Influencing Factors and Benefits of Use

Among the participants that have tried to use the WeBuild application, we see that 54.5% partly agree/totally agree that the application is easy to use, 60.3% agree/totally agree that it has a functionality that is well adapted to the discipline's needs, and 60.4% answer partly agree/totally agree that it is a tool supporting their work. Further we were interested to see whether or not there were some differences in these variables among the active versus inactive WeBuild users and among those received training or not.

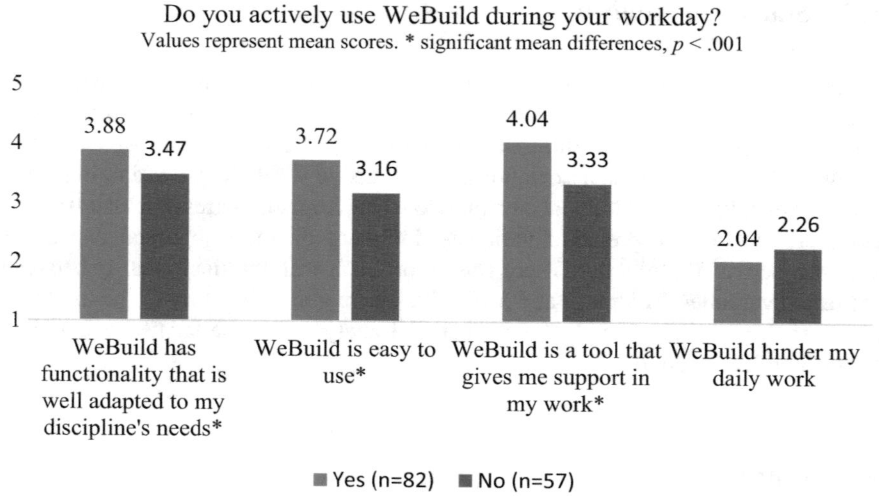

Do you actively use WeBuild during your workday?
Values represent mean scores. * significant mean differences, $p < .001$

Fig. 1 Difference between the active WeBuild use and inactive WeBuild use and four influencing factors

Among the influencing factors tested, some significant mean differences were found between the active WeBuild users compared to inactive WeBuild users. On allegations regarding functionality fit and usability, the results show higher averages for active users than inactive users (Fig. 1). On the following allegations, we found differences among active users and inactive users that were statistically significant: WeBuild has functionality that is well adapted to my discipline's needs $t(137) = 3.27, p < .001$, [95% CI (.16–.65)], Hedges' $g = .56$; WeBuild is easy to use $t(137) = 3.48, p < .001$, [95% CI (.23–.89)], Hedges' $g = .57$; and WeBuild is a tool that gives me support in my work $t(137) = 4.63, p < .001$, [95% CI (.40–1)], Hedges' $g = .77$. The value of Hedges' g for the three significant differences represents strong effect sizes.

Among the participants who have used WeBuild, it is interesting to test whether training has an effect. Among those 139 answering "Yes" on the question whether they have tried and used WeBuild, 59% of the participants have received training and 48.8% not. Among the 58 participants answering "Yes, but no longer," 46% have received training, and 54% have not received training. We found no significant mean differences on the group receiving training compared to those not receiving training on the four influencing factors same as those presented in Fig. 1. But as stated in RQ1, we are interested to see whether training can act as an influencing factor for daily and active use of WeBuild during their workday.

According to a crosstab, 67.1% of the active users have received training. In line with our results obtained from chi-square analysis, training affects active use. There was a significant association between training or not and whether the persons have a daily active use of the WeBuild application $\chi^2 (1) = 5.40, p < .05$. Based on odds ratio (OR), the odds of active use were 2.27 times higher if received training than

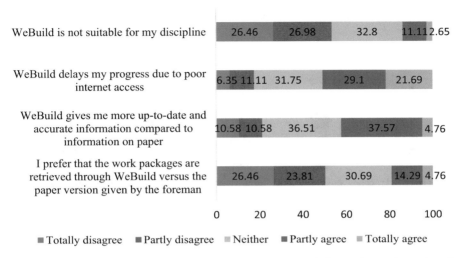

Fig. 2 Frequencies of some experience with WeBuild and its relation to the work process of number of deliverables among 189 participants who have tried WeBuild

not. Further, we found that 75.4% of the active users have received the chance of influencing the functionality of the WeBuild application, and results of the chi-square analysis indicate that being involved by getting the chance to influence functionality also affects active use of WeBuild $\chi^2(1) = 8.50, p < .01$. Based on OR, the odds of active use were 3.74 times higher when the department had been involved and got the chance to influence the functionality of the application.

50.80% reported partly/totally agree that WeBuild delays progress because of poor Internet access (wireless connectivity) (Fig. 2). Further, the figure shows that 42.33% partly/totally agree that WeBuild gives more up-to-date and accurate information compared to information on paper; however, only 19.05% partly/totally agree to the fact that they prefer their work packages are handed out through WeBuild instead of the paper version by the foreman.

Logistic regression was used to test the final hypothesis stating that training and suited functionality, together with stable Internet access (wireless connectivity), would predict active and daily use (Table 1). The independent variables explain

Table 1 Logistic regression of the predictive value of training, functionality, and Internet access on the dependent variable active WeBuild use

Variable	b(SE)	Wald	OR [Exp (b)]	95% CI for OR
Constant	−5.05(1.31)			
1. Training	.89*(.38)	5.48	2.45	[1.16–5.17]
2. Functionality well adapted to the discipline's need	.94**(.27)	12.19	2.57	[1.51–4.36]
3. Wireless connectivity	.42*(.17)	6.15	1.52	[1.09–2.12]

Note: *$p < .001$, **$p < .05$. Model $\chi^2(3) = 23.33, p < .001$. −2log likelihood 164.84*
Cox & Snell's $R^2 = .16$, Nagelkerke's $R^2 = .21$

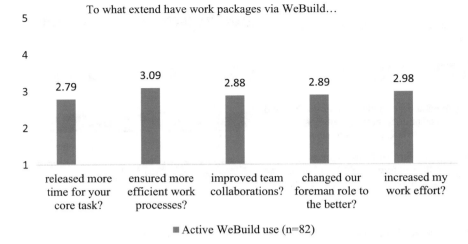

Fig. 3 Mean of five experienced benefits of WeBuild among active WeBuild users: 1, to a very small extent, to 5, to a very large extent

16–21% of the variance of active WeBuild use and the model is significant. All independent variables significantly contributed; however, functionality was the strongest predictor. The OR of 2.57 indicates that if the experience of *functionality is well adapted to the discipline's need* increase, 2.57 greater chance of active use would occur.

Figure 3 illustrates some of the benefits the participants experience when receiving their work packages via the application. For instance, the participants have to some degree experienced that WeBuild has ensured more efficient work processes ($M = 3.09$). The results indicate that those participants using WeBuild actively experience different positive effects, but the mean scores were low.

5 Discussion

From the classical theories of technology acceptance, such as TAM, we know that *perceived usefulness* and *perceived ease of use* are important determinants that influence the intention to use the technology [7]. From UTAUT, the four constructs that could explain user intention and behavior are performance expectancy, effort expectancy, social influence, and facilitating conditions. We used these determinants as our starting point when we analyzed the data with respect to functionality and usability.

5.1 Training and User Involvement

Training is not only important for the end users of the technology to understand the user interface and functionality of the technology; it can also have a positive impact on engagement and perceived usefulness [19]. Moreover, implementing training along with new software and IT technologies can help alleviate frustrations during the transition process, making adoption easier and less painful [26]. An interesting finding in our study is that users who have received training and those who have not seem to consider the functionality of the application as equally intuitive. Nevertheless, those who have received training use WeBuild more frequently during work than the other group. This may indicate that training has served as an internal promotion mechanism during implementation and perhaps contributed to more commitment and a better understanding of the overall objectives. This finding may also indicate that the user interface in WeBuild is relatively easy to understand and that there are other factors that are more important in terms of explaining active use. Regardless, the management of Akso believes that training is absolutely essential for successful implementation and has realized that the training process has not been sufficient so far. Accordingly, they are currently working on developing a better training program consisting of an online course with video lectures that will be available for all employees and good follow-up routines. During the training phase, the management will also have the opportunity to explain how WeBuild is part of the process of digitally transforming the business operations, by producing relatively large changes in terms of work processes and also contributing to increased organizational flexibility that makes it easier to enter new market segments. Such dissemination of information is particularly important in large and complex organizations with context-dependent work routines in the subdivisions and where the employees have been working in almost the same way for decades.

Companies are often in a challenging trade-off situation when trying to develop and adopt new technology. On the one hand, they have to emphasize the functionality needs and technical requirements in order to satisfy the demands of the end users. On the other hand, they must make sure they have financial means and capacity to develop and implement a good training program to succeed with adoption. This situation can be very difficult for companies to handle as they usually have limited resources. As a consequence, functionality and technological requirements often end up being prioritized, while training is somewhat neglected or "set aside for later."

In conversations with project managers in Akso, it became clear that functionality and technical requirements were prioritized as "must-win battles" regarding the WeBuild project. In many ways, this approach is understandable as the application must work as intended and respond to the needs of the end users. However, by prioritizing development and functionality, less resources were unfortunately allocated to training and follow-up procedures. Akso managed nevertheless to create some engagement among some of the employees, and the figures show that a relatively large proportion of employees use the application in the departments where it has been introduced. Particularly, super-users that were involved during the development phase have been positive toward the application. The super-users have also been central in the dissemination of WeBuild as well as in training their fellow colleagues [23].

Hence, the results indicate that better and more thorough training is needed to reach out to the early and late majority and turn them into active users. That being said, adoption of a new technology in this order of magnitude usually takes time—it requires significant changes in work practices and routines and even a shift of mentality. It reminds us that digital transformation should be thought of as a marathon, not a sprint. When planning for change, we therefore encourage practitioners to design a process and timeline with sufficient resources. This could include allocating enough time for training, preparing a timeline for change of work practices, and engaging ambassadors/change-agents ("super-users"). Further, the process needs to be continually evaluated so that it is possible to make adjustments during the period of establishing new work practices and routines.

5.2　Functionality Fit and Usability

As described in the results section, 75.4% of the active users had the opportunity to influence the functionality of the WeBuild application, and the OR told us that active use was 3.74 times higher when the department had been involved and got the chance to influence the functionality of the application. From the logistic regression analysis in Table 1, we found that functionality adapted to the needs of the respondents' respective disciplines was the strongest predictor of active use. All these findings show that functionality is a very important factor in explaining the active use of WeBuild.

The results from the survey indicate that the respondents find WeBuild relatively easy to use and that the functionality of the application is largely adapted to the different disciplines at the yard. Nevertheless, we have uncovered some interesting contradictions in the data material. For instance, a relatively large proportion of the respondents believe that WeBuild gives them more updated and correct information compared to information received on traditional paper sheets. At the same time, and slightly contradicting with the previous finding, more than half of the respondents still want to receive their work packages manually from foremen in paper format. This finding can be interpreted in several ways. It may indicate that some parts of the application's functionality are considered better than others or that receiving work packages digitally is perceived as little useful and practical by the users. From Fig. 3, we see that the active users of WeBuild experience different positive effects with regard to receiving work packages from the application. However, the mean scores are quite low which are telling us that the perceived benefits are somewhat limited when it comes to this functionality. Further, several respondents said in the section with open-ended questions that the working drawings in particular are better suited for paper format, because of limitations regarding size and readability of the digital representations (images) on their personal smartphones. This finding is further supported by information retrieved from interviews with project participants conducted in advance of the survey [21]. Larger screens (e.g., tablets) could have been a potential solution to this problem, but it seems rather unrealistic that Akso would invest in personal tablets for the time being, especially as they quite recently bought personal smartphones to their entire workforce.

Regarding the challenges described above, we believe it is important to emphasize the following point: it naturally takes time to change people's habits and work practices. The operators at Akso have been handed their work packages from the foremen for decades; thus, this procedure is incorporated into their daily routine. In a transition phase from an analog to a digital procedure, it may be appropriate to allow for a coexistence between new and old tools/routines. This could make the operation less vulnerable to glitches in the digital solution (WeBuild) and prevent potential interruptions in production [22].

While some of the changes in work practices that the WeBuild application entail are quite easy to achieve, others are much more challenging. The example with "the digitalization of work packages" shows that transforming work practices by utilizing digital technologies often requires significant efforts and some patience from project managers and the organization as such. Measures of effectiveness and the constant need to deliver business profit can act as a barrier to both the development and the implementation of digital tools [22]. In some digital projects, it is difficult to show the instant effect or the return of investment because new work practices need to be in place before it can be documented to increase productivity and efficiency. Sometimes, patience for long-term effects rather than shutting down initiatives with lack of short-term effects is a better organizational practice.

5.3 IT Infrastructure: A Neglected Necessity in Digital Transformation?

Digital technologies and a mobile application such as WeBuild depend on proper IT infrastructure to work optimally and as intended. Slow wireless download/upload speeds, instability, software freezes, and delayed systems reactions are common sources of annoyance and key barriers for implementation of ICT [17]. We do not discuss how all of the components of IT infrastructure are affecting the implementation of WeBuild. However, we emphasize the basic infrastructural need of wireless connectivity and explain why this particular need may cause challenges at Akso's yards.

Within the construct of *facilitating conditions* in the UTAUT framework, you find the sub-level of technical infrastructure (which IT infrastructure is part of) and that this is a direct determinant of user behavior. Our findings suggest that poor Internet access in certain parts of the yard makes it challenging to use WeBuild and other digital solutions relying on Internet access. In Fig. 2, we see that more than

50% of the users of WeBuild report that their progress is delayed due to poor Internet access, and in the section with open-ended questions, a large proportion of the respondents claimed that poor Internet access was a "major issue at several locations at the yard and caused the application to work very slowly." In addition, several of the respondents have stated that the mobile data that Akso pays for is nowhere near sufficient if the intention is that this data should be used to execute tasks via WeBuild and other digital solutions. Thus, many of the employees believe that the wireless connectivity must be improved at the yard and that end users must be provided with more mobile data.

The management of Akso is aware of this challenge and takes it seriously. They hope to solve some of the challenges associated with poor Internet access by installing more and better routers and other equipment in some of the exposed areas. However, one may have to reckon that parts of the yard will have slightly poorer Internet access than others and thus influence the use of WeBuild and other digital technologies. For instance, ensuring good Internet access in the department of prefabrication can be easier than doing it in some places at the department of construction, for example, inside the massive concrete structures that form the foundation of oil platforms. It is important to remember that a yard of this size is quite different from a traditional factory in manufacturing and that it may be more problematic to put in place the necessary IT infrastructure in this particular industrial environment.

It is beyond dispute that poor Internet access and issues related to IT infrastructure can have a negative impact on the intention to use WeBuild and other digital technologies. Hence, when implementing the mobile application in more departments, Akso should emphasize the challenges related to wireless connectivity and do their best to solve them. Therefore, we highlight the importance of involving those managing the underlying IT infrastructure early in the design and development process. This is important to ensure that the underlying network is able to support quality of experience (QoE) requirements [27]. Resources for expanding network capabilities need to be budgeted. And, if discovered that wireless connectivity is not feasible in certain locations or environments, the system needs to adopt different coping strategies and techniques to be able to still adhere to user expectations.

6 Conclusion

Our research shows that training and user involvement, functionality and usability, and technical infrastructure (IT infrastructure) are important determinants which influence the active use of the WeBuild application. The findings are indicating that the user interface in WeBuild is relatively easy to understand, which may indicate that training has served as an internal promotion mechanism during implementation and perhaps contributed to more commitment. Thus, the importance of adequate training and follow-up procedures cannot be overstated. Furthermore, our findings suggest that poor Internet access in certain parts of the yard makes it challenging to use WeBuild and other digital solutions. Poor Internet connection will naturally cause the application to run slower, which in turn becomes an annoyance to the end user and have negative consequences for the intention to use. Moreover, the mobile data that Akso pays for is nowhere near sufficient according to many respondents. This is a challenge that is important to investigate further as the application runs on 4G. With regard to functionality, our findings show that functionality adapted to the needs of the respondents' respective disciplines was the strongest predictor of active use. The vast majority of the respondents find the functionality sufficient and that WeBuild is useful for many purposes. However, for some of the procedures/tasks that have been digitalized through WeBuild, a large proportion of the employees prefer the old way of doing things. For instance, more than half of the respondents still want to receive their work packages manually from foremen in paper format. This tells us that digitalization is not necessarily suitable for all work processes and that companies should think about this in advance. Regarding receiving work packages digitally via WeBuild, we believe that this will gradually become part of the employees' routine. However, companies should recognize that digital transformation requires a great deal of effort and time, as it implies to change employee's habits and work practices. TAM and UTAUT can be used as practical tools and give guidance to the organization about where the challenges are. For instance, it is possible to conduct surveys which are built upon this literature and ascertain the perceived usefulness, perceived ease of use, or other factors (constructs). The findings can be used to evaluate the organizations' overall attitude toward the technology and as a basis to carry out targeted measures to make improvements. However, these theories do not tell us how to ensure use of digital technology, establish new work practices, and make other changes that transform the organization. Future research should therefore give more attention toward the implementation of digital tools and how organizations should work to succeed with implementation processes. There is also a need for a more thorough understanding of how digital transformation is aligned with the establishment of new work practices.

References

1. Majchrzak, A., Markus, M. L., & Wareham, J. (2016). Designing for digital transformation: Lessons for information systems research from the study of ICT and societal challenges. *MIS Quarterly, 40*(2), 267–277.
2. Gobble, M. M. (2018). Digitalization, digitization, and innovation. *Research-Technology Management, 61*(4), 56–59.
3. Nambisan, S., Wright, M., & Feldman, M. (2019). The digital transformation of innovation and entrepreneurship: Progress, challenges and key themes. *Research Policy, 48*(8), 103773.
4. Vial, G. (2019). Understanding digital transformation: A review and a research agenda. *The Journal of Strategic Information Systems, 28*(2), 118–144.
5. Romero, D., et al. (2016). *Towards an operator 4.0 typology: A human-centric perspective on the fourth industrial revolution technologies.* Proceedings of the international conference on computers and industrial engineering (CIE46), Tianjin, China.

6. Hermann, M., Pentek, T., & Otto, B. (2016). Design principles for industrie 4.0 scenarios. In *2016 49th Hawaii international conference on system sciences (HICSS)*. IEEE.
7. Davis, F. D., Bagozzi, R. P., & Warshaw, P. R. (1989). User acceptance of computer technology: A comparison of two theoretical models. *Management Science, 35*(8), 982–1003.
8. Mathieson, K., Peacock, E., & Chin, W. W. (2001). Extending the technology acceptance model: The influence of perceived user resources. *ACM SIGMIS Database: The DATABASE for Advances in Information Systems, 32*(3), 86–112.
9. Venkatesh, V., et al. (2003). User acceptance of information technology: Toward a unified view. *MIS Quarterly*, 425–478.
10. Alexopoulos, K., et al. (2018). An industrial Internet of things based platform for context-aware information services in manufacturing. *International Journal of Computer Integrated Manufacturing, 31*(11), 1111–1123.
11. Landmark, A. D., et al. (2019). Situation awareness for effective production control. In *IFIP International Conference on Advances in Production Management Systems*. Springer.
12. Liu, T., et al. (2017). The perceived benefits of apps by construction professionals in New Zealand. *Buildings, 7*(4), 111.
13. Thun, S., et al. (2019). Industry 4.0: Whose revolution? The digitalization of manufacturing work processes. *Nordic Journal of Working Life Studies*.
14. Al Aufa, B., et al. (2020). An application of the Unified Theory of Acceptance and Use of Technology (UTAUT) model for understanding patient perceptions on using hospital mobile application. *Enfermería Clínica, 30*, 110–113.
15. Saghafian, M., Laumann, K., & Skogstad, M. R. (2021). Stagewise overview of issues influencing organizational technology adoption and use. *Frontiers in Psychology, 12*, 654.
16. Kierkegaard, P. (2015). Interoperability after deployment: Persistent challenges and regional strategies in Denmark. *International Journal for Quality in Health Care, 27*(2), 147–153.
17. Alghazi, S. S., et al. (2021). For sustainable application of mobile learning: An extended UTAUT model to examine the effect of technical factors on the usage of mobile devices as a learning tool. *Sustainability, 13*(4), 1856.
18. Molino, M., Cortese, C. G., & Ghislieri, C. (2020). The promotion of technology acceptance and work engagement in industry 4.0: From personal resources to information and training. *International Journal of Environmental Research and Public Health, 17*(7), 2438.
19. Marler, J. H., Liang, X., & Dulebohn, J. H. (2006). Training and effective employee information technology use. *Journal of Management, 32*(5), 721–743.
20. Escobar-Rodríguez, T., & Bartual-Sopena, L. (2015). Impact of cultural factors on attitude toward using ERP systems in public hospitals. *Revista de Contabilidad, 18*(2), 127–137.
21. Gartner Inc. *Gartner Glossary*. Undated. https://www.gartner.com/en/information-technology/glossary/it-infrastructure.
22. Thun, S., Bakås, O., & Storholmen, T. C. B. (2021). Development and implementation processes of digitalization in engineer-to-order manufacturing: Enablers and barriers. *AI & SOCIETY*, 1–19.
23. Klemets, J., & Storholmen, T. C. B. (2020). Towards super user-centred continuous delivery: A case study. In *International Conference on Human-Centred Software Engineering*. Springer.
24. Eisenhardt, K. M., & Graebner, M. E. (2007). Theory building from cases: Opportunities and challenges. *Academy of Management Journal, 50*(1), 25–32.
25. Yin, R. K. (2003). *Case Study Research Design and Methods* (Applied Social Research Methods Series) (3rd ed., p. 181). SAGE.
26. Maali, O., et al. (2020). Change management practices for adopting new technologies in the design and construction industry. *Journal of Information Technology in Construction, 25*, 325–341.
27. Seufert, A., Schröder, S., & Seufert, M. (2021). Delivering user experience over networks: Towards a quality of experience centered design cycle for improved design of networked applications. *SN Computer Science, 2*(6), 1–18.

Part II
Public Enterprises

Digital Transformation in NAV IT 2016–2020: Key Factors for the Journey of Change

Hulda Brastad Bernhardt

Abstract The directorate of Labor and Welfare Administration in Norway (NAV) is responsible for one of the most complex system portfolios in Norway. Since the establishment of the directorate in 2006, NAV has had the ambition of modernizing IT systems, but the development has been slow. In the last 4 years, however, there have been major changes in the way NAV works with digital development and modernization. The purpose of the study is to describe the changes that have taken place in the NAV IT department in the period from 2016 to 2020. The survey identifies four key changes that have had a major effect on the IT department in NAV. These key factors are changed organizational design to support *the creation of teams and product areas,* changed sourcing strategy and *insourcing* of services, changed technological direction toward a *modern application platform and a changeable application architect*, as well as changes in working method from waterfall to *agile product development.* The IT department has moved from being a management-oriented, static organization structured by function to having a flat and dynamic organizational structure with dedicated areas of expertise. NAV replaced all supplier contracts on development and management with capacity agreements, regained ownership of its solutions, recruited programmers, and developed NAV's internal competence. By developing its own application platform for deployment, NAV IT made it possible for teams to automatically deploy to production whenever they wanted. NAV IT has developed an increasingly agile organization where autonomous teams and empowered employees are a key factor.

H. B. Bernhardt (✉)
Directorate of Labor and Welfare, Oslo, Norway
e-mail: hulda.brastad.bernhardt@nav.no

© The Author(s) 2022
P. Mikalef, E. Parmiggiani (eds.), *Digital Transformation in Norwegian Enterprises,*
https://doi.org/10.1007/978-3-031-05276-7_7

115

1 Introduction

During the last 4–5 years, the Directorate of Labor and Welfare Administration in Norway (NAV) has changed the way they work with modernization and development of digital solutions for users while at the same time changing and renewing working methods, technology, and framework conditions for employees.

The purpose of this case study is to describe the digital transformation in NAV, in specific IT department. The case's empirical framework is to identify changes in the period from 2016 to 2020. The case study was part of a master's thesis [1] where findings and observations about the current organizational structure (team/product areas) and working methods (agile methodology) have affected the organization's ability to solve the crisis and the extreme digital challenges for which the organizations were responsible for solving during the pandemic in 2020.

Digital transformation is often described as changes and improvements in an organization's operations and work processes by using digital tools [2, 3]. Development of new tools opens up for changes in business practices, business model, and value system [4]. By utilizing these, organizations can operate with more transparency and increase efficiency. According to Unruh and Kiron [5], this also applies to the public sector. At the organizational level, this means that business models and strategies must be adapted to the new changes [5].

There have been few relevant studies about organizational changes in NAV, considering management structure, the introduction of management tools in the form of measurements, the establishment of new NAV offices, and the introduction of new IT tools (see, e.g., Parslow [6], Thilageswaran [7], Vågen [8], and Grung et al. [9]) but no relevant research considering digital transformation so far.

NAV manages a massive portfolio of services for the Norwegian population. The Directorate's social mission is to secure work for the Norwegian population, provide good living conditions for the most disadvantaged, secure financial rights through good performance management, and offer services with good service. This requires an enormous organizational structure and a correspondingly complex system portfolio that ranges from the most hard-coded mainframe "Infotrygd" to the most easygoing microservices. A total of 1400 employees work in NAV Directorate, and about 800 of them are located at the IT Department. NAV is probably one of Norway's most complex organizations, and one of the interview objects described it as "an onion." There are layers upon layers of organizational levels, lines, and structures, and it is too extensive to use the entire NAV as a backdrop in this case. Therefore, the case is limited to primarily concerning the IT department in NAV.

The case is further limited in time to the period 2016–2020. During this period, major changes were made in the IT department, organizationally, technologically, contractually, and working methods/way of working. The time span has been chosen because it represents a period in which there has been a significantly greater breadth and speed of change initiatives than previous periods. Organizationally, the start was made at the end of 2015, with the formal start of a major organizational development project in 2016.

2 The Case Study

This case study presents an analysis of the changes the IT department has had in the last 4–5 years, both through the formal change of the organization and the more informal changes that have taken place. The data collection mainly consisted of interviews with relevant employees in NAV and the IT department, as well as document studies of available written documentation.

Using document analysis, available documents relating to the journey of change in the IT department have been examined. Relevant documentation has been sought that provides information on any formal changes to organizational structures, other decisions, and decisions that have had an impact on the changes that have taken place. The following written documentation is included in the study:

- A selection of organizational maps from the period 2016–2020
- Case basis for organizational change in 2017 (OU project) and 2019/2020 (IT-2020)
- Relevant strategies (including Cloud Strategy and Sourcing Strategy)
- A team overview from 2018
- Case basis for changing competence profiles 2018
- Case basis for the establishment of product area 2019
- Overview of the development in the number of employees per competence profile (2016–2020)

To enrich this data material and to gain a greater knowledge of what experiences employees in NAV have had related to changes in the organization in the last 4–5 years, the study included a series of interviews (video interview according to COVID restrictions). A total of ten informants were strategically selected so that they could express themselves in a reflective manner on the topic in question [10]. In this thesis, the main criteria were that the informants had been employed in the NAV/IT department in the period 2016–2020 and that they had worked actively with the implementation of digital transformation and/or the work with handling the Corona crisis (Table 1).

Table 1 List of informants

Informant	Male/Female	Role	Years employed	IT Dep.
A1	F	Product manager	17	No
B2	M	Developer	4	Yes
C3	M	Middle management	21	No
D4	M	Developer	3.5	Yes
E5	M	Top management	4	Yes
F6	F	Top management	9	No
G7	M	Top management	14	No
H8	M	Middle management	9	Yes
I9	F	Product manager	6	Yes
J10	F	Top management	1.5	No

3   The Digital Transformation Process

The objective of the case study was to identify changes that have taken place in NAV IT in the period 2016–2020. During the case study, four categories of change were observed that manifested themselves during the study period. These were changes in the organizational structures, changed sourcing strategy, changed technological direction, and changed working method.

3.1   Organizational Changes

The following sections provide a brief account of NAV IT's organizational change journey 2016–2020. A full-fledged review of changes in organizational structure and the emergence of teams in NAV IT is available in the master's thesis [1].

The organization of NAV's IT department has been the subject of many changes and reorganizations since its inception in 2006. Organization chart (Fig. 1) from January 2016 shows an ICT department that consisted of 3 subdivisions, 8 sections, and 26 offices, of which 9 were in the management section.

This organizational structure was designed to support massive IT projects with external suppliers, quarterly main deliveries with change assignments on the entire system portfolio, and follow-up of management agreements with external suppliers. This became particularly visible through the organization of the project section and the management section, with separate offices for follow-up of external suppliers. There were also separate offices for planning, verification, and coordination.

During 2016, a major organizational development project was initiated with the aim of redesigning the organizational structure in the IT department. An organizational model was established to create a more comprehensive dialogue and better collaboration with the professional side, provide room to establish flexible delivery teams, support different delivery models, and facilitate user orientation and business-driven development and innovation. A new organizational structure was implemented in 2017 and entailed a complete reorientation of the organization (Fig. 2). The number of subdivisions increased from three to nine, and teams now appeared in the organizational structure.

In the autumn of 2019, a major reorganization project was initiated by the IT department. The reason for this was the need to better support and adapt to the changes in the way NAV develops technological solutions and services. The goal of reorganizing the IT department was to establish a structure that maintained the operational responsibility of IT and supported the digital transformation of NAV. The new organization should support NAV's preferred way of working with product development in interdisciplinary and cross-functional teams.

An organizational model (Fig. 3) was therefore adopted that distinguished sharply between competence departments and IT delivery areas. The competence

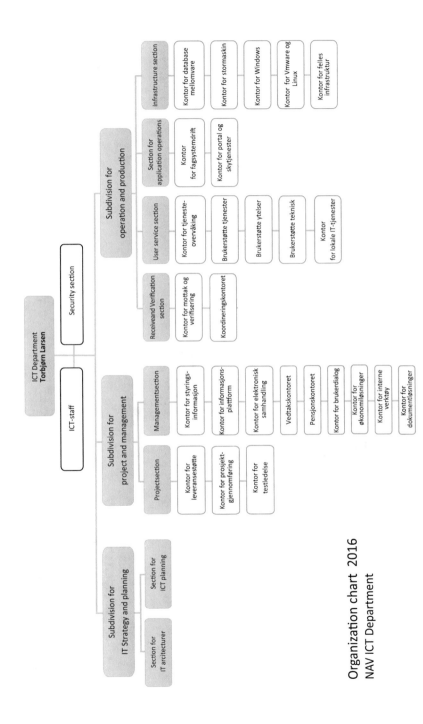

Organization chart 2016
NAV ICT Department

Fig. 1 Organizational chart 2016

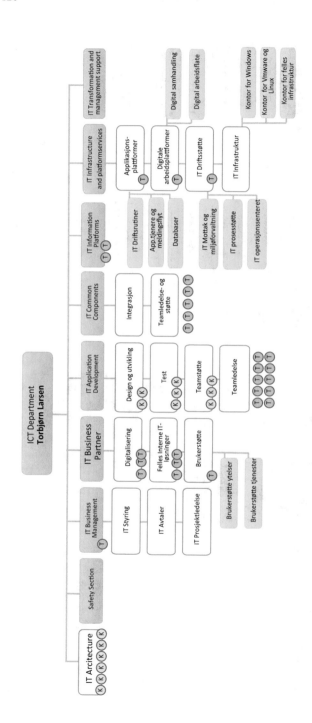

Fig. 2 Organizational chart 2017

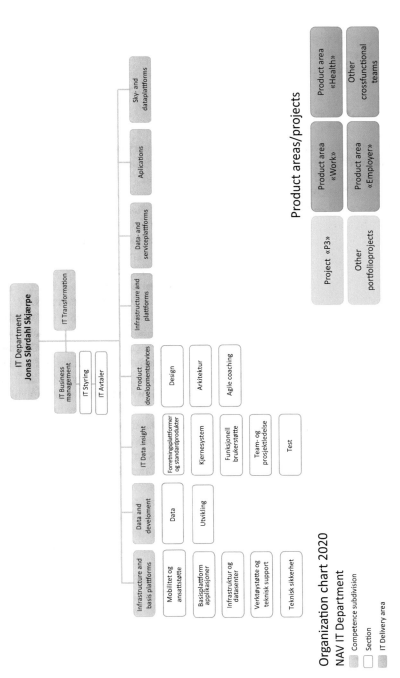

Fig. 3 Organizational chart 2020

departments combined competence and capacity and form the stable structure of the IT department. The delivery dimension was organized in IT areas and platform areas.

Overall, the IT department has changed from being a deep management-oriented and static organization structured by function to having a flat and dynamic organizational structure with dedicated areas of expertise.

3.1.1 Cross-Functional Teams

Working in groups consisting of different complementary competences is not new to NAV, but working with interdisciplinary teams with defined roles, agile working methods, and overall responsibility for products and deliverables was something new. This was formalized through the first major reorganization in 2017.

In the years 2015–2017, documentation of teams was good at the unit level, and the team's updated information on the team's own information pages. However, there was little aggregated information about the development and distribution of teams, and it is not possible to present a complete statistic on the prevalence of the number of teams, etc. One of the informants stated that in 2015 there were seven teams in the IT department. In excess of these seven early teams, it has not been possible to obtain documentation of the prevalence of teams before 2017. The information presented in this case is based on information about team development that has been visible in organization charts (2017 and 2018) and a static team overview from 2019. From 2020, there is data from a digital team directory/database.

In the organization chart from 2017 (Fig. 2), 42 teams are visualized. Fourteen of these are clusters of expertise, while 28 are teams. The category "team" was immature in 2017, and there was great variation in how the teams were organized, delivery models, what work processes and development methodology they used, and what sourcing strategy applied to the team. The case study shows that there has been awareness and maturation on how the organization perceives the team concept and that there is a need for a differentiation of team types in team topologies [11].

In 2019, the number of teams has increased, but they have now been removed from the organization chart. A team overview has been established, and the number of delivery teams in NAV IT has increased to 45 teams in 2019. In March 2020, a digital team catalogue was launched that gave an overview of all delivery teams in NAV and their affiliation to a product area/IT delivery area. The purpose of the Team Catalogue was to provide a reliable and up-to-date overview of all delivery teams in NAV.

As of December 1, 2020, 1167 employees were registered in 132 teams across 16 areas. Of these, 58 were product teams, 33 IT teams, 5 management teams, and 3 project teams, as well as 22 teams categorized as "other" (Fig. 4).

The development of teams in NAV has continued with a sharp increase in the number of teams even after the survey period. In August 2021, 173 teams were registered in the team directory, showing how fast this organization develops.

Team categories

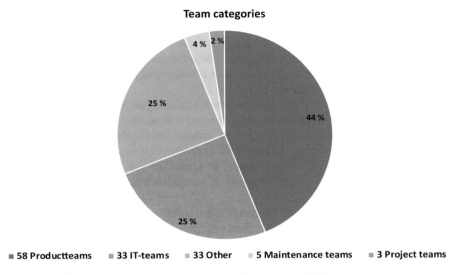

■ 58 Productteams ■ 33 IT-teams ■ 33 Other ■ 5 Maintenance teams ■ 3 Project teams

Fig. 4 Distribution of team types, from the Team Directory Dec. 2020

3.1.2 Product Areas

From 2016 to 2017, most of the product development was done in teams and projects, but from 2018, NAV IT started focusing on how NAV could work differently to better meet users' needs. Until now, modernization and development initiatives had been organized through large projects, but because NAV wanted to take greater ownership of the entire process from needs, development, operation, and management to sanitation, it was decided to establish product areas to manage product development.

In 2018, it was decided to pilot a product area "Health"; the product area itself was established in 2019. During 2019, the product area "Work" was also established. In 2020, the product areas "Employer" and "Pension" were established. In a product development idea, the IT department not only wanted to "bring people and code together" in product teams but also bring together product teams working on the same domain, life event, or user group in product areas. The tasks of the product areas are to ensure holistic service development for a better user-centric perspective.

During the period 2016–2020, there have been several major changes in NAV IT. The first major move came in 2017 and was a complete redesign of the organizational structure. This was done to facilitate the establishment of flexible delivery teams and support various delivery models, user orientation, and business-driven development and innovation. During 2017 and 2018, the IT department found that the organizational design did not contribute sufficiently to building strong competence environments and that it was not clear which deliveries the IT department was responsible for. As a result, an organizational model was launched from 2020 with a distinction between competence departments and IT delivery areas. This is to ensure that the IT department could better support and adapt to the changes in the way NAV develops solutions. Major changes in a business model are often shown in how an organization changes its services through new digital tools [4]. When society is constantly changing, it also affects users' demands and expectations. This has an impact on business models because organizations must adapt to their customers/users to a greater extent [4, 12].

The review has shown that the organization has changed significantly from 2016 to 2020. The IT department has gone from being a deep management-oriented and static organization structured by function to having a flat and dynamic organizational structure with dedicated areas of expertise. Delivery units have been established in the IT department that develop, operate, and manage products within the same domain/category. The employees have their competence home in the departments and work in teams.

NAV IT has established a broad competence environment for development, data, and design during the period. The number of internal developers and programmers increased by almost 250 employees in the years 2017–2019. This corresponds to almost a third of the IT department's total number of employees (a total of 785 employees in 2020). By redesigning the organizational structure and building up interdisciplinary teams and product areas, NAV has facilitated an increasingly comprehensive service development. There has been an extensive process of change, which has had consequences for all parts of the organization.

3.2 Insourcing

An important choice NAV made was to take stronger responsibility and ownership for its own development processes. One of the key changes during the case period was to change the company's sourcing strategy. NAV's first sourcing practice was established in 2007. From then until 2016, NAV had an established practice of using external suppliers through service purchase agreements for detailed design and application development (new and further development, error correction, testing, and documentation) of NAV's IT systems.

Sourcing is about retrieving resources from different places and is commonly explained as producing services yourself or buy services abroad. Insourcing and outsourcing is about moving services into or out of the business. A sourcing strategy can thus be defined as a plan for which services the company is to produce itself with its own employees and which services are to be purchased from external suppliers [13].

In 2017, a comprehensive sourcing strategy was decided for the development and maintenance of NAV's IT systems. The new strategy was to take greater internal ownership in the development and management of IT solutions. Continuous development of digital solutions was no longer a side activity in NAV, but part of the core of solving the greater social mission. In practice, it was decided to establish a separate technology environment and move away from outsourcing development and management assignments to external consulting houses. The consequence of this was that one had to build strong internal competence to ensure delivery precision from the IT department. The advantages of this were that NAV took leadership and ownership of its own solutions at the same time as they used their own employees and developed NAV's internal competence. There was an increased potential for delivering better and cheaper services to users and better direction management for the solutions.

A broad effort was therefore initiated to recruit developer capacity and exchange external consultants with their own developers in 2017. Over time, NAV has terminated almost all supplier contracts on development and management and replaced this with capacity agreements in the areas needed. In practice, NAV IT has terminated all management agreements and taken over ownership of its own solutions. One of the prerequisites for success in this has been to be able to recruit a large number of employees in developmental and programming disciplines. In this way, there has been a marked shift in the composition of competence in the IT department in the period 2016–2020 (Fig. 5). During the survey period, the number of *designers* has increased from 11 to 50 employees, and the number of *developers/ programmers* has increased from 64 to 298 in-house developers (Fig. 6). Some of this is due to internal competence shifts, but mainly this is recruitment of new employees with developer expertise over the past 2–3 years.

The number of employees in roles as architects and advisors has been relatively stable, while the number of employees in roles such as technicians and support functions has decreased significantly over the period. In parallel with a reduction in support functions, there has been a marked increase in development-related roles.

Such a large shift in the composition of competence in an organization can have consequences for the organizational culture. Almklov and Antonsen [14] argue that outsourcing can lead to employees having reduced ownership of work processes, especially in a crisis [14]. In this survey, all informants refer to a deep commitment and a spirit of voluntary work throughout the organization. This is exemplified during the months after the pandemic shut Norway down; there were 650 employees working around the clock to keep all services up and make sure the wheels went around despite a massive pressure on all services. In Almklov and Antonsen's article, outsourcing creates less ownership and engagement [14], and in this survey, it appears that insourcing has created more ownership and engagement. For NAV IT, a clearly communicated trust in employees may also have contributed to increased ownership and a desire to help the organization achieve its central goals.

3.3   Technology and Infrastructure

Technologically, NAV IT has made major leaps during the survey period. NAV has taken over responsibility for the management and further development of most of its solutions. The most important technological change moves have been to establish a modern application platform and a changeable application architecture. NAV IT has

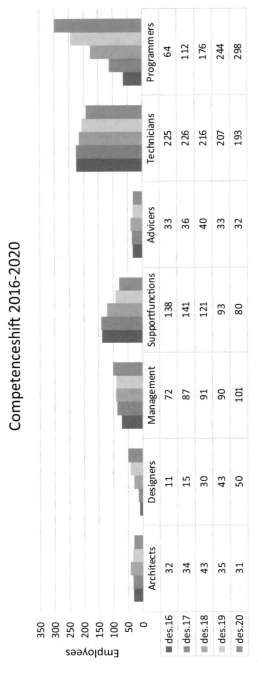

Fig. 5 Competence shift

Number of employees 2016-2020

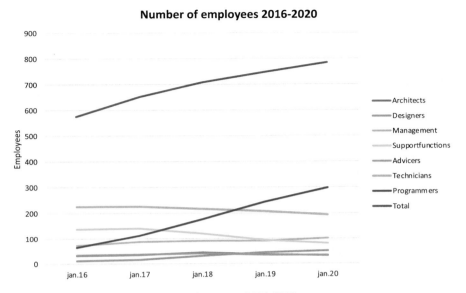

Fig. 6　Number of employees in the IT department 2016–2020

increasingly moved from closed source code to open code, from on premise to cloud, as well as a mobility solution that enables all employees in the IT department to interact and perform their ordinary work tasks from laptop regardless of location.

By developing its own application platform for deployment/production setting (NAIS), NAV IT gained a modern application platform that allowed teams to automatically deploy to production whenever they wanted. The average number of deploys has increased every week since 2017. In 2016, there were less than 50 deploys a week, while in 2020, there are between 750 and 1000 deploys. One consequence of this was that coordination needs were reduced and that changes could be delivered continuously—and not through huge main deliveries.

By building a changeable application architecture, teams were able to build small parts of a solution that could be quickly and easily replaced (microservices), without making major changes to their systems. In addition, a platform was built for collecting and exchanging data.

Another important step has been to introduce a mobile workplace. Employees in NAV have for many years used landline and thin client in their daily work. In 2015, a pre-project was started to facilitate a more flexible mobile solution, where one primarily wanted to facilitate the use of laptops. In 2017, this was formalized and intensified, and the mobility project was established. In 2019, all NAV IT employees were on the mobility platform, computer, and mobile phone. During 2020, the rest of NAV was also moved to the mobility solution, which meant that the IT department in this field was well shod when the COVID-19 pandemic brought all employees to home office for 18 months.

3.4   Way of Working

NAV has been developing digital solutions ever since the "Central National Insurance System" was launched in 1967, and the large bedrock Infotrygd (IBMz Mainframe) has been delivering steadily for many decades. Traditionally, IT solutions have been developed through large waterfall projects, IT projects funded over the central government budget. One major challenge using project methodology was that there was traditionally a long runway from start-up to delivery in a long-term project. In the early phase, there was a lot of time spent planning, specifying, and detailing, and with an ever-increasing need for coordination when NAV was making changes. This delivered yesterday's technology when the final solution was put into production. This plan-build-run model followed the IT department until 2017 where it was decided to adopt agile development methodology.

From 2017 to 2020, NAV has moved from project development to ongoing product development in interdisciplinary/cross-functional product teams. NAV IT works according to agile development methodology, where agile software development is central. The Agile Manifesto defines common focus areas for agile software development. This manifesto covers the essence of all agile methods regardless of whether it is software, products, or services to be developed [15].

Since the agile manifesto was published in 2001, the software development field has, according to Dybå and Dingsøyr, experienced major changes [16]. As a result, new software development methods, tools, techniques, and practices have been introduced. Rajlich [17] describes agile development as a paradigm shift in software development from the traditional plan-driven methodologies.

The goal of an agile development is to be flexible and customer-focused and deliver products frequently and with the greatest possible value for the customer. Few or no requirements are set for how to achieve the goal, but most methods use teams consisting of experienced people who together can meet the expected challenges. Agile methodology is based on the philosophy that you do not know everything at the start of the project and that the framework for the assignment or project is likely to change along the way [18].

In recent years, NAV IT has developed an increasingly agile organization where autonomous teams and empowered employees are a key factor. Agility in an organization is both about the ability to quickly act on changes and new information and the ability to increase process flow and resource efficiency. According to Sherehiya and Karwowski, an agile organization is better able to adapt to changing environments: "Organization agility refers to an enterprise's ability to quickly respond and adapt in response to continuous and unpredictable changes of competitive market environments" ([19], p. 471).

According to Cohn [20], one of the hallmarks and strengths of an agile approach is that you work in tight-knit empowered teams. Teams as a way of working have become the strategic choice for organizations when they face complex and challenging tasks [21]. The formation of a work team is usually motivated by the benefits it brings, such as increased productivity, innovation, and employee satisfaction [22].

A clear finding in this study has been the emergence of teams in the IT department. In the period from 2015 to 2020, the organization has seen a very large increase in the number of teams from 7 to 132, and in 2021 the number has increased further to 173 teams. There is a wide variation in team types and their framework conditions. An interdisciplinary team can be understood as a team that builds on principles of interdependence and responsibility in the work to achieve common goals. According to Eckstein [23], interdisciplinary teams consist of all the roles/functions needed to complete a product or complement a service.

Wageman [24] has a somewhat broader definition and believes that autonomous teams take responsibility for the result of the team's work, monitor, and seek data on the team's effectiveness and change work processes without waiting for the message from others that it needs to be done. A self-directed or autonomous team can decide for themselves how they want to organize their work to achieve their goals. They have more freedom to choose for themselves how they want to work, and they distribute tasks and responsibilities based on what is effective [25].

In the agile method, teams seek the greatest possible autonomy and want leadership based on needs and not as leadership by default [26]. Thus, through a tight-loose-tight approach, teams have a clear purpose for the work or task they are to solve—and a clear requirement for results/delivery. But managing how the team solves the task is up to the team to decide. This leadership approach gives teams room for maneuver and autonomy, and employees gain ownership and motivation to help solve the task [27].

Most NAV teams are interdisciplinary/cross-functional, and the goal is for the teams to be autonomous [28]. A team directory has been established that provides information about the team, but there is no assessment of the condition, maturity, or the extent to which the teams themselves feel that they have real autonomy [26]. The informants talk about different maturities in the teams, where some are highly empowered and autonomous, while others do not have conditions or prerequisites for becoming one. Furthermore, the informants talk about different priorities between the teams. Teams in product areas have better conditions in terms of the right expertise, funding, and agency. Teams that are in IT regions or stand-alone teams do not have the same favorable conditions. When there is a different degree of maturity in the teams, they also have different opportunities to help streamline work processes in and around their team.

3.4.1　Discussion

This case study has tried to describe the digital transformation in NAV. Through the framework of Unruh and Kiron [5], we learn that a digital revolution has three levels: digitization, digitalization, and digital transformation. Digital transformation requires the organization to adopt digital tools [2, 3, 29] and that this not only results in more efficient work processes but also leads to significant changes in the work processes [5]. The survey has shown that it has gradually adapted the organization to support increased digitalization.

An organization has been established to facilitate product development in teams and product areas to improve internal work processes. But this does not apply to all the other departments in the organization. Thus, IT has initiated an organizational change to support a digital transformation without the entire organization doing the same. The danger of this is that it becomes a battle site in an organization where some have progressed further in their development, while others have come shorter in their path. This asynchronous organizational development is also reflected in the establishment of product areas and creates friction.

The precondition for making significant changes in the work processes is that the organization facilitates the desired change. Several of the informants highlight a situation where the IT department has "run *ahead, and we were necked behind*" G7, head of department. If the organization does not pull together in the desired direction, one will not achieve the desired effect. Turning a complex organization around has not been without challenges. The informants have problematized that the teams were freed from structure and frames, and several used the phrase "the pendulum may have swung too far" about this. Dingsøyr, Moe, and Seim [30] have investigated experiences with coordination of/between teams in large-scale agile organizations. They find that there is an increasing need for horizontal coordination mechanisms; the organizations they examined used many different mechanisms and that these constantly changed.

Change and journeys of change are common in all organizations and take place in all sectors and industries [31]. Based on Ven and Poole, a definition of change in organizations can be an empirical observation of the difference in shape, quality, or condition over time in an organizational unit [32]. Change is shown in different categories; among other things, this may involve changing technology that means that an organization can find new ways to perform existing tasks (ibid.). Change may vary in scope and can be divided into radical and incremental change [33]. Radical change entails a clear violation of previous practice, while incremental change occurs by improving and refining what is already decided in a step-by-step process (ibid.). The study has shown that the change in NAV is a combination of these categories of changes, where some major radical steps have been made (e.g., organizational changes), while there are regularly small incremental changes related to, for example, new ways of work and gradually competence shift.

Considering this, one might say that the journey of change described in this study does not represent a total digital transformation [5]. Rather, it is part-stage of a larger digitalization process, where it is not only used as a support tool but that IT becomes part of the company's DNA [4]. But the next step from digitalization is digital transformation, and to this one of the informants says: "The revolution in NAV is not that we should automate case processing. It saves money, but it's when we have automated case processing that we get a basis for creating good tools—that's when we can create better services. Then you can call it digital transformation" (D4, developer).

4 Conclusion

In 2016–2017, NAV IT underwent a complete organizational redesign. The organization went from being function-oriented and specialized in coordination and follow-up of external suppliers to an organizational structure that would provide better interaction with the subject side and provide room for maneuver to establish flexible delivery teams and better facilitate user orientation and business-driven development and innovation. During the period, the number of teams grew from about 7 to about 132, and 4 product areas were established. In 2020, the organization was further changed, and dedicated areas of expertise and delivery areas were separated.

During the period, NAV IT has moved from giant projects and plan-build-run to agile product development in interdisciplinary product teams. Four key changes have been identified that have had a major effect on the IT department in NAV (Fig. 7). These are:

1. Changed organizational design to support *the creation of teams and product areas*
2. Changed sourcing strategy and *insourcing* of services
3. Changed technological direction toward a *modern application platform and a changeable application architect*
4. Changed in working method from waterfall to *agile product development*

At a superior level, the key changes in NAV IT can be illustrated with this model:

These key changes have collectively contributed to increased interdisciplinarity and collaboration across the organization. It has led to an increased focus on technology and tools that promote teamwork and agile product development. IT

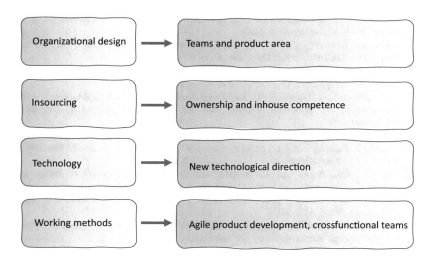

Fig. 7 Major key changes at NAV IT

has led to increased ownership of own systems and solutions, a shift in competence toward developer-oriented roles, and a sharp distinction between competence and the delivery dimensions in the organization. And a small, but important step is that it has detached employees from physical infrastructure and facilitated a mobile workforce that can work anywhere.

As a real acid test of whether the changes have influenced the organization, one can in retrospect say that when the corona situation escalated in March 2020, it was teams and product areas that did the job. There were no proprietary suppliers or coordinating intermediaries. The teams had the advantage of being able to reuse modern solutions or quickly deliver newly developed solutions without downtime or fierce testing regimen. The teams had the expertise and capacity to work continuously. And they could do the job from home. From that perspective, the identified changes have had a major effect on the organization's ability to change.

References

1. Bernhardt, H. B. (2021). *Endringsreisen I NAV IT 2016-2020. En studie av den digitale transformasjonen i NAV IT og endringenes effekt på håndteringen av Koronakrisen.* Masteroppgave. Norges teknisk-naturvitenskapelige universitet.
2. Horlacher, A., Klarner, P., & Hess, T. (2016). *Crossing boundaries: Organization design parameters surrounding CDOs and their digital transformation activities.* AMCIS: Surfing the IT Innovation Wave – 22nd Americas Conference on Information Systems.
3. Libert, B., Beck, M., & Wind, J. (2016). *The network imperative: How to survive and grow in the age of digital business models.* Harvard Business Review Press.
4. Andersen, E., & Sannes, R. (2017). Hva er digitalisering? *Magma - Tidsskrift for økonomi og ledelse, 6,* 18–24.
5. Unruh, G., & Kiron, D. (2017, November). Digital transformation on purpose. *MIT Sloan Management Review, 6.*
6. Parslow, A. (2016). *Endringsledelse i det offentlige. En casestudie av innføringen av et nytt IT-verktøy i NAV.* Masteroppgave, UIO.
7. Thilageswaran, S. (2015). *Endringsledelse: Omstilling til Enhetlig ledelse i NAV Alna/Oslo.* Masteroppgave, Diakonhjemmet Høgskole, Oslo.
8. Vågen, L. E. (2012). *Mål og resultatstyring i NAV. En casestudie av målekortet.* Masteroppgave, Universitetet i Stavanger, Stavanger.
9. Grung, C., Johnsen, I., Hansen, H.-T., Lundberg, K., & Syltevik, L. J. (2014). *Implementering av Nav-reformen ved to lokale Nav-kontorer sett fra ansattes perspektiv.* Uni Research Rokkansenteret.
10. Tjora, A. (2017). *Kvalitative forskningsmetoder i praksis* (3. utg). Gyldendal Norsk Forlag AS.
11. Skelton, M., & Pais, M. (2019). *Team topologies: Organizing business and technology teams for fast flow.* IT Revolution Press.
12. Mikalef, P., Pateli, A., & van de Wetering, R. (2021). IT architecture flexibility and IT governance decentralisation as drivers of IT-enabled dynamic capabilities and competitive performance: The moderating effect of the external environment. *European Journal of Information Systems, 30*(5), 512–540.
13. Seip, Å. A. (2020). *Sourcingstrategier for IKT i offentlig sektor. Om skytjenester og digitale veivalg i fire statlige virksomheter og fire kommuner.* Fafo-rapport 2020:17.
14. Almklov, P. G., & Antonsen, S. (2010). The commoditization of societal safety. *Journal of Contingencies and Crisis Management, 18,* Issue 3.

15. Wysocki, R. K. (2009). *Effective project management traditional, agile, extreme* (5th edn). Wiley.
16. Dybå, T., & Dingsøyr, T. (2008). Empirical studies of agile software development: A systematic review. *Information and Software Technology, 50*(9).
17. Rajlich, V. (2006). Changing the paradigm of software engineering. *Communications of the ACM, 49*(8).
18. Wysocki, R. (2006). *Effective software project management* (1st edn). Wiley. Paperback.
19. Sherehiya, B., & Karwowski, W. (2014). *The relationship between work organization and workforce agility in small manufacturing enterprises. International Journal of Industrial Ergonomics, 44*(3).
20. Cohn, M. (2009). *Succeeding with agile: Software development using scrum.* Addison-Wesley Professional.
21. Salas, E., Stagl, K. C., Burke, C. S., & Goodwin, G. F. (2007). *Fostering team effectiveness in organizations: Toward an integrative theoretical framework* (Vol. 52). Nebraska Symposium on Motivation.
22. Moe, N. B., Dingsøyr, T., & Dybå, T. (2010). A teamwork model for understanding an agile team: A case study of a Scrum project. *Information and Software Technology, 52*(5).
23. Eckstein, J. (2010). Roles and responsibilities in feature teams. In D. Šmite, N. B. Moe, & P. J. Ågerfalk (Eds.), *Agility across time and space implementing - agile methods in global software projects.* Springer.
24. Wageman, R. (1997). Critical success factors for creating superb self-managing teams. *Organizational Dynamics, 26*(1).
25. Hjertø, K. B. (2015). *Team.* Fagbokforlaget Vigmostad Bjørke AS. (2. opplag).
26. Dyer, W., & Dyer, J. H. (2013). *Team building: Proven strategies for improving team performance* (Jossey-Bass Business & Management Series) (5th ed.). JosseyBass.
27. Sagie, A., Zaidman, N., Amichai-Hamburer, Y., Teeni, D., & Schwartz, D. (2002). An empirical assessment of the loose–tight leadership model: Quantitative and qualitative analyses. *Journal of Organizational Behavior, 23.*
28. Campion, M., Medsker, G., & Higgs, A. (1993). Relations between work group characteristics and effectiveness: Implications for designing effective work groups. *Personnel Psychology, 46*(4), 823–847.
29. Conboy, K., Mikalef, P., Dennehy, D., & Krogstie, J. (2020). Using business analytics to enhance dynamic capabilities in operations research: A case analysis and research agenda. *European Journal of Operational Research, 281*(3), 656–672.
30. Dingsøyr, T., Moe, N. B., & Seim, E. A. (2018). Coordinating knowledge work in multi-team programs: Findings from a large-scale agile development program. *Project Management Journal, 49,* 64–77.
31. Jacobsen, D. I. (2012). *Organisasjonsendringer og endringsledelse.* Fagbokforlaget.
32. Ven, A. H., & Poole, M. S. (1995). *Explaining development and change in organizations. The Academy of Management Review, 20*(3).
33. Jacobsen, D. I., & Thorsvik, J. (2013). *Hvordan Organisasjoner Fungerer* (4th ed.). Fagbokforlaget.

Improving Digitization of Urban Mobility Services with Enterprise Architecture

Anthony Bokolo ⓘ, Sobah Abbas Petersen ⓘ, and Markus Helfert ⓘ

Abstract Cities are actively deploying modern digital technologies to foster digitalization due to the emergence of data-driven innovations. Through modern digital technologies, municipalities aim to enhance services performance. Despite prior studies that focused on digital transformation in smart cities, there have been few studies aimed at managing service transformation and complexities needed to support cities in getting smarter. Also, as the deployment of information technology (IT) continues to grow within urban environment, there has been little research conducted that develops data-driven approach for digital services within urban environment. Additionally, cities are exploring methods of providing seamless mobility services based on collaboration among several enterprises and stakeholders in urban environment while achieving seamless data-driven services. Therefore, this study explores the adoption of Enterprise Architecture (EA) for digital transformations to achieve seamless urban mobility services. Qualitative data was collected using case study by interview from an organization that employs distributed ledger technology (DLT) to deploy digital services in smart cities. Findings from the interview sessions were modelled in ArchiMate language to illustrate the application of digital payment solution via DLT toward digitization of urban mobility services. The findings reveal that EA supports digital transformation of cities and manages data integration and alignment. Besides, findings from this study propose an EA approach to support urban planners and developers in understanding the actions required to implement digital transformation of their city services in becoming smarter.

A. Bokolo (✉) · S. A. Petersen · M. Helfert
Department of Computer Science, Norwegian University of Science and Technology,
Trondheim, Norway
e-mail: anthony.j.bokolo@ntnu.no; sap@ntnu.no

P. Mikalef, E. Parmiggiani (eds.), *Digital Transformation in Norwegian Enterprises*,
https://doi.org/10.1007/978-3-031-05276-7_8

135

1 Introduction

Digitization is the conversion of analog information to a digital format into zeros and ones such that computers can retain, process, and transmit such information. Digitization also refers to the transformation of analog to digital tasks [1]. Practically, it is the integration of information technology (IT) to existing tasks, and more specifically it is the enabler or development of IT. Hence, digitization entails the process of changing analog information into digital information [1]. Digitalization is a prevalent topic for both practitioners and researchers mostly seen as a driver toward the modernization of public sectors such as in smart healthcare, smart cities, etc. [2]. Digitization provides an instrument for the development of innovative business models and services [3]. In urban context, information system modelling approaches such as enterprise architecture (EA) are being adopted as a practice to support detailed description, design, and analysis of the enterprise's information and communications technology (ICT) and business structures enterprise [4].

Accordingly, EA is an artifact which comprises of models, principles, and methods employed to design and deploy institutional structures, information systems alignment, and business processes of an enterprise [5]. One of the goals of EA is to improve the management of complex information systems deployed in enterprise. Extant literature maintains that EA enhances an enterprise's IT capabilities and is seen as an important approach that enhances organizational agility [6]. EA enables the actualization of integrated solutions with the city from isolated silos system creating seamless service deployment. Hence, EA is considered as an important approach for successful digitalization of urban services [2]. EA is an established governance planning tool employed to help institutions manage constant change to align organizational resources toward a mutual goal [7]. Accordingly, EA is often adopted in organizations to manage the complexity of enterprise's structures in facilitating the integration of IT and business strategy with stakeholders' requirements [8].

Practically, enterprises holistically adopt EA to enable interoperability, support resource sharing across organizations, and decrease incurred cost of business and IT operations by specifying duplications and opportunities for reuse of IT and business services, thus enabling actualization of seamless services and development of shared data stream [4]. Presently, EA is adopted in organization based on enterprise architecture framework (EAF) which is usually developed based on prior EAF such as Zachman framework, The Open Group Architecture Framework (TOGAF), The Department of Defense Architecture Framework (DoDAF), etc. Such EAFs provide models to describe the process of planning and designing EA languages for representing of organizational, human, and infrastructural aspects across different EA perspectives such as business, application, data, and technologies [4]. Therefore, to contribute to existing body of knowledge, this study poses the following research question:

- How to achieve seamless urban mobility services in smart cities toward digitization?

To provide answer to this research question, this study presents an enterprise architecture framework that captures the technical and human resources required for digital transformations of electric mobility to achieve seamless urban mobility services. We draw on qualitative data collected during a case study via semi-structured interviews. Findings from the interview was received as feedback and was modelled in ArchiMate to show how the organization implements a digital payment solution via DLT toward digitization of urban mobility services. Additionally, findings from the analyzed data are used for modelling of seamless urban mobility services which help enterprises providing services to citizens in smart city digitalize their service. Besides, findings from this study suggest that EA can be utilized for analysis, design, and plan execution, aiding in transition from an as-is state to a to-be state of cities. EA manages information systems alignment with business interests. This alignment process is an important component that supports the success and continued digitalization of cities services. This study is structured as follows: Sect. 2 presents the literature review. Next, the methodology is presented in Sect. 3. In Sect. 4, the findings from the case study are presented. Section 5 presents the discussion and implications of the study. Finally, the conclusion is presented in Sect. 6.

2 Literature Review

This section discusses the overview of enterprise architecture, background of smart cities, and prior studies that employed EA in urban/smart city context.

2.1 Overview of Enterprise Architecture

Architectures or computer architecture as a term has been in use in IT domain since the early 1960s, where it denotes the basics underlying the design of computer operating systems and hardware [5]. According to the definition provided by an IEEE working group, architecture is defined as the fundamental organization of a system in relation to the deployed components, their relationships to each other, and the deployed environment, as well as the principles controlling its design and evolution [9]. Likewise, the definition from The Open Group defined an architecture as a detailed plan of a system formal or a description guide of a system component implementation [9]. In information systems domain architectures are typically described in terms of architectural models such as an ICT architecture, service-oriented architecture, enterprise architecture, etc. [10, 11].

This study is more concerned with enterprise architecture which provides a holistic aggregated view of the business to ICT alignment within an enterprise encompassing its organizational structure, IT infrastructure, software and data, strategic aspects, as well as business processes [12]. EA is the description of a high-level representation of an organization's IT systems and business processes and their interrelationships and the degree to which these systems and processes are shared by diverse parts of the organization. EA mainly aims to define the anticipated future state of the enterprise's IT systems and business processes and provide a roadmap for realizing this target from the present state [13]. EA supports enterprise operations, reflecting standardization and integration requirements of the organization [14]. Thus, providing a strategic top-down and holistic view of an enterprise to enable decision-making for business executives, business managers, IT architects, software engineers, and IT technicians to coherently integrate, coordinate, and conduct enterprise activities seamlessly [15].

2.2 Background of Smart Cities

The course of urbanization has importantly improved modern economy and enhanced human capability to transform society and achieve increase in standard of living [16]. However, the progression of urban development around the world also brings new issues, such as pollution, depletion of natural resources, etc. [8]. To resolve these issues, the idea of "Smart City" was coined to denote the process by which a city can make appropriate changes to reduce those issues [17]. The progression of smart cities started in the 1990s when the phrase was proposed to highlight urban development toward globalization, technology, and innovation [18]. In 2009, discussion on smart cities received more attention when IBM cultivated and published their report on corporate initiative of Smarter Planet, which then received wide acceptance from enterprises, governments, universities, and other partners around the world [19].

Ever since, smart city has developed as a term for pervasive implementation of ICT deployed to enhance various areas of urban surrounding [20]. Besides, a smart city can be referred to as a complex ecosystem embodied by the intensive use of technologies to make cities more sustainable and attractive [21]. Additionally, a smart city is a city in which ICT provides technological, business, and social support to address city challenges and enhance attractiveness of citizens' experiences [22]. In such cities, private and public services are deployed in an affordable, integrated, and sustainable way [23]. ICT can support city's vision of becoming smart by providing a unified and integrated system that manages huge volumes of data to improve city services [24].

2.3 Prior Studies on EA Adoption in Smart City/Urban Context

Due to the potential of EA in managing IT and business component, it has been employed in a smart city/urban context. A few studies have employed EA in their research; among these studies, Gobin-Rahimbux et al. [25] carried out a review on existing ICT architectures for smart governance in a local council. The study is elicited toward the overall transformation of a city to achieve smart city initiatives. Jindal et al. [26] developed an ICT architecture to facilitate supplementary services in future energy distribution networks. The authors further implemented a dashboard based on the architecture to support communication and to allow management of the grid. Jnr et al. [11] presented a big data-based multi-tier architecture to enhance electric mobility as a service in smart cities. The authors focused to achieve interoperability and foster the sharing of data among deployed infrastructures needed for electric mobility services.

Additionally, Anthony et al. [27] presented an architecture based on an EAF for management of big data generated to promote energy prosumption service in smart community districts. Based on a multi-case study, the authors offered help for cities to design their energy platforms. The presented architecture can be employed as a guide to help cities in making decisions toward energy services and energy prosumption development. Similarly, Anthony and Petersen [28] presented an architecture to support electric mobility as a service in smart cities. The authors employed Application Programming Interfaces (APIs) to enhance interoperability of mobility-associated data. Tanaka et al. [29] designed a proposal toward an ICT governance framework with a focus on EA aimed at achieving a smart city. A case study was employed in the educational sector to illustrate the view in ArchiMate language. After which, a questionnaire was used to collect data to assess the maturity level of the city.

Strobbe et al. [30] presented an ICT architecture to manage demand response in a residential area. The architecture is designed to support sharing of energy metering data and providing flexibility information to citizens and demand response balancing of renewable energy within the distribution grids. Janssen [31] provided a sociopolitical approach and adopted EA as a tool to advance e-government, create rationality, and enhance interoperability. Their study aimed at reducing the gap between complex policies in enterprises and less-complex adoption of information systems. Scheibmayer and Deindl [32] designed an ICT architecture to aid business processes achieve Internet of Energy in smart city. Thus, a smart architecture was developed as a decentralized method to connect diverse stakeholders involved in the energy sector toward supporting flexible and open communication.

Furthermore, Toh et al. [33] presented an ICT and business architecture based on EA for a logistics city. EA was adopted in the study to facilitate the development of a collaborative business model to improve productivity based on social, environmental, and economic factors. Evidence from the reviewed ten studies suggest that EA is adopted to facilitate different services in smart cities. However, there are fewer studies that investigated how EA can be employed to achieve seamless urban mobility services in smart cities toward digitization. Thus, this current study aims to address these shortcomings.

3   Methodology

3.1   Designed Enterprise Architecture Framework

To achieve seamless urban mobility services in smart cities toward digitization, EA is employed. Grounded on prior studies [11, 27], an EA framework was presented as seen in Fig. 1.

The EA framework comprises of different layers. Each of which are discussed below.

Context
This layer necessitates requirements that relate to stakeholders' wants, concerns, and associated key performance indicators (KPIs) that improve quality of life [22]. This layer comprises of the set of goals, constraints, principles, and main requirement related to smart city initiatives. The context layer also captures the interests of city stakeholders and citizens [11].

Service
This layer is responsible for presenting the city's action plans, resources, and capabilities [8]. It consists of high-level processes provided by the enterprises collaborating to provide new functionalities to citizens [34]. This layer also provides interfaces which deliver services to citizens. Thus, the service layer aims to effectively implement specified outputs and competently realizing specified key performance goals within the city such as digitalization of urban services [11].

Business
The business layer is responsible for listing all enterprises involved in providing functions and processes to deliver digital services to stakeholders [35]. Business layer involves activities that provide and deliver digital urban services [34]. Thus,

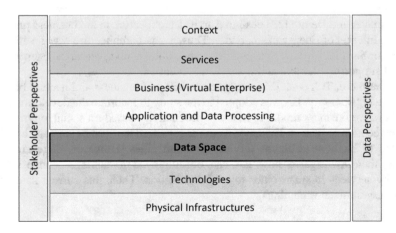

Fig. 1 Presented architecture adapted from [8]

this layer involves virtual enterprises that cooperate toward providing digital services to citizens to support in making urban services smarter [11].

Application and Data Processing
The application and data processing layer encompasses all systems deployed to provide digital services to stakeholders [36]. This layer collects data from the data space layer in providing digital services [11]. Moreover, this layer processes and transforms data into useful information to provide digital services and insights [34]. Hence, this layer provides applications that expose digital services to support the actualization of a smart city operations [8].

Data Space
This layer specifies which data are being utilized by the enterprises in providing digital services within the city [22]. The data space layer consists real-time data, online data, historical data, and third-party data form external sources [35]. Moreover, data space layer comprises of non-relational and relational databases that support city operations. The data space layer provides access to data sources through APIs [11].

Technologies
The technological layer comprises all the technologies deployed across the city such as ubiquitous computing, big data, processing, cloud computing, service-oriented architecture, etc. The technology layer provides the required software and hardware infrastructures needed to provide digital services in smart cities [34]. This layer consists of infrastructures needed to collect, process, handle, and store urban data.

Physical Infrastructures
This layer comprises of physical assets within the city that generates data [34]. Physical infrastructures layer produces real-time data generated from physical sources that is transferred to the technology layer [22]. This layer comprises of physical infrastructures such as sensors, metering devices, IoT devices, and sensing device deployed within the city that generates data [11].

Figure 1 also comprises of the data perspectives and stakeholders' perspectives. Stakeholders' perspective includes policies and regulations, data ownership and access, and privacy and trust, whereas data perspective comprises of data standards, data interoperability, risk assessment, security, and data governance.

3.2 Research Approach

A qualitative research approach was employed for this study similar to a prior study by Gregor et al. [37]. This method allowed data to be triangulated across multiple secondary sources such as from interview, observation, and document review of publicly available archival documents [38, 39]. Documents that provided information on the technology specification and requirements for implementing urban mobility services were provided by the organization discussed in Sect. 4.1, and

Table 1 Overview of participants

Current position and years of experience	Education	Current role and responsibilities
Junior Project Manager with >5 years' experience	M.Sc.	• Focuses on digital technology and its benefits within IoT and industry 4.0 to design testbeds for future full-scale deployment • Works on formal parts of project management for communication, reporting, documenting, etc.
Head of Infrastructure Development with >3 years' experience	PhD	• Focuses on research and development in IoT and data in enterprise and smart cities • Contributes in achieving trust infrastructure for creation of novel data sharing ecosystem • Experienced in managing stakeholder initiatives to address real-world challenges
Senior Technical Analyst with >3 years' experience	M.Sc.	• Experience knowledge in mobility within cities • Focuses in creation, prototyping, and deployment of digital services
Business Development Director with >5 years' experience	M.Sc.	• Involved in development of digital ecosystem toward achieving synergies among multi-stake-holders • Focuses on smart energy, electric mobility, and sustainability

qualitative data was collected from four participants (see Table 1), during an online interview conducted on the 26th of November 2019, on how the organization implements micropayment to support electric mobility services in smart cities.

In the second online interview, data was also collected concerning the technical specifications and requirements for DLT payment module to be integrated to foster urban mobility services. The use case was modelled in the presented EA framework (see Fig. 2). The model was sent to participants (see Table 1) in the organizations, and feedback was provided on September 3, 2020. The feedback provided helped refine the modelled in providing a final use case illustrated in Fig. 2.

3.3   Overview of Modelling Language

A modelling language comprises of notation, syntax, and semantics that provide the required modelling needed to design a model within an EA framework [40]. Modelling language provides graphical modelling languages that facilitate communication among stakeholders [11]. One of such modeling tools employed in the literature is ArchiMate tool which introduces a language for describing EA. ArchiMate is a modelling language developed based on Unified Modelling Language (UML) class diagram but tailored and modified to a limited set of modelling parameters for simplicity of use and learning [40]. Besides, ArchiMate provides a standard set of

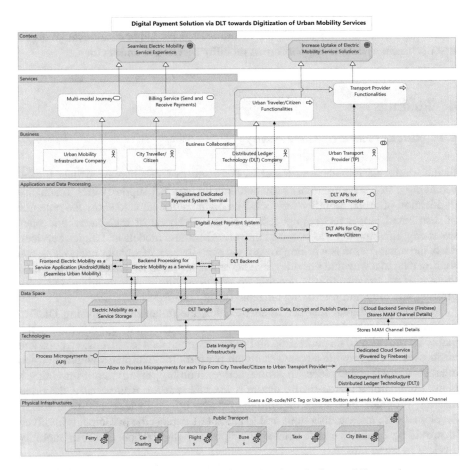

Fig. 2 Meta-modeling of the digital payment for digitization of urban mobility services

objects and relationships with their associated icons for illustration of architecture descriptions [29].

Thus, ArchiMate can be utilized to model EA in an intelligible way while adapting the content for different stakeholders. However, ArchiMate language does not support automatic reasoning as it comprises of basic concepts, objects, and relationships that are suitable mainly for enterprise architecture modelling purposes [40]. ArchiMate is mostly used for modelling EA as it aligns with the TOGAF framework, and it also provides concepts for designing use case model that fits to TOGAF architecture (business, application, and technology) layers. In this study, qualitative data was collected, and ArchiMate was the language utilized to capture the content for urban mobility services modelled as a use case to elicit requirements needed for achieving digitization of urban mobility services based on the feedback provided by the participants. The designed use cases as seen in Fig. 2 reflect the current and potential future functionalities related to an innovative digital asset payment system to support urban mobility services in smart cities.

4 Findings

4.1 Background of Case Study

In this study, an organization based in Germany that provides open data toward achieving a smarter community provided data on how EA support cities to enhance digitization of urban mobility services. The organization aims to show the potential of distributed ledger technology (DLT) as the backbone of transparent and open smart city infrastructures to support innovative business models and digital services. Also, the organization is working toward the actualization of smarter cities using and sharing data in a way that provides insights and is useful to all stakeholders in a city. Presently, the organization is opening up and providing access to urban data silos offering visibility and improving citizens' quality of life.

In improving digital services in smart cities, the organization is using DLT to enable permissionless open data innovations. The organization supports the municipality by providing data generation and access to urban data to citizens, visitors, and businesses. It can provide a common digital platform for enterprises within a city to interact with all stakeholders in infrastructure, mobility, energy, etc., providing a mutual standardized open secure platform for data sharing. Additionally, the organization provides incentives capabilities offered by its feeless, real-time token, developed with microtransactions and IoT. Table 1 depicts the participants involved in providing qualitative data related to improving digitization of urban mobility services in smart city.

Table 1 depicts that data collected from four participants as recommended by [8, 41] where the researchers recommended that data should be collected from more than three participants in a single case study. During the interview session, data was collected from an organization that provides distributed ledger technology in smart cities as previously stated. The data was provided as comments and during three semi-structured interviews and follow-up discussions which lasted for up to 2 h in duration. The interview questions were based on the usefulness of the presented enterprise architecture framework as shown in Fig. 1. The feedback from the interview was later modelled in ArchiMate modelling tool.

4.2   Modeling of Use Case for Digitalization of Urban Mobility Services

Findings from the interview session are modelled in ArchiMate as seen in Fig. 2 as a use case for the innovative digital asset payment system implemented to support digital payment via DLT toward improving digitization of urban mobility services.

Figure 2 depicts the modelled use case in ArchiMate for a seamless electric mobility service supported by a digital asset payment system modelled in the presented enterprise architecture framework (see Fig. 1). The digital asset payment system was implemented by the organization discussed in Sect. 4.1 as a proof of concept to enable citizens to reserve and make payment for several journeys provided by different mobility providers seamlessly in one step. Findings also indicate that the digital asset payment system is deployed with infrastructure to support users that utilize electric mobility services application to directly reserve and pay for urban mobility services with DLT micropayment's native digital asset.

As seen in Fig. 2, the physical infrastructures comprise of all urban mobility options that can be employed by citizens for transportation within the city. The technologies layer comprises of real-time data that is transmitted from public transports to DLT micropayment infrastructure via dedicated Masked Authenticated Messaging (MAM) channel. The MAM is a layered data communication protocol which aids to encrypted data stream DLT infrastructure. Besides, in the layers, the data integrity infrastructure aids citizens to book and record travel data on the DLT Tangle. Using Application Programming Interfaces (API), DLT offers audit trail to enforce integrity of payments distributed to urban transport provided within smart city. Considering the data space, all related urban data both historical and real time are retained in this layer in relational and non-relational database. Next, the application and data processing layer captures all systems that seamlessly connect to provide urban mobility services. This layer also comprises of API that provides data.

The business layer comprises of stakeholders and enterprises that collaborate to provide and utilize digital payment for the urban mobility services provided to citizens. As seen in Fig. 2, the business layer comprises of urban transport provider who is the organization that provides mobility services to citizens and city travelers. The urban transport provider receives payment for the journey performed by the citizens and city travelers, the urban mobility infrastructure company provides urban mobility data, and DLT company processes the payment. The service layer comprises of digital services provided by the digital asset payment solution to support urban mobility services as seen in Fig. 2. These digital services are provided to the city traveler/citizen and transport provider within the city. The context layer comprises of the main goal of urban mobility to be achieved in the city which is the seamless electric mobility service experience and increase uptake of electric mobility service solutions as a sustainable transportation means.

5   Discussion and Implications

5.1   Discussion

EA provides an outline of the as-is state of the city and facilitates digital transformation to a to-be state for the city by reducing the gap between IT deployed and
business strategies employed within the city. In urban environment, EA includes use
case models developed to help manage the continuous development transformation,
implementation, and migration plan to a future state of the city being a smart city.
Therefore, EA provides the rules, blueprint, and standards required with planning the
transition of urban services to a digitalization state. This study builds upon earlier
work of Anthony et al. [27] and Jnr et al. [11] who presented an EA framework to
support cities in becoming smarter. Accordingly, findings from this research show
the adoption of enterprise architecture for digital transformations to achieve seamless
urban mobility services. EA supports urban strategy by guiding the digitization
processes of enterprises that provide digital services within cities. EA improves
enterprise capabilities and links isolated systems and data sources to achieve seamless services toward digitalizing urban core services.

EA plays a vital role in ensuring that IT can deliver value in aligning business
strategies of enterprises in smart cities [42]. As stated by Kluge et al. [43], EA
comprises of a methods, models, and principles that are used in the development of
institutional structure, information systems, infrastructure, and business processes.
Findings reveal that EA supports digitalization of cities mobility services toward
managing data integration and alignment to provide electric mobility services similar
to prior studies [11]. Besides, findings from this study suggest that EA supports
developers and urban planners in understanding the actions required toward digitalization of their city services in becoming smarter. Additionally, findings from this
study are analogous with results from the literature [3] which suggested that EA
provides a critical role in deploying the vision of digitalization. EA captures the
business processes and IT infrastructure and entails how to align business and IT
components in relation to the strategies and objectives of cities. Thus, EA aligns IT
and business processes toward management of urban process.

5.2   Implications of the Study

Findings from this study have several contributions to digitalization research and
practice. Theoretical findings from this study show how EA can contribute to the
digitalization toward enhancing city's agility. The presented enterprise architecture
framework (see Fig. 1) assists cities in anticipating and assessing the business and
technological infrastructures required for successful EA adoption for digitalization
of urban mobility services. This study extends research on the emerging literature on

EA by providing an empirically validated understanding of the role of EA anchoring as a critical constituent for digitalization of cities grounded on qualitative data.

Besides, this study provides a comprehensively designed and verified EA framework that helps cities alike to rigorously deploy digital payment via DLT toward digitization of urban mobility services. This research contributes to practice by taking a broader view of the usefulness of EA, illustrating how EA-based capabilities across urban environment can be attained. Thus, this research provides insights into the potential benefits of EA in making cities smarter.

6 Conclusion

This current research extended previous EA studies by presenting an approach that supports the seamless mobility services based on collaboration among several enterprises and stakeholders in urban environment while achieving seamless data-driven services. An enterprise architecture framework was presented that can be employed by cities to support the digitalization of urban mobility services. Furthermore, qualitative research approach was employed for this study, and data was collected using semi-structured interview from four participants during an online interview and archival documents provided on how the interview participant's organization implements micropayment for the electric mobility services in smart cities. The collected data was modelled in ArchiMate language as a use case illustrated (see Fig. 2). Although this study provides several contributions, there are a few limitations that need to be addressed. First, data was collected from only one organization.

Second, only qualitative data was employed in this study; no quantitative data was used in this study. Third, the data perspectives and stakeholders' perspectives in the present EA framework were not modelled or captured in the modelled use case. Last, in this study, only a use case related to digital payment via DLT toward digitization of urban mobility services was modelled. Future works will consider collecting data from more than two organizations in Norway where EA is adopted for digitalization services. Moreover, survey questionnaires will be used to collect data from practitioners that employ EA for digitalization of cities. Further work will consider the data perspectives and stakeholders' perspectives in modelling of use cases. Finally, more use case related to energy prosumption, community engagement, decision support tool, and monitoring and evaluation of smart city services will be modeled as use cases in ArchiMate.

References

1. Verhoef, P. C., Broekhuizen, T., Bart, Y., Bhattacharya, A., Dong, J. Q., Fabian, N., & Haenlein, M. (2021). Digital transformation: A multidisciplinary reflection and research agenda. *Journal of Business Research, 122*, 889–901.
2. Ajer, A. K., & Olsen, D. H. (2018). Enterprise architecture challenges: A case study of three Norwegian public sectors. In *Twenty-Sixth European Conference on Information Systems (ECIS2018), Portsmouth, UK* (pp. 1–18).
3. Härting, R. C., Reichstein, C., & Sandkuhl, K. (2018). Determinants to benefit from enterprise architecture management–A research model. In *International Conference on Business Information Systems* (pp. 101–111). Springer.
4. Ojo, A., Janowski, T., & Estevez, E. (2012). Improving government enterprise architecture practice–Maturity factor analysis. In *45th Hawaii International Conference on System Sciences* (pp. 4260–4269).
5. Jnr, A. (2021). Managing digital transformation of smart cities through enterprise architecture–A review and research agenda. *Enterprise Information Systems, 15*(3), 299–331.
6. Pattij, M., van de Wetering, R., & Kusters, R. (2019). From enterprise architecture management to organizational agility: The mediating role of IT capabilities. *Bled eConference*, 31.
7. Niemi, E. I., & Pekkola, S. (2016). Enterprise architecture benefit realization: Review of the models and a case study of a public organization. *ACM SIGMIS Database: the DATABASE for Advances in Information Systems, 47*(3), 55–80.
8. Jnr, B. A., Petersen, S. A., Helfert, M., Ahlers, D., & Krogstie, J. (2021). Modeling pervasive platforms and digital services for smart urban transformation using an enterprise architecture framework. *Information Technology & People*. https://doi.org/10.1108/ITP-07-2020-0511
9. Arbab, F., de Boer, F., Bonsangue, M., Lankhorst, M., Proper, E., & van der Torre, L. (2007). Integrating architectural models-symbolic, semantic and subjective models in enterprise architecture. *Enterprise Modelling and Information Systems Architectures (EMISAJ), 2*(1), 40–57.
10. Anthony Jnr, B. (2020). Applying enterprise architecture for digital transformation of electro mobility towards sustainable transportation. In *Proceedings of the 2020 on Computers and People Research Conference* (pp. 38–46).
11. Jnr, B. A., Petersen, S. A., Ahlers, D., & Krogstie, J. (2020). Big data driven multi-tier architecture for electric mobility as a service in smart cities. *International Journal of Energy Sector Management., 14*(5), 1023–1047.
12. Aier, S. (2014). The role of organizational culture for grounding, management, guidance and effectiveness of enterprise architecture principles. *Information Systems and e-Business Management, 12*(1), 43–70.
13. Tamm, T., Seddon, P. B., Shanks, G., & Reynolds, P. (2011). How does enterprise architecture add value to organisations? *Communications of the Association for Information Systems, 28*(1), 10.
14. Brosius, M., Aier, S., Haki, K., & Winter, R. (2018). Enterprise architecture assimilation: An institutional perspective. In *Thirty ninth International Conference on Information Systems, San Francisco* (pp. 1–17).
15. Gilliland, S., Kotzé, P., & van der Merwe, A. (2015). Work level related human factors for enterprise architecture as organisational strategy. In *2015 International Conference on Enterprise Systems (ES)* (pp. 43–54).
16. Ju, J., Liu, L., & Feng, Y. (2018). Citizen-centered big data analysis-driven governance intelligence framework for smart cities. *Telecommunications Policy, 42*(10), 881–896.
17. Wenge, R., Zhang, X., Dave, C., Chao, L., & Hao, S. (2014). Smart city architecture: A technology guide for implementation and design challenges. *China Communications, 11*(3), 56–69.
18. Bokolo, A. J., & Petersen, S. A. (2019). A smart city adoption model to improve sustainable living. *Norsk konferanse for organisasjoners bruk av informasjonsteknologi*.

19. Anthony Jnr, B., Abbas Petersen, S., Ahlers, D., & Krogstie, J. (2020). API deployment for big data management towards sustainable energy prosumption in smart cities-a layered architecture perspective. *International Journal of Sustainable Energy, 39*(3), 263–289.
20. Vögler, M., Schleicher, J. M., Inzinger, C., Dustdar, S., & Ranjan, R. (2016). Migrating smart city applications to the cloud. *IEEE Cloud Computing, 3*(2), 72–79.
21. Bokolo, A. J., Majid, M. A., & Romli, A. (2018). A trivial approach for achieving Smart City: A way forward towards a sustainable society. In *21st Saudi Computer Society National Computer Conference (NCC)* (pp. 1–6).
22. Petersen, S. A., Pourzolfaghar, Z., Alloush, I., Ahlers, D., Krogstie, J., & Helfert, M. (2019). Value-added services, virtual enterprises and data spaces inspired Enterprise architecture for smart cities. In *Working Conference on Virtual Enterprises* (pp. 393–402).
23. Schleicher, J. M., Vögler, M., Inzinger, C., & Dustdar, S. (2017). Modeling and management of usage-aware distributed datasets for global Smart City Application Ecosystems. *PeerJ Computer Science, 3*, e115.
24. Santana, E. F. Z., Chaves, A. P., Gerosa, M. A., Kon, F., & Milojicic, D. S. (2017). Software platforms for smart cities: Concepts, requirements, challenges, and a unified reference architecture. *ACM Computing Surveys (Csur), 50*(6), 1–37.
25. Gobin-Rahimbux, B., Cadersaib, Z., Chooramun, N., Sahib-Kaudeer, N. G., Khan, M. H. M., Cheerkoot-Jalim, S., ... Elaheeboccus, S. (2020). A systematic literature review on ICT architectures for smart Mauritian local council. *Transforming Government: People, Process and Policy, 14*(2), 261–281.
26. Jindal, A., Kronawitter, J., Kühn, R., Bor, M., de Meer, H., Gouglidis, A., ... Mauthe, A. (2020). A flexible ICT architecture to support ancillary services in future electricity distribution networks: an accounting use case for DSOs. *Energy Informatics, 3*(1), 1–10.
27. Anthony, B., Petersen, S. A., Ahlers, D., Krogstie, J., & Livik, K. (2019). Big data-oriented energy prosumption service in smart community districts: A multi-case study perspective. *Energy Informatics, 2*(1), 1–26.
28. Anthony, B., & Petersen, S. A. (2019). A practice based exploration on electric mobility as a service in smart cities. In *European, Mediterranean, and Middle Eastern Conference on Information Systems* (pp. 3–17). Springer.
29. Tanaka, S. A., de Barros, R. M., & de Souza Mendes, L. (2018). A proposal to a framework for governance of ICT aiming at smart cities with a focus on Enterprise architecture. In *Proceedings of the XIV Brazilian symposium on information systems* (pp. 1–8).
30. Strobbe, M., Vanthournout, K., Verschueren, T., Cardinaels, W., & Develder, C. (2015). Deploying the ICT architecture of a residential demand response pilot. In *2015 IFIP/IEEE International Symposium on Integrated Network Management (IM)* (pp. 1041–1046).
31. Janssen, M. (2012). Sociopolitical aspects of interoperability and enterprise architecture in e-government. *Social Science Computer Review, 30*(1), 24–36.
32. Scheibmayer, M., & Deindl, M. (2010). An ICT architecture to support business processes in the Internet of Energy. In *eChallenges e-2010 Conference* (pp. 1–8).
33. Toh, K. T. K., Nagel, P., & Oakden, R. (2009). A business and ICT architecture for a logistics city. *International Journal of Production Economics, 122*(1), 216–228.
34. Berkel, A. R., Singh, P. M., & van Sinderen, M. J. (2018). An information security architecture for smart cities. In *International Symposium on Business Modeling and Software Design* (pp. 167–184).
35. Anthony Jnr, B. (2021). Exploring data driven initiatives for smart city development: Empirical evidence from techno-stakeholders' perspective. *Urban Research & Practice*, 1–32. https://doi.org/10.1080/17535069.2020.1869816
36. Jnr, A., & Petersen, A. (2021). Examining the digitalisation of virtual enterprises amidst the COVID-19 pandemic: A systematic and meta-analysis. *Enterprise Information Systems, 15*(5), 617–650.
37. Gregor, S., Hart, D., & Martin, N. (2007). Enterprise architectures: Enablers of business strategy and IS/IT alignment in government. *Information Technology & People, 20*(2), 96–120.

38. Jnr, B. A. (2021). Green campus paradigms for sustainability attainment in higher education institutions–A comparative study. *Journal of Science and Technology Policy Management., 12*(1), 117–148.
39. Junior, B. A., Majid, M. A., Romli, A., & Anwar, S. (2020). Green campus governance for promoting sustainable development in institutions of higher learning-evidence from a theoretical analysis. *World Review of Science, Technology and Sustainable Development, 16*(2), 141–168.
40. Hinkelmann, K., Gerber, A., Karagiannis, D., Thoenssen, B., Van der Merwe, A., & Woitsch, R. (2016). A new paradigm for the continuous alignment of business and IT: Combining enterprise architecture modelling and enterprise ontology. *Computers in Industry, 79*, 77–86.
41. Yin, R. K. (2013). Validity and generalization in future case study evaluations. *Evaluation, 19*(3), 321–332.
42. Shanks, G., Gloet, M., Someh, I. A., Frampton, K., & Tamm, T. (2018). Achieving benefits with enterprise architecture. *The Journal of Strategic Information Systems, 27*(2), 139–156.
43. Kluge, C., Dietzsch, A., & Rosemann, M. (2006). How to realise corporate value from enterprise architecture. In *Proceedings of the 14th European conference on information systems* (pp. 1–12).

Operating Room of the Future (FOR) Digital Healthcare Transformation in the Age of Artificial Intelligence

Cristina Trocin ⓘ, Jan Gunnar Skogås ⓘ, Thomas Langø, and Gabriel Hanssen Kiss ⓘ

Abstract New technologies are emerging under the umbrella of digital transformation in healthcare such as artificial intelligence (AI) and medical analytics to provide insights beyond the abilities of human experts. Because AI is increasingly used to support doctors in decision-making, pattern recognition, and risk assessment, it will most likely transform healthcare services and the way doctors deliver those services. However, little is known about what triggers such transformation and how the European Union (EU) and Norway launch new initiatives to foster the development of such technologies. We present the case of Operating Room of the Future (FOR), a research infrastructure and an integrated university clinic which investigates most modern technologies such as artificial intelligence (AI), machine learning (ML), and deep learning (DL) to support the analysis of medical images. Practitioners can benefit from strategies related to AI development in multiple health fields to best combine medical expertise with AI-enabled computational rationality.

1 Introduction

Artificial intelligence (AI) implementation in healthcare organizations as part of digital transformation initiatives is an area with growing interest and accelerating implementation [1, 2]. AI can be leveraged to analyze big volume, variety, and velocity data and in supporting evidence-based decision-making while reducing

C. Trocin (✉) · G. H. Kiss
Department of Computer Science (IDI), Norwegian University of Science and Technology (NTNU), Trondheim, Norway
e-mail: Cristina.trocin@ntnu.no; Gabriel.Kiss@ntnu.no

J. G. Skogås
Operating Room of the Future, Trondheim, Norway
e-mail: Jan.Gunnar.Skogas@stolav.no

T. Langø
SINTEF Digital, Trondheim, Norway
e-mail: Thomas.Lango@sintef.no

© The Author(s) 2022
P. Mikalef, E. Parmiggiani (eds.), *Digital Transformation in Norwegian Enterprises*,
https://doi.org/10.1007/978-3-031-05276-7_9

medical errors and improving care coordination [3]. Because AI can automate various tasks that previously required human judgment such as reasoning, risk assessment, and decision-making, it appears to edge closer and closer to human capabilities generating new human-AI hybrid collaboration that opens completely new questions for work and organizing [4]. Thus, the introduction of AI in organizations is posing significant challenges such as doubting the diagnosis when making professional judgements with AI [2].

Initial studies on AI and the future of work focused on the evolution of professions and the economic impact, expecting that knowledge work would be substituted by intelligent machines [5]. Yet, acknowledging that organizations will thrive by combining the best of both worlds, humans with machines [6], several scholars started to investigate how the nature of work is changing with AI and with what implications for management and organizations [7]. For example, deep machine learning can perform cognitive work by learning from large high-quality data sets to improve the resolution of cardiovascular imaging, to develop pattern recognition, and to make automated predictions of cardiovascular diseases months in advance compared to traditional diagnostics [8].

AI is therefore predicted to affect almost every aspect of the work that medical professionals need to perform. However, little is known about what triggers such transformation and how the European Union (EU) and Norway launch new initiatives to foster the development of such technologies. Moreover, it is unclear how medical work is changing with the introduction of algorithms that process information and provide predictions. Additionally, AI implementation poses many challenges concerning the nature of medical work, professions that predominantly relied on human knowledge and judgement, and ethical concerns, which call for new approaches such as responsible AI. As a result, the repercussions on medical work have emerged as a major issue when considering AI implementation, since health professions tend to utilize a plethora of advanced technologies that shape work content, process, and organizational structures [9]. This prompts the issue that health professionals need to navigate the transition from "human-based" to "human-AI hybrids" collaborations during their work activities.

This chapter presents the Operating Room of the Future (FOR), which is a research infrastructure and an integrated university clinic developed from a multidisciplinary collaboration between St. Olav Hospital in Norway and the Norwegian University of Science and Technology (NTNU) and key initiatives related to AI technology. The main goal of these projects is to support medical professionals to combine their expertise with novel AI technology for improving their work performance. In the next sections, we present important notions about digital transformation in healthcare with a focus on AI technology. Then, we discuss the strategies and policies developed in EU and in Norway as part of digital transformation.

2 Digital Transformation in Healthcare

Digital transformation (DT) had and is continuing to have a profound impact on the way we create our social reality [10]. The word *digital* is omnipresent in everyday activities, and it is *transforming* the way organizations operate in the new virtual reality [11, 12]. We refer to digital transformation as "a process that aims to improve an entity by triggering significant changes to its properties through combinations of information, computing, communication, and connectivity technologies" [13]. Recently, DT has shifted its influence from the mere technicalities of creating a virtual tool toward human-electronic devices interaction, which requires specific attention and investigation for being able to exploit its opportunities and to be aware of its challenges [1]. Given the unprecedented amount of digital technologies and pervasive information, organizations need to understand the way such technologies have been developed, the way they are implemented in organizations, and with what consequences for management [14].

Several examples show how digital technologies are transforming multiple industries. For instance, telecommunication focused on the operating system platforms like Android and iOS and on the development of mobile applications to gain value and maintain own position on the marketplace [15, 16]. Another example refers to dynamics within the travel industry that took another path with the advent of peer-to-peer digital platforms such as Airbnb, TripAdvisor, Booking.com, and others, which shifted the power of control from the providers toward the final customers during the pre- and post-acquisition process [11, 17]. Indeed, the customer evaluation acquired not only social but also economic impacts on many companies in several industries, acting as an electronic word of mouth always available online [18]. Therefore, digital platforms are changing the way people interact [19], and new payment platforms are reconfiguring payment methods making them available anytime everywhere. Another example refers to the healthcare industry, which by definition is a knowledge-intensive and information-intensive industry and is making progress by rendering available medical information through electronic health records [20, 21], mobile health applications [22], and more in general with health information exchange platforms (HIE) [20, 23].

The implementation of digital technologies in healthcare gives new opportunities to improve the quality of healthcare services and to decrease the costs through data processing and intelligent sharing of information [10, 20, 24]. Digital technologies are particularly beneficial for improving internal and external processes of healthcare facilities and for managing large amount of medical information [25, 26]. Therefore, the generation, storage, and processing of digital information is the lifeblood of digital transformation. This allows to exploit different advantages of intra- and inter-organizational distribution of limited resources with a patient-centered perspective [27], to facilitate the interactions between multiple healthcare actors, and to optimize internal processes [10, 23].

The digital transformation in healthcare does not involve only few countries, but it has an international or better said global magnitude. For example, the European

Union developed a Digital Health and Care Innovation initiative in the context of the Digital Single Market Strategy 2021–2027[1] to enhance the interoperability of healthcare systems, its quality, and access across European counties. New Zealand Health Strategy 2017–2027[2] defined the four core components that will guide the strategic digital investments for the next years. Australian digital health strategy[3] outlined seven strategic priorities to foster a patient-centered system and to provide choice, control, and transparency. The policy at a global level provides financial investments to foster digital transformation in healthcare. Among the global initiatives, electronic healthcare records (EHR) and more in general the development of healthcare platforms played a strategic role [28]. Its main aim is to store digital medical information over time and share it with authorized healthcare actors [29]. They are implemented as vehicles to improve the communication between actors and to increase the coordination at high levels of reliability. Their implementation is valuable also for administrative purposes and patient transactions as they contain personal information of patients and are available across time and space [30]. EHR has the possibility to combine clinical and financial data to contain costs and improve the care quality, which is also supported by political initiatives to support digital transformation of healthcare.

3   Artificial Intelligence Technology as Part of Digital Transformation in Healthcare

New initiatives are emerging under the umbrella of digital transformation in healthcare such as artificial intelligence (AI) and medical analytics to develop deeper and better insights beyond the abilities of human experts by delivering granular, micro-targeted insights [31]. AI is extensively used for cleaning and analyzing structured and unstructured data from multiple sources. Since data analysts spend most of their time cleaning and organizing data, AI has been extensively used to accelerate this process while saving time and making the process more efficient [32]. AI can autonomously generate insights for taking actions based on information extracted from datasets to reach a set of objectives. We refer to AI as "the ability of a system to identify, interpret, make inferences, and learn from data to achieve predetermined organizational and societal goals" [33].

In line with this definition, artificial intelligence has been increasingly used for analyzing vast amounts of medical information collected through digitized devices from multiple sources across healthcare units to offer IT infrastructure, operational, organizational, managerial, and strategic benefits [34, 35] and to enable the shift

---

[1] https://digitalhealtheurope.eu/overview/

[2] https://www.hrc.govt.nz/resources/nz-health-research-strategy-2017-2027

[3] https://www.digitalhealth.gov.au/about-us/national-digital-health-strategy-and-framework-for-action

toward value-based care over volume [36], whereas the term "medical analytics" refers to descriptive and interpretive analysis of digitized data with advanced statistical, data mining, and machine learning methods for problem-solving and algorithmic (supporting or driving) decision-making [37]. Analytics have the potential to make sense of the information created by individuals defined also as "walking data generators" [38]. They are promising for their ability to collect not only structured but also unstructured data to identify connections and patterns across vast datasets [39], to track and profile fine-grained behaviors of patients [40], and to make algorithm-driven predictions [41].

Previous studies investigated this phenomenon by focusing on its inherent duality. On one side, advanced analytics have been effective in increasing firms' competitiveness [42], making better predictions and more informed decisions [43]. On the other side, they have been criticized for breach of privacy as they distort the power relationship on personal information [44], exploit individuals for data collection purpose [45], share information with other organizations beyond the purposes of individuals' given consents [46], and restrict their choices through algorithms for profiling individuals [47]. Despite the promising benefits, the aggregation and use of the information extracted from vast datasets challenges accepted social and ethical norms [40]. Specifically, ethical concerns are stemming from the sensitivity of data and from unlimited and unknown opportunities that may arise from identified patterns and connections across vast datasets, which might limit or totally obscure these promised benefits [48].

Ethical concerns became even more pervasive because social processes, business transactions, and governmental decisions are increasingly delegated to advanced analytics such as algorithms, machine learning, deep learning, and big data analytics [49]. The promise of making sense of the information collected in big datasets is also coupled with discrimination against disadvantaged groups, uncertainty over how and why algorithm-driven decisions has been achieved (explainability), which rules have been applied, and to which specific information in the datasets as analytics has the capacity of tweaking operational parameters and rules. Therefore, more challenges and ethical concerns arose with the analytics' complexity and their interaction with others' results [49]. Authors developed a map for a rigorous diagnosis of ethical concerns emerged with algorithms. They discussed three epistemic types of ethical concerns that refer to the quality of the evidence provided by the algorithms and two normative kinds of ethical concerns, which refer to the "fairness" of the actions taken based on algorithms results and its effects. This framework was used to conduct a synthesis of prior literature and provide a research agenda for future studies to develop responsible AI for digital health [50].

Moreover, AI technology often provides results that are significantly different from those elaborated by experts, the so-called AI opacity problem [51]. In these circumstances, when experts try to compare the reasoning behind their results with the logic and the procedures followed by algorithms, it is difficult or almost impossible not only for the experts but also for the developers of algorithms due to the black box issue. A recent study highlighted the issue of training and evaluating algorithms only on know-what aspects of knowledge, while experts use rich know-how practices in their daily work [9]. Although more information is captured digitally that can contribute to make more informed and evidence-based decisions, at the same time, algorithms can actually reduce the transparency of the outcomes as they provide black box outputs. On the one hand, AI comes with the promise of more objectivity and fairness by mitigating human biases. On the other hand, AI raises significant ethical challenges related to the quality of the evidence provided that might be inconclusive, inscruble, or misguided, leading to unfair outcomes and unexpected transformative effects [50]. For example, the introduction of hiring algorithms in organizations shapes the notion of fairness in different ways by confirming and contesting it in different phases of implementation [4].

Medical analytics are characterized by unique features such as the capability to aggregate, process, and analyze huge volumes of medical information for transforming it into actionable information [52]. To materialize this feature in the healthcare context, an in-depth understanding of the information lifecycle management (ILM) is necessary. Among the several definitions of analytics capability, our study embraces the perspective offered by Wang and Hajli [52], which defined it as "the ability to acquire, store, process and analyse large amounts of health data in various forms, and deliver meaningful information to users, which allows them to discover business values and insights in a timely fashion" (p. 290). Consequently, analytics are increasingly used in the process of knowledge creation by collecting, elaborating, and displaying valuable information for decision-making [51]. There are several categories of medical analytics [35, 52] in healthcare (Table 1).

Descriptive capability refers to summarization of historical data in digital formats, where a high-speed parallel processing helps better understand what happened in the past. Although the capability used to quickly synthesize vast amounts of health data to compare medical interventions across settings of care enables care actors to improve the quality of care services by providing patient-centered care, few studies discussed descriptive analytics [55]. A recent review highlighted the importance to collect and analyze data with analytical methods to describe specific situations of specific patients, to understand what happened to them through the categorization of knowledge from vast datasets [34]. The techniques of profiling and classifying individuals into groups based on any given characteristic to support realistic public health interventions are widely used techniques to make actionable and interpretable recommendations [54]. Based on the categorization of this information, small patterns or correlations are calculated, which created clusters of groups according to their behavior, preferences, and other characteristics [53, 56].

Predictive capability relies on a set of sophisticated statistical tools to develop models and estimations to forecast the future for a specific variable, which helps understand what will happen in the future. The use of advanced analytics to predict future patterns of care behavior was the most popular capability in healthcare because predictions in healthcare seem to be considered more valuable than explanation since algorithms results are measured in lives [34, 39, 65, 66]. For example, an algorithm can calculate patients' individual therapeutic goals and preferences, hospital staffing (including staff members' experience and performance), resource constraints, and external conditions such as whether other hospitals are diverting

Table 1 Artificial intelligence capabilities (Adapted from Wang et al. [35] and Wang & Hajli [52])

	Analytics capabilities	Explanation	References
Wang and Hajli [52]	Descriptive capability	Descriptive capability describes data collected in digital forms, summarizes historical data, and identifies patterns and meanings. This is useful to understand past patient behaviors based on the data collected in EHR databases. It provides high-speed parallel processing, scalability, and optimization features to respond to the question: what happened in the past?	Cohen et al. [53]; Galetsi & Katsaliaki [34]; Garattini et al. [54]; Gray & Thorpe [55]; Maher et al. [56]; Mittelstadt et al. [57]; Morley et al. [58]
	Predictive capability	Predictive capability is the process of using a set of sophisticated statistical tools to develop models and estimations to forecast the future for a specific variable, based on the estimation of probability. It helps identity causalities, patterns, and hidden relationships between the target variables for future predictions. It uses techniques, such as business rules, algorithms, machine learning, and computational modelling procedures to provide potential responses to the question: what will occur in the future?	Cohen et al. [53]; Floridi et al. [48]; Galetsi & Katsaliaki [34]; Henriksen & Bechmann [41]; Mittelstadt [59]; Mittelstadt et al. [57]; Mittelstadt & Floridi [40]; Morley et al. [58]; Wang et al. [35]
	Prescriptive capability	Prescriptive capability enables users to automatically improve prediction accuracy by taking in new datasets to develop more thorough decisions regarding the diagnoses and treatments. With a combination of structured, unstructured patient data, and business rules, it offers potential optimal solutions or possible courses of action to help users respond to the question: what to do in the future?	Galetsi & Katsaliaki [34]; Mittelstadt et al. [57]
Wang et al. [35]	Analytical capability for patterns of care	Analytical capability processes massive healthcare records (structured data collected inside the healthcare units) to identify patterns of care and discover associations. It allows healthcare organizations to parallel process large data volumes, manipulate	Cohen et al. [53]; Galetsi & Katsaliaki [34]; Garattini et al. [54]; Gray & Thorpe [55]; Henriksen & Bechmann [41]; Mittelstadt & Floridi [40]; Morley et al. [58]; Wang et al. [35]

(continued)

Table 1 (continued)

Analytics capabilities	Explanation	References
	real-time or near-real-time data, and capture all patients' visual data or medical records	
Unstructured data analytical capability	Unstructured data analytical capability processes massive healthcare data (unstructured and semi-structured data gathered across multiple healthcare units, so do not fit into predefined data models) to identify unnoticed patterns of care. This data is stored from multiple sources in multiple formats in real time (e.g., XML-based EHRs, clinical images, medical transcripts, lab results). This data is stored in NoSQL databases and made visually accessible to facilitate decision-making	Varlamov et al. [60]; Wang et al. [35]
Decision support capability	Decision support capability produces reports about daily healthcare services to aid managers' decisions and actions. It shares information and knowledge such as historical reporting, executive summaries, drilldown queries, statistical analyses, and time series comparisons. It provides a comprehensive view for evidence-based medicine, for detecting advanced warnings for disease surveillance, and for developing personalized patient care	Astromskė et al. [61]; Galetsi & Katsaliaki [34]; Gray & Thorpe [55]; Henriksen & Bechmann [41]; Kaplan [62]; Martin [63]; Mittelstadt [59]; Mittelstadt et al. [49]; Morley et al. [58]; Wang et al. [35]; Woolley [64]
Traceability	Traceability tracks output data from the system's IT components throughout the organization's service units. Examples of healthcare-related data are cost data, clinical data, pharmaceutical R&D data, patient behavior and sentiment data from payers, healthcare services, pharmaceutical companies, consumers, and stakeholders outside healthcare. It facilitates monitoring the relation between patients' needs and possible solutions by tracking the	Galetsi & Katsaliaki [34]; Morley et al. [32, 58]; Wang et al. [35]

(continued)

Table 1 (continued)

Analytics capabilities	Explanation	References
	datasets provided by the various healthcare services or devices	

patients in the emergency department in the case of a disaster [53]. Algorithms that make predictions and suggest decisions based on probabilities were considered an ideal application because AI-controlled algorithm predicts the admission trajectory significantly better than medical officers, who have an average error rate of about 30% [41]. They were intensively used also to make treatment recommendations to improve overall health outcomes in a population. However, these recommendations may conflict with physicians' ethical obligations to act in the best interests of individual patients [53].

Prescriptive capability enables users to automatically improve prediction accuracy by taking in new datasets to develop more thorough decisions regarding the diagnoses and treatments. Next, Wang et al. [35] identified additional categories, which are more advanced and sophisticated. *Analytical capability* processes massive healthcare records (structured data collected inside the healthcare units) to identify patterns of care and discover associations. It allows healthcare organizations to parallel process large data volumes, manipulate real-time or near-real-time data, and capture all patients' visual data or medical records. *Unstructured data analytical capability* processes massive healthcare data (unstructured and semi-structured data gathered across multiple healthcare units, so do not fit into predefined data models) to identify unnoticed patterns of care.

Decision-making capability shares information and knowledge such as historical reporting, executive summaries, drilldown queries, statistical analyses, and time series comparisons. It provides a comprehensive view for evidence-based medicine, for detecting advanced warnings for disease surveillance, and for developing personalized patient care. Artificial intelligence systems were commonly used to gather structured and unstructured data to automatically assist medical decision-making based on the recommendations done through pattern recognition [3, 32, 53, 59]. One of the main benefits referred to the possibility to compare data from multiple sources and to identify potential solutions visible in the forms of trees. AI was intensively used to create deeper knowledge and to identify the logics underlying AI predictive modelling [54]. New insights extracted from health-related data were extremely helpful to detect a disease and to decide the treatment(s) to follow [67]. Therefore, the decision-making process was partially delegated to advanced analytics. This delegation has been translated also in the design of algorithms by inscribing developers vision of who will be responsible for mistakes through the degree of social embeddedness and reflection permitted in use [68]. The decision-making capability is coupled with "reporting capability," for organizing the collected data in easily understandable ways, such as describing the information contained in the datasets for specific purposes [34].

Surveillance capability offers the opportunity to survey and monitor past actions based on the information collected indirectly such as the time, the care actor who did that action, the notes taken in databases, and the information consulted based on specific accounts and other. For example, patients now have the possibility to own health information anytime and take decisions in everyday life concerning healthcare, disease prevention, and health promotion [69]. Although they do not possess the expertise for the physician to interpret the information received from the previous medical visits and cannot make an auto-diagnosis, the patient is empowered to the information collected, which requires a higher patient involvement and also some digital and health literacy. Patients are not considered passive receivers of the healthcare services anymore. This aspect was already inscribed in the design of analytics for more transparency for being able to perform those actions [58, 67] as recognized also by policy-makers [64]. From this indirect data, it was possible also to understand the assumption of the actions done, which might help the traceability.

The *capability to correct mistakes* offers the opportunity to adjust the erroneous results of algorithms that contributed to a larger decision [68]. The results of advanced analytics were prone to errors as will be discussed in the next section. Therefore, such capability will be extremely beneficial for correcting the results provided by algorithms. It will increase the awareness of potential errors created by AI systems, which will be trained to detect such errors to correct them or to take them into account when making the decision. Therefore, designers will need to develop the ability to question the results provided by AI tools, and this can be achieved by analyzing the process AI followed and by extracting meaningful information for future reflections. Lastly, *traceability* tracks output data from the system's IT components throughout the organization's service units. Examples of healthcare-related data are cost data, clinical data, pharmaceutical R&D data, patient behavior and sentiment data from payers, healthcare services, pharmaceutical companies, consumers, and stakeholders outside healthcare.

Artificial intelligence and medical analytics have the potential to generate multiple benefits, but at the same time, they are coupled with significant ethical challenges [50, 70] as the "walking data generators" (individuals) are often unaware of how their data are used, for which purposes, and by whom [37]. Therefore, the increasing use of big data containing personal, sensitive information and the growing reliance on algorithms to make sense of this data and identify behavioral patterns raise concerns of fairness, responsibility, and human rights [70]. Scholars shifted their attention from technological means toward the content (information) created by these technologies, which is composed of different moral dimensions. Information is increasingly used as evidence to make decisions and choices, whose outcomes are calling for ethical approaches to address the information creation, sharing, storage, use, and protection. However, ethics concerns first the collections, aggregation, use, and analysis of large datasets and then the information, thus creating a semantic shift [40].

4 Digital Healthcare Transformation in Europe and in Norway

To appreciate the digital transformation in healthcare, it is helpful to understand broader initiatives developed by the European Union (EU) and Norway that are engaged with policies and actions to provide top-quality digital services. The final aim is to empower citizens to build a healthier society and to offer citizen-centered health services. The maximum aspiration is to help citizens take care of their health and prevent future disease. Indeed, one of the most desirable solutions to decrease care costs is to prevent any kind of disease. This means to educate citizens to develop healthy lifestyles and to avoid bad behaviors in the present, which might lead to potential disease in the future. If the aim of *empowering citizens towards the prevention* will not achieve the desired outcomes, citizen will receive innovative health services to respond to their health demand following a *citizen-centered* approach.

The European Union focuses on three priorities.[4] The first one is to provide citizen *secure* access to personal health data across EU borders; the second refers to the implementation of *personalized medicine* through shared European data infrastructure, while the third one focuses on increasing *citizen empowerment* to encourage people to take care of their health and to stimulate interactions between patients and care providers. The aim is to become more resilient, accessible, and effective in providing quality care for European citizens.[5] The implementation of new technologies aims at fostering organizational changes in different departments and for alternative work activities. Digital tools are co-created, co-distributed, and co-used involving directly the end users and consciously fostering a highly collaborative environment. Indeed, the contribution of patients and of other active actors represents the keystone for an interactive digital healthcare ecosystem. A continuous state of evolution and a steady contribution from end users create unexpected changes, which may enable new patterns of communication and interaction.

Digital transformation of healthcare can foster the transition toward new care models focused on patients' need. Patients' contribution represents a keystone for creating useful and usable services for everyday activities and at the same time ends up with enriching the construction of a new healthcare digital ecosystem. The innovativeness lies in the integration of different needs of all involved categories in an open space for dialogue, listening, co-creating, and negotiating toward proposals for common innovative solutions [30]. The aim is to offer tailored digital health services and to give access to dematerialized medical information, to manage personal medical information, to monitor the process of personal continuous healthcare, to be aware of the healthcare process, to understand how healthcare

---

[4] https://ec.europa.eu/health/ehealth/home_en

[5] https://healthmanagement.org/c/healthmanagement/issuearticle/digital-health-transformation-in-europe-recommendations-are-on-the-horizon

system works (transparency), and to be responsible for the personal medical data management (patient empowerment and awareness).

Patient-centered care system can be seen as a partnership among caregivers and care receivers to diagnose and prescribe a suitable treatment. Six aspects are fundamental to define this concept, which are shared decision-making, psychosocial support, access to information, access to care, coordination of care, and self-management [71]. With the use of new digital technologies, a new healthcare paradigm emerges, which transforms the delivery of healthcare services to bring them closer to the patient guided by the following strategies. (1) Efficiency aims at reducing healthcare costs by avoiding unnecessary diagnostic interventions and increasing communication between healthcare institutions and the patient. At the same time, it is committed to ensuring the quality of health services through comparisons between different suppliers to enhance the delivered quality (2). Encourage the empowerment of patients (3) by making personal data, medical records, diagnosis, and treatment accessible through digital platforms and by making more responsible the care information process. Increasing the quality of the doctor-patient relationship to facilitate shared decision-making is a direct consequence of patient empowerment [27]. The digital transformation of healthcare sector increases the probability to maintain and further improve these strategies. The healthcare quality is not only a medical concern, but it is also about the process to reach outstanding care results, which is one of the high priorities of the Norwegian healthcare system.

Norway is one of the most innovative and technological countries, and it is constantly engaged with transforming health and welfare system with new tools, services, or technologies. Key initiatives refer to the development of electronic health record (EHR), ePrescriptions, and algorithms. Ellingsen and Monteiro [72] provided a chronological perspective of the EHR as follows. In the mid-1980s, a group of laboratory technicians in a central hospital highlighted the need of creating a system to support internal work processes by sharing files necessary to perform daily tasks. For the next 10 years, this group and other hospitals continued to develop a network of computers and other important features such as writing clinical documents of each patient and sharing it with the network. In 1997, a limited company was established to follow the implementation of the new system in smaller hospitals. The number of users and hospitals that adhered to this initiative increased, more employees have been hired, and new challenges mined the internal coordination. In 2002, the Norwegian health system established regional health authorities, which were in charge of managing the acquisition of new systems in hospitals with public bids for tenders. This triggered new needs for different types of users at the regional level, which were difficult to meet. Such changes led to redesign the process of EHR software and to redefine the content in the EHR in a dynamic way. A project management approach was used to work on new activities, which was increasingly used in the next years.

The process of transforming the healthcare system continued during 2000 with the eNorway plan,[6] which enabled patients to communicate with their doctors and the hospital through digital platforms such as electronic healthcare record (EHR). This gave the citizens freedom to choose the family doctor online, to receive online medical results from the hospital, and to have access to own medical data with referrals and medical records at any time. The eNorway plan offered telemedicine solutions by implementing broadband in hospitals and primary health services. It was an essential service during the COVID-19 pandemic. Healthcare public system provided telehealth consultations since the 1990s; thus, it could rely on prior experience to further improve this technology to share high-quality medical images to help make diagnoses.

From 2022, Norway plan to implement a new unified EHR, called EPIC, the regional Health Platform program [73]. The new system was acquired with a bid-and-tender process in order to unify the disparate patient records systems used currently in healthcare organizations. The aim is to reduce information fragmentation and facilitate cross-sectoral coordination. EPIC will be implemented first in Trondheim municipality and then in other municipalities in Central Norway. It is important to note that GPs offices are private business, and they have the possibility of deciding whether to implement it or not.

ePrescriptions are another key initiative of the digital transformation in healthcare sector in Norway, which started to be widely adopted from 2011 [74]. The digital prescriptions aim to support general physicians with the activity of prescribing patients medicines or medical visits with hospitals or other healthcare organizations. The first drafts of the prescriptions were developed since the 1990s; however, the results were discouraging. Only in 2011, a large-scale deployment achieved positive outcomes. Until 2013, ePrescriptions have been implemented in General Physicians' (GPs) offices and pharmacies in all municipalities.[7]

Norwegian healthcare system has been a model for other countries around the world, and it is developing new healthcare models based on digital data and advanced technologies in order to move toward a more preventative approach presented in The Nordic Health 2030.[8] In line with this, Norway developed a national strategy for artificial intelligence in order to create a good basis for AI for enhancing innovation capacity in multiple sectors such as healthcare.[9] Another way to trigger digital healthcare transformation in Norway is by constructing operating rooms that use most advanced technologies to support medical work in critical times. In the next section, we present the case of Operating Room of the Future (FOR) in Trondheim, Norway.

---

[6] https://www.regjeringen.no/no/dokumenter/enorway-action-plan/id105562/

[7] https://www.regjeringen.no/en/dokumenter/digital-agenda-for-norway-in-brief/id2499897/?ch=8

[8] http://nordichealth2030.org/

[9] https://www.regjeringen.no/en/dokumenter/nasjonal-strategi-for-kunstig-intelligens/id2685594/?ch=6

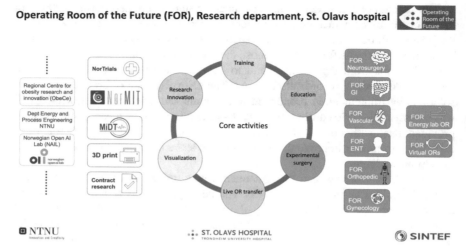

Fig. 1 Operating Room of the Future (FOR) structure and core activities. Source: St. Olav hospital, Trondheim, Norway

5   What Is the Operating Room of the Future?

The Operating Room of the Future (FOR) is a research infrastructure and an integrated university clinic developed from a multidisciplinary collaboration between St. Olav Hospital in Norway,[10] the Norwegian University of Science and Technology (NTNU),[11] and the not-for-profit and independent research institute SINTEF.[12] The three entities developed the basis for the infrastructure in terms of funding proposals, scientific content, logistics, and others between 2003 and 2005. From 2006 to 2012, two operating rooms have been developed for laparoscopic surgery and vascular diseases close to the existing operating department. An interactive lecture room was equipped with HD transmission to watch the operative procedures and to communicate directly through dedicated audio and video channels. From 2013 to present, new operating rooms have been developed within surgical disciplines such as neurosurgery, gastrointestinal, ear-nose-and-throat diseases (ENT), orthopedic, and genecology (Fig. 1). FOR is now a department under the director of research and development at St. Olav's hospital and Department of Circulation and Medical Imaging, Faculty of Medicine, NTNU.

Various stakeholders such as clinicians, PhD candidates, technologists, scientists, and industry conduct cutting-edge research in these six operating rooms. They are unique "laboratories" for developing, testing, and implementing new technologies

---

[10] https://stolav.no/en

[11] https://www.ntnu.edu/

[12] https://www.sintef.no/en/

and new treatment modalities with a focus on minimal invasive image-guided patient treatment and medical technology [75]. This arena for research and development investigates most modern medical equipment such as artificial intelligence (AI), machine learning (ML), deep learning (DL), neural networks, and integration of advanced visualization tools, robotic arms, and others. The six FOR operating rooms have become an important clinical research platform for minimally invasive therapy and for the development of medical technology. The overarching aim is to improve patient care, to develop more efficient logistics and a better architecture of operating departments. The Research Council of Norway financially supported the development of FOR; it is part of the national research infrastructure NorMIT (Norwegian centre for Minimally invasive Image guided Therapy and medical technologies)[13] and cooperates with the Intervention Centre at the National Hospital, Oslo.

There is an increasing number of research projects conducted in the Operating Room of the Future (FOR) in several fields. Decision support in lung cancer diagnostics[14] is an ongoing project that integrates and implements new tools for image analysis and decision support in patient care for lung cancer. A multidisciplinary team (MDT) is developing a digital technology to support patient assessment and treatment [76]. Artificial intelligence (machine learning) is used to analyze patient's CT and PET-CT for finding normal anatomy and pathology (tumor). It is especially used for automatic detection and segmentation of mediastinal anatomical structures and potentially malignant lymph nodes for accurate lung cancer diagnosis.

In line with cancer diagnostic, FOR recently developed the project entitled IDEAR: Improving Cancer Diagnostics in Flexible Endoscopy Using Artificial Intelligence and Medical Robotics in collaboration with Craiova University, Romania.[15] This project is developing an advanced prototype of a medical software and robotic platform for improving cancer diagnostics in flexible endoscopy using AI and medical robotics. The researchers are creating a platform to allow concomitant visualization of the anatomical target(s), the neighboring anatomy, and the CT/MRI image. The project allows performing both diagnostic and treatment during the same procedure using an advanced smart robotic system and customized instruments with dual electromagnetic-optical tracking.

Deep convolutional neural networks (CNNs) are increasingly used for digital analysis of histopathological images. A research team is developing and implementing an open-source platform for deep learning-based research and decision support in digital pathology [77]. *FastPathology* is a new platform using the FAST framework and C++ to minimize memory usage for reading and process whole-slide microscopy images (WSIs). This offers an efficient visualization and processing of WSIs in a single application, including inference of CNNs with real-time display of the results.

---

[13] http://normit.no/en/

[14] https://www.sintef.no/en/projects/2020/decision-support-in-patient-care-for-lung-cancer/

[15] https://www.sintef.no/en/projects/2020/idear/

6 Conclusions

This chapter presents key initiatives of digital transformation in the healthcare sector in the age of artificial intelligence, where the line between virtual and physical reality is pretty thin. We started with a general overview of digital transformation in healthcare. Then, we discussed the emergence of new technologies such as artificial intelligence (AI) and medical analytics as part of digital transformation. In this section, we highlighted the main capabilities that differentiate these technologies from the previous ones and how they contribute to "triggering significant changes to the properties of entities through combinations of information, computing, communication, and connectivity technologies" [13]. After presenting two specific examples of digital health transformation in Europe and in Norway, we conclude with Operating Room for the Future (FOR), an outstanding research infrastructure and an integrated university clinic, which is developing AI technology to support medical tasks in specific health fields such as pulmonology, digital pathology, cardiology, and others.

Due to digital pervasiveness of new technologies, it is pivotal to understand the mechanisms of organizational processes, multi-sided platforms, healthcare applications, and social networks as they have the potentiality to lead toward an effective design, management, and implementation of digital health information systems. Moreover, we believe that the materialization of this opportunity depends on the engagement of the actors involved in this process. It is important to investigate topics at the intersection of work, technology, and information systems and for a broader academic audience such as medicine, computer science, and sociology of work. Such a focus will contribute to the understanding of the development of AI technology in the workplace and to the literature on knowledge creation [14, 78, 79]. Next, there is the need to investigate the challenges doctors are facing with the introduction of AI such as disputing what is worth knowing, what actions matter to acquire new knowledge, and who has the authority to make decisions. This will provide new insights into how and why AI is reconfiguring work boundaries of healthcare professionals and with important consequences for their jurisdictions, skills, status, and visibility. Lastly, it is important to highlight the ways AI tools are used in medical work by paying equal attention to the actions performed by doctors and their social interactions as well as to the machines that are part of the medical workplace [11, 80].

The digital transformation of the healthcare sector is driven by multiple mechanisms, such as the transformation of the population demand for health services, the changes in the relationship between patients and care providers, the pervasive use of digital technologies, and the emergence of new technologies that significantly differ compared to the previous ones. The digitalization of the care paths, increased interoperability among actors, organizational communication, tools, and organizations offer new models for knowledge management, which can be beneficial for individual performance and organizational efficiency, but it also raises several concerns related to privacy, security, and responsibility. A dynamic and digital environment of an ecosystem composed of often-conflicting interests requires a better understanding of the logic and opportunities of a plethora of virtual tools to match them with everyday requirements. The activity of matching the digital solutions with specific and context-dependent needs composes the puzzle of managing the Health Information Systems in current times. The main objectives refer to increasing the quality of service delivery, empowering the citizen-patient that fosters a patient-centered ecosystem.

References

1. Baptista, J., Stein, M.-K., Klein, S., Watson-Manheim, M. B., & Lee, J. (2020). Digital work and organisational transformation: Emergent Digital/Human work configurations in modern organisations. *Journal of Strategic Information Systems*, 101618. https://doi.org/10.1016/j.jsis.2020.101618

2. Lebovitz, S., Levina, N., & Lifshitz-Assaf, H. (2021). Is AI ground truth really "true"? The dangers of training and evaluating AI tools based on experts' know-what. *Management Information Systems Quarterly*.

3. Bjerring, J. C., & Busch, J. (2020). Artificial intelligence and patient-centered decision-making. *Philosophy & Technology*. https://doi.org/10.1007/s13347-019-00391-6

4. van den Broek, E., Sergeeva, A., & Huysman, M. (2021). When the machine meets the expert: An ethnography of developing AI for hiring. *MIS Quarterly*.

5. Frey, C. B., & Osborne, M. A. (2017). The future of employment: How susceptible are jobs to computerisation? *Technological Forecasting and Social Change, 114*, 254–280. https://doi.org/10.1016/j.techfore.2016.08.019

6. McAfee, A., & Brynjolfsson, E. (2017). *Machine, platform, crowd: Harnessing our digital future*. WW Norton.

7. Raisch, S., & Krakowski, S. (2020). Artificial intelligence and management: The automation-augmentation paradox. *Academy of Management Review*.

8. Choi, E., Schuetz, A., Stewart, W. F., & Sun, J. (2017). Using recurrent neural network models for early detection of heart failure onset. *Journal of the American Medical Informatics Association, 24*(2), 361–370.

9. Lebovitz, S., Lifshitz-Assaf, H., & Levina, N. (2022). To engage or not to engage with AI for critical judgments: How professionals deal with opacity when using AI for medical diagnosis. *Organization Science*.

10. Karahanna, E., Chen, A., Liu, Q. B., & Serrano, C. (2019). Capitalizing on health information technology to enable digital advantage in US hospitals. *MIS Quarterly, 43*(1), 113–140. https://doi.org/10.25300/misq/2019/12743

11. Orlikowski, W. J., & Scott, S. V. (2015). The algorithm and the crowd: Considering the materiality of service innovation. *MIS Quarterly, 39*(1), 201–216. https://doi.org/10.25300/MISQ/2015/39.1.09

12. Orlikowski, W. J., & Scott, S. V. (2021). Liminal innovation in practice: Understanding the reconfiguration of digital work in crisis. *Information and Organization, 31*(1), 100336. https://doi.org/10.1016/j.infoandorg.2021.100336

13. Vial, G. (2019). Understanding digital transformation: A review and a research agenda. *The Journal of Strategic Information Systems, 28*(2), 118–144. https://doi.org/10.1016/j.jsis.2019.01.003

14. Benbya, H., Pachidi, S., & Jarvenpaa, S. L. (2021). Special Issue Editorial: Artificial intelligence in organizations: Implications for information systems research. *Journal of the Association for Information Systems, 22*(2), 281–303.

15. Spagnoletti, P., Resca, A., & Lee, G. (2015). A design theory for digital platforms supporting online communities: A multiple case study. *Journal of Information Technology, 30*(4), 364–380.
16. Ye, H. (Jonathan), Kankanhalli, A., & National University of Singapore. (2018). User service innovation on mobile phone platforms: Investigating impacts of lead userness, toolkit support, and design autonomy. *MIS Quarterly, 42*(1), 165–187. https://doi.org/10.25300/MISQ/2018/12361
17. Ciborra, C., Braa, K., Cordella, A., Dahlbom, B., Hepsø, V., Failla, A., Hanseth, O., Ljungberg, J., & Monteiro, E. (2000). *From control to drift: The dynamics of corporate information infrastructures.* Oxford University Press on Demand.
18. Orlikowski, W. J., & Scott, S. V. (2014). What happens when evaluation goes online? Exploring apparatuses of valuation in the travel sector. *Organization Science, 25*(3), 868–891. https://doi.org/10.1287/orsc.2013.0877
19. Sæbø, Ø., Federici, T., & Braccini, A. M. (2020). Combining social media affordances for organising collective action. *Information Systems Journal, 30*(4), 699–732. https://doi.org/10.1111/isj.12280
20. Adjerid, I., Adler-Milstein, J., & Angst, C. (2018). Reducing Medicare spending through electronic health information exchange: The role of incentives and exchange maturity. *Information Systems Research, 29*(2), 341–361. https://doi.org/10.1287/isre.2017.0745
21. Volkoff, O., & Strong, D. M. (2013). Critical realism and affordances: Theorizing IT-associated organizational change processes. *MIS Quarterly, 37*(3), 819–834. https://doi.org/10.25300/MISQ/2013/37.3.07
22. Fox, G., & Connolly, R. (2018). Mobile health technology adoption across generations: Narrowing the digital divide. *Information Systems Journal, 28*(6), 995–1019. https://doi.org/10.1111/isj.12179
23. Chen, L., Baird, A., Georgia State University, USA, Straub, D., & Temple University, USA. (2019). An analysis of the evolving intellectual structure of health information systems research in the information systems discipline. *Journal of the Association for Information Systems*, 1023–1074. https://doi.org/10.17705/1jais.00561
24. Hansen, S., & Baroody, A. J. (2020). Electronic health records and the logics of care: Complementarity and conflict in the US healthcare system. *Information Systems Research, 31*(1), 57–75. https://doi.org/10.1287/isre.2019.0875
25. Makowski, P. T., & Kajikawa, Y. (2021). Automation-driven innovation management? Toward Innovation-Automation-Strategy cycle. *Technological Forecasting and Social Change, 168*, 120723. https://doi.org/10.1016/j.techfore.2021.120723
26. Tschang, F. T., & Mezquita, E. A. (2020). Artificial intelligence as augmenting automation: Implications for employment. *Academy of Management Perspectives*, amp.2019.0062. doi: https://doi.org/10.5465/amp.2019.0062
27. Yaraghi, N., Gopal, R. D., & Ramesh, R. (2019). Doctors' orders or patients' preferences? Examining the role of physicians in patients' privacy decisions on health information exchange platforms. *Journal of the Association for Information Systems, 20*(7), 14. https://doi.org/10.17705/1jais.00557
28. Esmaeilzadeh, P. (2019). The process of building patient trust in health information exchange (HIE): The impacts of perceived benefits, perceived transparency of privacy policy, and familiarity. *Communications of the Association for Information Systems*, 364–396. https://doi.org/10.17705/1CAIS.04521
29. Kohli, R., & Tan, S. S.-L. (2016). Electronic health records: How can IS researchers contribute to transforming healthcare? *MIS Quarterly, 40*(3), 553–573. https://doi.org/10.25300/MISQ/2016/40.3.02
30. Anderson, C. L., & Agarwal, R. (2011). The Digitization of healthcare: Boundary risks, emotion, and consumer willingness to disclose personal health information. *Information Systems Research, 22*(3), 469–490.

31. Fan, W., Liu, J., Zhu, S., & Pardalos, P. M. (2018). Investigating the impacting factors for the healthcare professionals to adopt artificial intelligence-based medical diagnosis support system (AIMDSS). *Annals of Operations Research, 1–26*.
32. Morley, J., Machado, C., Burr, C., Cowls, J., Taddeo, M., & Floridi, L. (2019, November 13). The debate on the ethics of AI in health care: A reconstruction and critical review. *SSRN Electronic Journal*. https://doi.org/10.2139/ssrn.3486518
33. Mikalef, P., & Gupta, M. (2021). Artificial intelligence capability: Conceptualization, measurement calibration, and empirical study on its impact on organizational creativity and firm performance. *Information & Management, 58*(3), 103434. https://doi.org/10.1016/j.im.2021.103434
34. Galetsi, P., & Katsaliaki, K. (2020). A review of the literature on big data analytics in healthcare. *Journal of the Operational Research Society, 71*(10), 1511–1529. https://doi.org/10.1080/01605682.2019.1630328
35. Wang, Y., Kung, L., & Byrd, T. A. (2018). Big data analytics: Understanding its capabilities and potential benefits for healthcare organizations. *Technological Forecasting and Social Change, 126*, 3–13. https://doi.org/10.1016/j.techfore.2015.12.019
36. Agarwal, R., Dugas, M., Gao, G. G., & Kannan, P. K. (2020). Emerging technologies and analytics for a new era of value-centered marketing in healthcare. *Journal of the Academy of Marketing Science, 48*(1), 9–23. https://doi.org/10.1007/s11747-019-00692-4
37. Newell, S., & Marabelli, M. (2015). Strategic opportunities (and challenges) of algorithmic decision-making: A call for action on the long-term societal effects of 'datification'. *The Journal of Strategic Information Systems, 24*(1), 3–14. https://doi.org/10.1016/j.jsis.2015.02.001
38. McAfee, A., & Brynjolfsson, E. (2012). Big data: The management revolution. *Harvard Business Review, 90*(10), 9.
39. Floridi, L., Cowls, J., King, T. C., & Taddeo, M. (2020). How to design AI for social good: Seven essential factors. *Science and Engineering Ethics, 26*(3), 1771–1796. https://doi.org/10.1007/s11948-020-00213-5
40. Mittelstadt, B. D., & Floridi, L. (2016). The ethics of big data: Current and foreseeable issues in biomedical contexts. *Science and Engineering Ethics, 22*(2), 303–341. https://doi.org/10.1007/s11948-015-9652-2
41. Henriksen, A., & Bechmann, A. (2020). Building truths in AI: Making predictive algorithms doable in healthcare. *Information, Communication & Society, 23*(6), 802–816. https://doi.org/10.1080/1369118X.2020.1751866
42. Mikalef, P., Krogstie, J., Pappas, I. O., & Pavlou, P. (2020). Exploring the relationship between big data analytics capability and competitive performance: The mediating roles of dynamic and operational capabilities. *Information & Management, 57*(2), 103169.
43. Meyer, G., Adomavicius, G., Johnson, P. E., Elidrisi, M., Rush, W. A., Sperl-Hillen, J. M., & O'Connor, P. J. (2014). A machine learning approach to improving dynamic decision making. *Information Systems Research, 25*(2), 239–263.
44. Zuboff, S. (2015). Big other: Surveillance capitalism and the prospects of an information civilization. *Journal of Information Technology, 30*(1), 75–89.
45. Clarke, R. (2016). Big data, big risks. *Information Systems Journal, 26*(1), 77–90. https://doi.org/10.1111/isj.12088
46. Martin, K. E. (2015). Ethical issues in the big data industry. *MIS Quarterly Executive, 14*, 2.
47. Loebbecke, C., & Picot, A. (2015). Reflections on societal and business model transformation arising from digitization and big data analytics: A research agenda. *The Journal of Strategic Information Systems, 24*(3), 149–157.
48. Floridi, L., Luetge, C., Pagallo, U., Schafer, B., Valcke, P., Vayena, E., Addison, J., Hughes, N., Lea, N., Sage, C., Vannieuwenhuyse, B., & Kalra, D. (2019). Key ethical challenges in the European medical information framework. *Minds and Machines, 29*(3), 355–371. https://doi.org/10.1007/s11023-018-9467-4

49. Mittelstadt, B. D., Allo, P., Taddeo, M., Wachter, S., & Floridi, L. (2016). The ethics of algorithms: Mapping the debate. *Big Data & Society, 3*(2), 2053951716679679. https://doi.org/10.1177/2053951716679679

50. Trocin, C., Mikalef, P., Papamitsiou, Z., & Conboy, K. (2021). Responsible AI for digital health: A synthesis and a research agenda. *Information Systems Frontiers.* https://doi.org/10.1007/s10796-021-10146-4

51. Anthony, C. (2021). When knowledge work and analytical technologies collide: The practices and consequences of black boxing algorithmic technologies. *Administrative Science Quarterly*, 00018392211016755. https://doi.org/10.1177/00018392211016755

52. Wang, Y., & Hajli, N. (2017). Exploring the path to big data analytics success in healthcare. *Journal of Business Research, 70*, 287–299. https://doi.org/10.1016/j.jbusres.2016.08.002

53. Cohen, I. G., Amarasingham, R., Shah, A., Xie, B., & Lo, B. (2014). The legal and ethical concerns that arise from using complex predictive analytics in health care. *Health Affairs, 33*(7), 1139–1147. https://doi.org/10.1377/hlthaff.2014.0048

54. Garattini, C., Raffle, J., Aisyah, D. N., Sartain, F., & Kozlakidis, Z. (2019). Big data analytics, infectious diseases and associated ethical impacts. *Philosophy & Technology, 32*(1), 69–85. https://doi.org/10.1007/s13347-017-0278-y

55. Gray, E. A., & Thorpe, J. H. (2015). Comparative effectiveness research and big data: Balancing potential with legal and ethical considerations. *Journal of Comparative Effectiveness Research, 4*(1), 61–74. https://doi.org/10.2217/cer.14.51

56. Maher, N. A., Senders, J. T., Hulsbergen, A. F. C., Lamba, N., Parker, M., Onnela, J.-P., Bredenoord, A. L., Smith, T. R., & Broekman, M. L. D. (2019). Passive data collection and use in healthcare: A systematic review of ethical issues. *International Journal of Medical Informatics, 129*, 242–247. https://doi.org/10.1016/j.ijmedinf.2019.06.015

57. Mittelstadt, B. D., Stahl, B. C., & Fairweather, N. B. (2015). How to shape a better future? Epistemic difficulties for ethical assessment and anticipatory governance of emerging technologies. *Ethical Theory and Moral Practice, 18*(5), 1027–1047. https://doi.org/10.1007/s10677-015-9582-8

58. Morley, J., Machado, C. C. V., Burr, C., Cowls, J., Joshi, I., Taddeo, M., & Floridi, L. (2020). The ethics of AI in health care: A mapping review. *Social Science & Medicine, 260*, 113172. https://doi.org/10.1016/j.socscimed.2020.113172

59. Mittelstadt, B. (2017). Ethics of the health-related internet of things: A narrative review. *Ethics and Information Technology, 19*(3), 157–175. https://doi.org/10.1007/s10676-017-9426-4

60. Varlamov, O. O., Chuvikov, D. A., Adamova, L. E., Petrov, M. A., Zabolotskaya, I. K., & Zhilina, T. N. (2019). Logical, philosophical and ethical aspects of AI in medicine. *International Journal of Machine Learning and Computing, 9*(6), 868–873. https://doi.org/10.18178/ijmlc.2019.9.6.885

61. Astromskė, K., Peičius, E., & Astromskis, P. (2020). Ethical and legal challenges of informed consent applying artificial intelligence in medical diagnostic consultations. *AI & SOCIETY.* https://doi.org/10.1007/s00146-020-01008-9

62. Kaplan, B. (2016). How should health data be used?: Privacy, secondary use, and big data sales. *Cambridge Quarterly of Healthcare Ethics, 25*(2), 312–329. https://doi.org/10.1017/S0963180115000614

63. Martin, K. (2019). Ethical implications and accountability of algorithms. *Journal of Business Ethics, 160*(4), 835–850. https://doi.org/10.1007/s10551-018-3921-3

64. Woolley, J. P. (2019). Trust and justice in big data analytics: Bringing the philosophical literature on trust to bear on the ethics of consent. *Philosophy & Technology, 32*(1), 111–134. https://doi.org/10.1007/s13347-017-0288-9

65. Burr, C., Taddeo, M., & Floridi, L. (2020). The ethics of digital well-being: A thematic review. *Science and Engineering Ethics, 26*(4), 2313–2343. https://doi.org/10.1007/s11948-020-00175-8

66. Cath, C., Wachter, S., Mittelstadt, B., Taddeo, M., & Floridi, L. (2017). Artificial Intelligence and the 'Good Society': The US, EU, and UK approach. *Science and Engineering Ethics.* https://doi.org/10.1007/s11948-017-9901-7

67. Lankshear, G., & Mason, D. (2001). Technology and ethical dilemmas in a medical setting: Privacy, professional autonomy, life and death. *Ethics and Information Technology, 3*(3), 223–233. https://doi.org/10.1023/A:1012248219018

68. Martin, K. (2019). Designing ethical algorithms. *MIS Quarterly Executive*, 129–142. doi: https://doi.org/10.17705/2msqe.00012

69. Schmietow, B., & Marckmann, G. (2019). Mobile health ethics and the expanding role of autonomy. *Medicine, Health Care and Philosophy, 22*(4), 623–630. https://doi.org/10.1007/s11019-019-09900-y

70. Floridi, L., & Taddeo, M. (2016). What is data ethics? *Philosophical Transactions of the Royal Society A: Mathematical, Physical and Engineering Sciences, 374*(2083), 20160360. https://doi.org/10.1098/rsta.2016.0360

71. Zhou, Y., Kankanhalli, A., Yang, Z., & Lei, J. (2017). Expectations of patient-centred care: Investigating IS-related and other antecedents. *Information & Management, 54*(5), 583–598. https://doi.org/10.1016/j.im.2016.11.009

72. Ellingsen, G., & Monteiro, E. (2012). Electronic patient record development in Norway: The case for an evolutionary strategy. *Health Policy and Technology, 1*(1), 16–21. https://doi.org/10.1016/j.hlpt.2012.01.007

73. Hertzum, M., Ellingsen, G., & Melby, L. (2021). Drivers of expectations: Why are Norwegian general practitioners skeptical of a prospective electronic health record? *Health Informatics Journal, 27*(1), 1460458220987298. https://doi.org/10.1177/1460458220987298

74. Hanseth, O., & Bygstad, B. (2017). The ePrescription initiative and information infrastructure in Norway. In M. Aanestad, M. Grisot, O. Hanseth, & P. Vassilakopoulou (Eds.), *Information infrastructures within European health care: Working with the installed base* (pp. 73–87). Springer International. https://doi.org/10.1007/978-3-319-51020-0_6

75. Skogås, J. G., Myhre, H. O., Ødegård, A., & Kiss, G. (2016). Imaging for minimally invasive surgery. *Surgical Science, 7*(8), 333–341. https://doi.org/10.4236/ss.2016.78048

76. Bouget, D., Jørgensen, A., Kiss, G., Leira, H. O., & Langø, T. (2019). Semantic segmentation and detection of mediastinal lymph nodes and anatomical structures in CT data for lung cancer staging. *International Journal of Computer Assisted Radiology and Surgery, 14*(6), 977–986. https://doi.org/10.1007/s11548-019-01948-8

77. Pedersen, A., Valla, M., Bofin, A. M., De Frutos, J. P., Reinertsen, I., & Smistad, E. (2021). FastPathology: An open-source platform for deep learning-based research and decision support in digital pathology. *IEEE Access*, 1–1. https://doi.org/10.1109/ACCESS.2021.3072231

78. Faraj, S., Pachidi, S., & Sayegh, K. (2018). Working and organizing in the age of the learning algorithm. *Information and Organization, 28*(1), 62–70. https://doi.org/10.1016/j.infoandorg.2018.02.005

79. Pachidi, S., Berends, H., Faraj, S., & Huysman, M. (2021). Make way for the algorithms: Symbolic actions and change in a regime of knowing. *Organization Science, 32*(1), 18–41. https://doi.org/10.1287/orsc.2020.1377

80. Orlikowski, W. J., & Scott, S. V. (2016). Digital work: A research agenda. In *A research agenda for management and organization studies*. Edward Elgar.

Part III
Synthesis

A Framework for Digital Transformation for Research and Practice: Putting Things into Perspective

Patrick Mikalef ⬤ **and Elena Parmiggiani** ⬤

Abstract The past years of researching digital transformation and the accumulated experience of practitioners in deploying projects of novel digital technologies have allowed us to gain much valuable insight about the process. From this assembly of knowledge, there is a lot we can learn about how to conduct future research, as well as a depth of knowledge regarding best practices that can aid practitioners. In this chapter, we provide some key input on how research and practice can approach digital transformation and discuss some ideas that are likely to be central in the near future. We draw on some streams of literature which have yet to be fully integrated in the current discourse of digital transformation research and provide some practical guidelines that can aid practitioners at different levels. We conclude with a brief overview of some key technologies which are likely to be in the spotlight of attention in the upcoming years and discuss their implications for research and practice.

1   Introduction

In the cases presented in the previous chapters, there are some key takes that can contribute to both research and practice. In conjunction with the vast body of literature on the domain of digital transformation, we can adopt a reflective lens and identify some important themes that permeate recent academic studies and practice. In doing so, this chapter aims to present a future-looking framework for digital transformation which identifies some themes that are likely to be of increased

P. Mikalef
Department of Computer Science, Norwegian University of Science and Technology, Trondheim, Norway

Department of Technology Management, SINTEF Digital, Trondheim, Norway
e-mail: patrick.mikalef@sintef.no

E. Parmiggiani (✉)
Department of Computer Science, Norwegian University of Science and Technology, Trondheim, Norway
e-mail: parmiggi@ntnu.no

© The Author(s) 2022
P. Mikalef, E. Parmiggiani (eds.), *Digital Transformation in Norwegian Enterprises*,
https://doi.org/10.1007/978-3-031-05276-7_10

significance in the upcoming years. We therefore build a research framework which draws on some ongoing challenges for current and future research and provide some suggestions about how researchers could delve into these questions. Furthermore, we present a number of practical suggestions of how stakeholders at different levels within organizations should process in their digital transformation efforts, highlighting some recurring challenging issues that emerge and ways to overcome them.

Through some prominent literature reviews in the area of digital transformation [1–4], several prominent research themes have emerged. While there is some overlap between these research agendas, there is also significant variation between them as they adopt a different viewpoint on digital transformation. These differences stem from a focus on specific industries [5, 6], epistemological approaches [7], as well as scientific domains [8]. Similarly, when it comes to suggesting practical implications and key takes on digital transformation, the literature has ranged from selected case studies [9], guidelines and rulebooks [10], and use of best practices [11]. The objective of this chapter is to provide an overview of some of the most important research themes and practical recommendations when it comes to digital transformation. Extending on these, we discuss how emerging digital technologies are likely to change the competitive landscape and introduce new challenges and opportunities in relation to digital transformation.

In the section that follows, we present a framework for digital transformation that builds on some important research themes and discuss the implications of past findings for practice. The framework is rooted in an amalgamation of research and practice-oriented models of digital transformation, covering some key themes without being exhaustive. The final section follows some of the key trends and identifies hype cycles that are likely to occupy research and practice attention in the years to come and provides a brief overview of how they are likely to create shifts in the way organizations operate [12].

2 A Framework for Digital Transformation for Research and Practice

In the framework presented in Fig. 1, we identify four main phases that underpin digital transformation initiatives. These phases include among others the following activities: First, organizations must develop an in-depth understanding of the current competitive landscape and the dynamics that characterize their industries; decode the relationships with key business partners, customers, and other stakeholders; and identify technological shifts and disruptive new digital tools. Doing so enables organizations to have a better awareness of the landscape in which they operate and chart the different forces that shape ongoing and future initiatives. Second, digital transformation should be approached as a strategy that is pursued by the entire organization and deployed within organizations in a top-down approach. This requires that strategies should be adapted to the different levels they are relevant.

- Define organizational goals for different intervals
- Develop digitally transformed business model scenarios
- Define goal hierarchy and target prioritization
- Evaluate required information technology architectural changes and costs

- Develop action plan with milestones
- Design governance scheme with roles, processes and structures
- Plan training and initiate organizational change
- Mobilize and invest in complementary resources

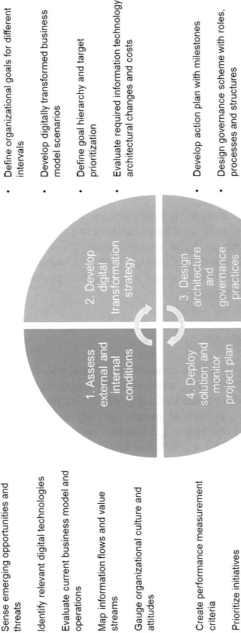

- Sense emerging opportunities and threats
- Identify relevant digital technologies
- Evaluate current business model and operations
- Map information flows and value streams
- Gauge organizational culture and attitudes

- Create performance measurement criteria
- Prioritize initiatives
- Move from proof-of-concept to production
- Monitor progress and rollout contingency plans
- Evaluate performance

Fig. 1 A framework for digital transformation

Third, new business models and strategies should be translated into concrete action plans and governance practices that dictate how the technological and other resources are leveraged. During this phase, organizations must mobilize and structure their resources in order to transition to digitally transformed operations. Fourth, it is important to monitor key performance indicators, develop a prioritization plan, and evaluate the progress of transformation efforts in order to ensure that they do not diverge from the set strategies. The framework is positioned in an iterative visualization denoting that digital transformation is not a process with an end goal, but rather a continuous process of identifying emerging opportunities in the new digital landscape and capitalizing on them.

2.1   Research Implications

While the framework presented above is predicated on a practice-based view of digital transformation, it can also be used by researchers to explore some emerging issues that still occupy research on digital transformation. These areas, or themes, can broadly be distinguished into the following: impact of technology, organizational change management, co-evolution, and non-economic performance effects. We briefly sketch out these themes next.

2.1.1   Impact of Technology

One of the underlying themes that have characterized digital transformation literature has been that the impact that is assumed is highly dependent on the type of digital technology at hand. A key consideration in this regard is that the emerging technologies are likely to have differential impacts not only on the types of performance measures used to evaluate their effect but also on the industries they will influence most. For example, RFID technologies have been instrumental in industries such as logistic, transport, and supply chain management, whereas the emergence of touch screen devices has created major shifts in the consumer electronics, gaming, and software industries. Hence, it is important for future studies to understand the specific shifts new digital technologies create for specific industries, or the processes to which they are likely to have a more pronounced effect. In this part, it is also important that there is a vision of how emerging digital technologies that have not been developed for any specific industry can be harnessed in a way that creates a competitive advantage. In doing so, it is important that researchers examine the role that consumers have in shaping such preferences of technology use and what type of pressure they exert on organizations to move in certain directions.

2.1.2 Organizational Change Management

A key understanding in practice is that digital transformation is an ongoing process that does not have a specific endpoint. This strongly contrasts the prevailing view in research where digital transformation is largely seen as a state that needs to be attained. As such, it is important that future studies engage more deeply with the process of enacting change in the organization as a result of digital transformation initiatives. Several sub-themes within this area are worthy of examination: what is the role of power distribution in enabling or inhibiting change, how does structure influence outcomes, and what changes do digital transformation necessitate? In addition, while there is some discussion on the phases that characterize technological deployment, there is limited research on the socio-organizational arrangements of digital transformation. In other words, we know very little about how to plan for preparing humans and teams to be open for change. Furthermore, a prominent theme is how to develop a culture that not only is open to change but also seeks it actively and is geared toward seeking digital innovations and piloting them in different operations. This essentially translated to building a digitally oriented culture which sees novel digital technologies as key components of remaining competitive and actively seeking ways through which to gain an edge by leveraging them appropriately.

2.1.3 Co-evolution

The notion of co-evolution in the context of digital transformation entails both internal synchronization with external shifts and the capacity to prompt change concurrently and in harmony with important business partners and other entities. While there is ample evidence highlighting the importance of creating digital interfaces with supplies, business partners, and even customers [13, 14], there is limited empirical research on how such ventures should co-evolve. Typically, digital transformation is seen as a process that has an impact on the abovementioned entities by redefining how focal organizations interact with them. Nevertheless, as organizations become increasingly embedded with their business partners and customers, it is important to understand how they can jointly engage in digital transformation that provides value for all. This becomes a challenging problem as different entities typically also have different requirements as well as oftentimes competing goals. To add to this challenge, organizations face a constant challenge of adapting to changing externa, conditions, which necessitate frequent repositioning of their competitive strategies and as a result of their business partners [15]. Therefore, the role of platform architectures in enabling such loose but not lax collaborations without compromising the ability to effectively co-create value is an important aspect of digital transformation that is likely to occupy future studies. Furthermore, the role of platform arrangements as either enablers or inhibitors of future change can create new opportunities in exploring the importance that technology has in eco-system formations [16, 17].

2.1.4 Non-economic Performance Effects

One of the criticisms of the extant literature on digital transformation is that it typically evaluates results and builds on a premise that economic outcomes are the primary objective that needs to be satisfied. Nevertheless, in recent years, there has been a move toward business models and strategies that promote sustainability principles, such as circular economy strategies. The use of digital technologies to support such strategies has been argued to create radical shifts in several industries [18, 19], transforming how operations are currently done and prompting changes that span entire industries. Nevertheless, despite a more comprehensive outlook on the non-economic effects that digital transformation can result in, there are still limited studies that take an empirical approach in examining how non-economic measures are fulfilled. Such measures can include the social and environmental impact that digital transformation has, as well as looking at phenomena at the micro- and meso-levels [20]. In addition, the recent work-from-home mandate due to the COVID-19 pandemic has placed a renewed emphasis on the human aspect, and especially the psychology and well-being of individuals [21]. As a result, it is important to understand what the effects on cognitive and emotional aspects of individuals are and how these influence other organizational outcomes.

2.2   Practical Implications

When it comes to the practical implications by reviewing findings on studies of digital transformation over the past two decades, there are several key points which can help guide practitioners at different levels. We summarize these in accordance with the framework presented in Fig. 1.

2.2.1   Assess External and Internal Conditions

One of the most important recurring findings of prior literature is that when organizations are planning their digital transformation strategies, it is important that they have an accurate assessment of the conditions that characterize their industries, country of operation, as well as their internal organizing. Doing so allows for a better positioning in terms of the business requirements and contingencies of the internal and external environment. Thus, any plans toward digitally transforming operations must take into account a thorough analysis of the immediate and long-term changes that are likely to emerge. Several useful tools have been developed to aid managers and other practitioners in this task, such as adapted digital transformation canvases, deciding on the right digital business models, design thinking, performing persona identification and developing empathy maps, as well as several other tools and methods that can increase understanding of the environment which organizations operate in [22–24]. In addition, organizations can utilize their existing tools, digital technologies, and data in order to identify emerging opportunities and threats and create an organization-wide sensing capability [25].

2.2.2 Develop Digital Transformation Strategy

A common theme among many IS researchers articles is that although digital transformation should be seen as an ongoing process, it should also be documented and tied to a clearly documented strategy [26]. This includes developing awareness about the transformative role of digital data across an organization's value chain [27]. Essentially, this translates into a necessity for top managers to consider the effects of digital transformation in their broader competitive strategy and to see emerging technologies as a means of developing unique and hard-to-imitate capabilities that are likely to give them a competitive edge. Therefore, it is important that there is a clear vision of how digitally transforming operations will provide an organization an edge over their rivals and prioritize the areas which are of higher importance in the new digital business strategies. As part of this planning, it is also important that organizations take into account the costs associated with different options, as well as the different ways through which they can realize their digital transformation initiatives. From the academic literature, the resource orchestration perspective can provide practitioners with an overview of the process of structuring, bundling, and leveraging the relevant resources to pursue competitive strategies [28, 29].

2.2.3 Design Architecture and Governance Practices

Following the definition of high-level objectives and goals, organizations must further detail their digital transformation processes by deciding the governance practices that will characterize their projects. Doing so entails defining roles and responsibilities, establishing and communicating processes, and setting up relational practices internally and externally [30]. This set of activities has also been defined as seizing by Teece [31], where organizations set out to mobilize their relevant resources in support of a given strategy. Within the information systems literature, there has been a lot of work focusing on approaches and practices for planning and mobilizing IT and other complementary resources [32], as well as on defining enablers and inhibitors of governance practices with their corresponding outcomes [33]. These studies provide an in-depth analysis of the value and associated risks with adopting specific approaches and document best practices of managing digital transformation [34]. One important point however is that such mobilization of resources does not only concern technical infrastructure and data, as human-related resources are equally as important. It is therefore critical that organizations make plans about how to secure employees with the necessary skills to drive digital transformation or to develop educational programs in order to re-train their current personnel [35].

2.2.4 Deploy Solution and Monitor Progress Plan

During the deployment of any new digital technology into production, it is important that organizations have established some key metrics to monitor effectiveness and performance and have placed feedback mechanisms in order to critically assess outcomes. Some prominent examples of digital transformation have shown that in the absence of such metrics, organizations suffer heavy losses due to misalignment with strategic objectives or novel technological solutions not functioning as anticipated [36]. Some practical solutions for avoiding such unintended consequences include gradually moving from proof-of-concept projects to production through carefully planned phase projects [37], as well as defining a priori a set of key performance indicators that can effectively monitor project performance. Furthermore, an important practical recommendation is to formulate contingency plans and have systems in place to avoid any disruptions in operations that might be caused by malfunctions of newly deployed technologies. This is particularly important in critical operations that require constant uptime. Finally, to develop a culture of learning from prior initiatives, it is important that organizations set up clear feedback mechanisms and identify aspects that worked well as well as those that caused delays or inhibited digital transformation.

3   Emerging Technologies and What Lies Ahead

In the previous sections, as well as in the chapters that preceded, we have discussed about what lessons can be learned from digital transformation in research and practice and placed a focus on the contingencies of the Norwegian context. Nevertheless, new trends in digital transformation projects are largely shaped by emerging technologies, which are then adopted and adapted by organizations. As such, it is important to examine how digital technologies that are in the early stage of development might influence different industries in the coming years. This analysis is solely based on how the authors envision organizational activities might change due to new emerging digital technologies.

First, the rapid pace at which AI-based applications are being adopted by organizations and their growing capabilities in conducting tasks previously performed by humans is likely to accelerate [38, 39]. Specifically, AI-augmented software engineering is likely to be a breakthrough in the upcoming years, where much of the manual coding and design of systems is now automated. This will lead to a greater access to custom-made software applications for organizations, as well as a significant reduction in cost developing such applications. Nevertheless, this is not the only areas where AI-based augmentation is likely to have a significant impact, as advances in the domain of generative AI are also likely to influence domains such as fashion, product and digital design, architecture, and art. For example, the music industry will be significantly disrupted with content being created by AI applications based on rich data collected over streaming services. Similarly, generative AI will likely create disruptions in the art industry, with a lot of content catering to different types of customers being fully or partially generated by AI algorithms.

Second, blockchain technologies are likely to see increased applications in several areas such as verifying product authenticity, establishing smart contracts, and as a means of transaction [40]. In fact, many governmental organizations have begun the process of designing their digital currencies, and blockchain technologies will become a major part of the infrastructure that supports such a transition [41]. This will result in transactions being executed directly without the requirement of an intermediary entity. In addition, tracking authenticity of products through supply chains is an application area where blockchain technology is already being implemented [42]. The value of blockchain in such applications is that it allows higher security and transparency and enables more precise authenticity tracking and trust. This is particularly important as global supply chains grow larger, more distributed, and complex. Nevertheless, blockchain technologies come at a cost, at least in their current status, of high environmental impact by requirement of vast amounts of energy.

Third, multi-experience applications that allow many different concurrent modalities such as touch, voice, and gesture, as well as the rapid maturation of augmented and virtual reality devices (AR/VR), create manifold opportunities for organizations in the entertainment industry, as well as in manufacturing, healthcare, and retail sectors, among others. We are already seeing a wave of applications that go beyond gaming, to VR meeting applications, collaboration tools, and immersive learning programs [43]. Such uses of AR/VR are likely to become increasingly common in many industries and for on-job training in professions that require direct exposure to physical locations and equipment. In addition, through the maturation of haptic devices, future applications are likely to include remote operations conducted by humans, as well as robotic training from humans.

While these are just a select few future digital technologies that are likely to disrupt entire industries, there are obviously many more which either we are currently unaware of or are still at very early stages of maturity. In closing this chapter, we wish to highlight the importance of both research and practice in being alert for novel technical developments. This requires considerable effort as it is difficult to discern the application areas of early prototypes; however, it will result in a forward-looking perspective that embraces change.

References

1. Vial, G. (2019). Understanding digital transformation: A review and a research agenda. *The Journal of Strategic Information Systems*.
2. Hanelt, A., Bohnsack, R., Marz, D., & Antunes Marante, C. (2021). A systematic review of the literature on digital transformation: Insights and implications for strategy and organizational change. *Journal of Management Studies, 58*(5), 1159–1197.
3. Reis, J., Amorim, M., Melão, N., & Matos, P. (2018). Digital transformation: A literature review and guidelines for future research. In *World conference on information systems and technologies* (pp. 411–421). Springer.
4. Henriette, E., Feki, M., & Boughzala, I. (2015). The shape of digital transformation: A systematic literature review. *MCIS 2015 Proceedings, 10*, 431–443.
5. Kutnjak, A., Pihiri, I., & Furjan, M. T. (2019). Digital transformation case studies across industries–literature review. In *2019 42nd International Convention on Information and Communication Technology, Electronics and Microelectronics (MIPRO)* (pp. 1293–1298). IEEE.
6. Filotto, U., Caratelli, M., & Fornezza, F. (2021). Shaping the digital transformation of the retail banking industry. Empirical evidence from Italy. *European Management Journal, 39*(3), 366–375.
7. Hausberg, J. P., Liere-Netheler, K., Packmohr, S., Pakura, S., & Vogelsang, K. (2019). Research streams on digital transformation from a holistic business perspective: A systematic literature review and citation network analysis. *Journal of Business Economics, 89*(8), 931–963.
8. Kutzner, K., Schoormann, T., & Knackstedt, R. (2018). Digital transformation in information systems research: A taxonomy-based approach to structure the field. *ECIS, 56*.
9. Correani, A., De Massis, A., Frattini, F., Petruzzelli, A. M., & Natalicchio, A. (2020). Implementing a digital strategy: Learning from the experience of three digital transformation projects. *California Management Review, 62*(4), 37–56.
10. Rogers, D. (2016). *The digital transformation playbook*. Columbia University Press.
11. Tabrizi, B., Lam, E., Girard, K., & Irvin, V. (2019). Digital transformation is not about technology. *Harvard Business Review, 13*(March), 1–6.
12. Shi, Y., & Herniman, J. (2022). The role of expectation in innovation evolution: Exploring hype cycles. *Technovation*, 102459.
13. Büyüközkan, G., & Göçer, F. (2018). Digital supply chain: Literature review and a proposed framework for future research. *Computers in Industry, 97*, 157–177.
14. Pappas, I., Mikalef, P., Giannakos, M., & Pavlou, P. (2017). Value co-creation and trust in social commerce: An fsQCA approach. In *The 25th European Conference on Information Systems (ECIS)*. Association for Information Systems.
15. Mikalef, P., Pateli, A., & van de Wetering, R. (2021). IT architecture flexibility and IT governance decentralisation as drivers of IT-enabled dynamic capabilities and competitive performance: The moderating effect of the external environment. *European Journal of Information Systems, 30*(5), 512–540.
16. Constantinides, P., Henfridsson, O., & Parker, G. G. (2018). Introduction—platforms and infrastructures in the digital age. *INFORMS, 29*, 381–400.
17. De Reuver, M., Sørensen, C., & Basole, R. C. (2018). The digital platform: A research agenda. *Journal of Information Technology, 33*(2), 124–135.
18. Kristoffersen, E., Blomsma, F., Mikalef, P., & Li, J. (2020). The smart circular economy: A digital-enabled circular strategies framework for manufacturing companies. *Journal of Business Research, 120*, 241–261.
19. Malhotra, A., Melville, N. P., & Watson, R. T. (2013). Spurring impactful research on information systems for environmental sustainability. *MIS Quarterly, 37*(4), 1265–1274.
20. Steininger, D. M., Mikalef, P., Pateli, A., de Guinea, A. O., & Ortiz-De, A. (2021). Dynamic capabilities in information systems research: A critical review, synthesis of current knowledge, and recommendations for future research. *Journal of the Association for Information Systems*.

21. Willems, T., & Hafermalz, E. (2021). Distributed seeing: Algorithms and the reconfiguration of the workplace, a case of 'automated' trading. *Information and Organization, 31*(4), 100376.
22. Muhtaroğlu, F. C. P., Demir, S., Obalı, M., & Girgin, C. (2013). Business model canvas perspective on big data applications. In *2013 IEEE International Conference on Big Data* (pp. 32–37). IEEE.
23. Osterwalder, A., Pigneur, Y., Bernarda, G., & Smith, A. (2015). *Value proposition design: How to create products and services customers want.* Wiley.
24. Lewrick, M., Link, P., & Leifer, L. (2018). *The design thinking playbook: Mindful digital transformation of teams, products, services, businesses and ecosystems.* Wiley.
25. Conboy, K., Mikalef, P., Dennehy, D., & Krogstie, J. (2019). Using business analytics to enhance dynamic capabilities in operations research: A case analysis and research agenda. *European Journal of Operational Research.*
26. Chanias, S., Myers, M. D., & Hess, T. (2019). Digital transformation strategy making in pre-digital organizations: The case of a financial services provider. *The Journal of Strategic Information Systems, 28*(1), 17–33.
27. Alaimo, C., & Kallinikos, J. (2022). Organizations decentered: Data objects, technology and knowledge. *Organization Science, 33*(1), 19–37.
28. Sirmon, D. G., Hitt, M. A., Ireland, R. D., & Gilbert, B. A. (2011). Resource orchestration to create competitive advantage: Breadth, depth, and life cycle effects. *Journal of Management, 37*(5), 1390–1412.
29. Parmiggiani, E., & Grisot, M. (2020). Data curation as governance practice.
30. Mikalef, P., Boura, M., Lekakos, G., & Krogstie, J. (2020). The role of information governance in big data analytics driven innovation. *Information & Management, 57*(7), 103361.
31. Teece, D. J. (2007). Explicating dynamic capabilities: The nature and microfoundations of (sustainable) enterprise performance. *Strategic Management Journal, 28*(13), 1319–1350.
32. Liu, D. Y., Chen, S. W., & Chou, T. C. (2011). Resource fit in digital transformation: Lessons learned from the CBC Bank global e-banking project. *Management Decision.*
33. Tallon, P. P. (2013). Corporate governance of big data: Perspectives on value, risk, and cost. *Computer, 46*(6), 32–38.
34. Cennamo, C., Dagnino, G. B., Di Minin, A., & Lanzolla, G. (2020). Managing digital transformation: Scope of transformation and modalities of value co-generation and delivery. *California Management Review, 62*(4), 5–16.
35. Mikalef, P., Giannakos, M. N., Pappas, I. O., & Krogstie, J. (2018). The Human Side of Big Data: Understanding the skills of the data scientist in education and industry. In *Global Engineering Education Conference (EDUCON), 2018 IEEE.* IEEE.
36. Loonam, J., Eaves, S., Kumar, V., & Parry, G. (2018). Towards digital transformation: Lessons learned from traditional organizations. *Strategic Change, 27*(2), 101–109.
37. Mikalef, P., van de Wetering, R., & Krogstie, J. (2020). Building dynamic capabilities by leveraging big data analytics: The role of organizational inertia. *Information & Management,* 103412.
38. Collins, C., Dennehy, D., Conboy, K., & Mikalef, P. (2021). Artificial intelligence in information systems research: A systematic literature review and research agenda. *International Journal of Information Management, 60*, 102383.
39. Enholm, I. M., Papagiannidis, E., Mikalef, P., & Krogstie, J. (2021). Artificial intelligence and business value: A literature review. *Information Systems Frontiers*, 1–26.
40. Antonucci, F., Figorilli, S., Costa, C., Pallottino, F., Raso, L., & Menesatti, P. (2019). A review on blockchain applications in the agri-food sector. *Journal of the Science of Food and Agriculture, 99*(14), 6129–6138.
41. Klein, M., Gross, J., & Sandner, P. (2020). *The digital euro and the role of DLT for central bank digital currencies.* Frankfurt School of Finance & Management GmbH, FSBC Working Paper.
42. Azzi, R., Chamoun, R. K., & Sokhn, M. (2019). The power of a blockchain-based supply chain. *Computers & Industrial Engineering, 135*, 582–592.

43. Hoppe, A. H., van de Camp, F., & Stiefelhagen, R. (2021). Shisha: Enabling shared perspective with face-to-face collaboration using redirected avatars in virtual reality. *Proceedings of the ACM on Human-Computer Interaction, 4*(CSCW3), 1–22.

The Way Forward: A Practical Guideline for Successful Digital Transformation

Elena Parmiggiani ⓘ **and Patrick Mikalef** ⓘ

Abstract This chapter presents key lessons learned and implications for practice resulting from the analysis of the empirical cases included in this book. We map emerging themes across five layers: unit or project, organization, organization ecosystem, ethical and environmental sustainability, and society. We identify two emerging trends: the co-evolution of organizational forms and new technologies and the fact that digital transformation increasingly happens on the organizational ecosystem level. This has consequences in terms of increased data work, new work processes, and the need to actively engage with sustainability policies. We highlight the need for a focus on the long-term effects of digital transformation initiatives with attention to their ripple effects over time.

1 Emerging Research Directions: A Way Forward

The aim of this book has been to present the theme of digital transformation and draw trajectories and present reflections along the journey in Norway so far. We started in Chap. 1 by pointing to the contextual nature of digital transformation, where its successful outcome is often the result of a jigsaw puzzle where bits that come in many "shapes and sizes" have to be combined and made to fit in a specific context. In the case of Norway, we observed that the evolution of ICT systems and infrastructures has been largely driven by pragmatic concerns related to specific applications, aimed to ensure the competitiveness of industrial and service

E. Parmiggiani (✉)
Department of Computer Science, Norwegian University of Science and Technology, Trondheim, Norway
e-mail: parmiggi@ntnu.no

P. Mikalef
Department of Computer Science, Norwegian University of Science and Technology, Trondheim, Norway

Department of Technology Management, SINTEF Digital, Trondheim, Norway
e-mail: patrick.mikalef@sintef.no

P. Mikalef, E. Parmiggiani (eds.), *Digital Transformation in Norwegian Enterprises*,
https://doi.org/10.1007/978-3-031-05276-7_11

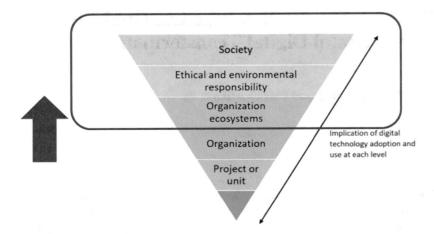

Fig. 1 Digital transformation unfolding at different organizational and social levels

organizations in the country against a very dynamic global market. Interestingly, this has also happened through public-private initiatives. A crucial aspect in this process is indeed the role of the state in maintaining a trust-based relation with its citizens and organizations, for example, by investing significantly in the digitalization of its public services as highlighted in Chap. 2. Chapters 3–9 contribute to further nuancing this picture and surfacing additional aspects across a variety of domains.

The most important observation that follows from the studies presented in the previous chapters is that digital transformation unfolds at different levels, moving from the unitary or project level, up toward organizations, and increasingly happening on the level of ecosystems of organizations, with implications for ethical and environmental concerns and for society at large (Fig. 1).

In the remainder of this chapter, we elaborate on the practical implications of this message based on a meta-analysis of the cases presented in this book. The emerging themes relate to different levels in Fig. 1 and are tightly interlinked as illustrated in Fig. 2.

On the level of single organizations, a first implication of the studies presented in this book is the *co-evolution of organizational forms and digital technologies*. In practical terms, this means that ways of working and digital technology influence and change each other. In general terms, this is not a new observation, as the fields of Information Systems (IS) and organization studies have long demonstrated [1, 2]. What is new in the current landscape is that successful digital transformation seems to be associated with the ability of aligning the way work and data are organized [3]. More in general, *organizations should plan for fluid and goal-oriented work practices, as opposed to rigid, department-based structures.* A vivid illustration of this is the case of the Norwegian Labor and Welfare Organization presented in Chap. 7, in which agile, project-based teams are replacing

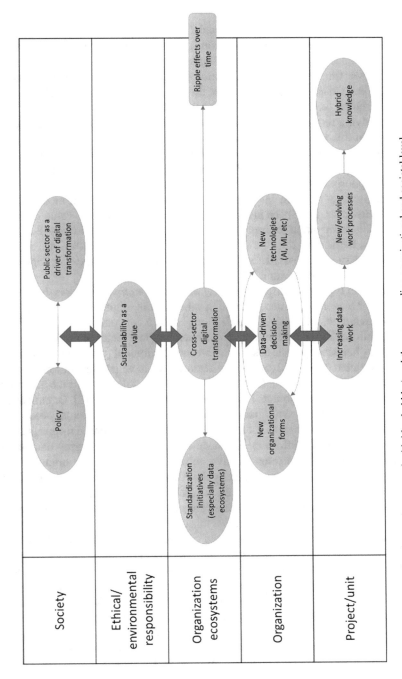

Fig. 2 Map of the emerging themes (represented with blue bubbles) and the corresponding organizational and societal level

a silo-based data and work structures, in connection with the implementation of a new digital platform.

The purposeful tuning of organizational forms and new technologies is a key enabler of data-driven digital transformation. This is particularly the case when some work processes become semi- or fully automated by means of novel algorithms and dashboards over time, as the cases of healthcare (Chap. 9), utility (Chap. 5), and oil and gas service (Chap. 6) demonstrate. On the level of single units or projects, data-driven algorithms (e.g., fueled by AI or ML) can learn from the available data, generate evolving results, and let new phenomena become visible as a result of that process [4]. In this process, the space between human and algorithmic work gives birth to increasingly hybrid [5] or meta-human [6] systems which are substantially changing the organization of work. A reason for this is that data-driven algorithms tend to work poorly when the underlying human knowledge work is characterized by high uncertainty, as research into the application of AI/ML tools in medical work shows [7]. However, this space is a still largely untapped source of value as digital transformation seems often to imply *increased data work* for employees [8, 9]. For organizations, harnessing the co-evolution of work processes and data-driven algorithms is an issue of governance, and new, flexible governance strategies are required to create business value [10].

Moving up in Fig. 2, *we observe that digital transformation increasingly happens at the level of organization ecosystems*. In other words, digital transformation not only involves single, innovative organizations but is a concerted process involving different public and/or private organizations operating in a sector or market segment, as is currently happening in the case of the oil and gas domain (Chap. 3). This has led to the development of data-driven service ecosystems, in which innovation practices do not only involve new technological and architecture solutions but the alignment of different actors who collaborate [11] around practical concerns [12]. Organizations should therefore consider synergizing with competitors in a particular sector in a more systematic way in order to promote the development of shared means (such as data infrastructures and platforms). Evidence demonstrates that sharing data across organizational boundaries creates positive network externalities for organizations, something which is currently leveraged by the Norwegian government in promoting an open data sharing policy (Chap. 2). These new means—as opposed to end products—become the new paths to create value and enhance organizational identity [13, 14] and value chains. For researchers, this could lead to further conceptualizing the blurred spaces between competition and collaboration in digital transformation.

An important corollary of this observation is that *organizations should perform a long-term analysis of the longitudinal, ripple effects associated with the consequences of the emergence of service ecosystems*. Orlikowski and Scott [15] show that cross-sector digital transformation processes transform business activities, and, in doing so, they tend to become disconnected from existing industry and service standards. On the long-term, the emerging new value chains generate new, de facto standards with surprising consequences for incumbent organizations and for society who adopt the digital products resulting from the new standards.

For researchers, this is an invitation to carry out longitudinal studies of digital transformation or historical reconstructions to capture the long-term trends and consequences of current digitalization initiatives. Chapters 3 and 4 in this book provide two examples in this direction.

Finally, *the societal, ethical, and environmental aspects are increasingly a core value for businesses that must be embraced in the fight against climate change and social inequalities*. For organizations, this warrants increased cooperation with national and supranational (e.g., the EU) governments on policy-related issues. In the public sector, this is evident in the ongoing investment in improving, for example, mobility services (Chap. 8). In this regard, the well-established cooperation between Norwegian organizations and the Norwegian government might be an inspiration (see Chap. 2).

For researchers, this requires a more explicit focus on what Jackson and colleagues call the "policy knot," namely, refrain from thinking of emerging technologies as an ex post solution to emerging ethical/environmental problems, but unpack how policy influences and impacts the design of new technologies and work practices [16]. Promising work in this direction is done in the Green IS field [17], but more research is needed to contribute to policy and politics [18].

To conclude, the journey of digital transformation in Norway illustrates that digital technology implementation and use overflow each of the layers and cut across at all other levels in Fig. 2. In sum, the most important message for future practice of digital transformation is therefore to take seriously the long-term ripple effects of digitalization initiatives across sectors and domains.

References

1. Orlikowski, W. J. (2000). Using technology and constituting structures: A practice lens for studying technology in organizations. *Organization Science, 11*, 404–428.
2. Baptista, J., Stein, M.-K., Klein, S., Watson-Manheim, M. B., & Lee, J. (2020). Digital work and organisational transformation: Emergent Digital/Human work configurations in modern organisations. *The Journal of Strategic Information Systems., 29*, 101618. https://doi.org/10.1016/j.jsis.2020.101618
3. Alaimo, C., & Kallinikos, J. (2022). Organizations decentered: Data objects, technology and knowledge. *Organization Science, 33*, 19–37. https://doi.org/10.1287/orsc.2021.1552
4. Monteiro, E., & Parmiggiani, E. (2019). Synthetic knowing: The politics of internet of things. *MIS Quarterly., 43*, 167–184.
5. van den Broek, E., Sergeeva, A., & Huysman, M. (2021). WHEN THE MACHINE MEETS THE EXPERT: AN ETHNOGRAPHY OF DEVELOPING AI FOR HIRING. *MIS Quarterly, 45*.
6. Lyytinen, K., Nickerson, J. V., & King, J. L. (2020). Metahuman systems = humans + machines that learn. *Journal of Information Technology*. https://doi.org/10.1177/0268396220915917
7. Lebovitz, S., Levina, N., & Lifshitz-Assa, H. (2021). Is AI ground truth really true? The dangers of training and evaluating AI tools based on experts' know-what. *MISQ., 45*, 1501–1526. https://doi.org/10.25300/MISQ/2021/16564

8. Bossen, C., Pine, K. H., Cabitza, F., Ellingsen, G., & Piras, E. M. (2019). Data work in healthcare: An introduction. *Health Informatics Journal, 25*, 465–474. https://doi.org/10. 1177/1460458219864730

9. Parmiggiani, E., Terracino, E. A., Huysman, M., Jones, M., Mueller, B., & Mikalsen, M. (2020). OASIS 2019 Panel Report: A glimpse at the 'Post-Digital'. *Communications of the Association for Information Systems, 47*, 583–596.

10. Mikalef, P., Pateli, A., & van de Wetering, R. (2020). IT architecture flexibility and IT governance decentralisation as drivers of IT-enabled dynamic capabilities and competitive performance: The moderating effect of the external environment. *European Journal of Information Systems, 0*, 1–29. https://doi.org/10.1080/0960085X.2020.1808541

11. Nambisan, S. (2018). Architecture vs. ecosystem perspectives: Reflections on digital innovation. *Information and Organization, 28*, 104–106. https://doi.org/10.1016/j.infoandorg.2018. 04.003

12. Parmiggiani, E., & Monteiro, E. (2016). A measure of 'environmental happiness': Infrastructuring environmental risk in oil and gas off shore operations. *Science & Technology Studies, 29*, 30–51.

13. Vial, G. (2019). Understanding digital transformation: A review and a research agenda. *The Journal of Strategic Information Systems*. https://doi.org/10.1016/j.jsis.2019.01.003

14. Wessel, L., Baiyere, A., Ologeanu-Taddei, R., Cha, J., & Blegind-Jensen, T. (2020). Unpacking the difference between digital transformation and IT-enabled organizational transformation. *Journal of the Association for Information Systems*.

15. Scott, S. V., & Orlikowski, W. J. (2021). The digital undertow: How the corollary effects of digital transformation affect industry standards. *Information Systems Research*.

16. Jackson, S. J., Gillespie, T., & Payette, S. (2014). The policy knot: Re-integrating policy, practice and design in CSCW studies of social computing. In *Proceedings of the 17th ACM Conference on Computer Supported Cooperative Work & Social Computing* (pp. 588–602). ACM. https://doi.org/10.1145/2531602.2531674

17. Watson, R., Elliot, S., Corbett, J., Farkas, D., Feizabadi, A., Gupta, A., Iyer, L., Sen, S., Sharda, R., Shin, N., Thapa, D., & Webster, J. (2021). How the AIS can improve its contributions to the UN's sustainability development goals: Towards a framework for scaling collaborations and evaluating impact. *Communications of the Association for Information Systems., 48*. https://doi. org/10.17705/1CAIS.04841

18. King, J., & Kraemer, K. (2019). Policy: An information systems frontier. *Journal of the Association for Information Systems., 20*, 842–847. https://doi.org/10.17705/1.jais.00553

Concluding Remarks and Final Thoughts on Digital Transformation

Patrick Mikalef ⓘ and Elena Parmiggiani ⓘ

Abstract While we have accumulated much knowledge over the past decades about how organizations engage in digital transformation, future developments are likely to make a lot of this knowledge at least partially obsolete. New forms of working and organizing, along with an increased collaboration between human and machine, are likely to give rise to new forms of digital transformation, novel practices and approaches, and significantly different strategies. Nevertheless, such changes are likely to be gradual. This is due to the fact that emerging technologies require time to mature and to be assimilated in organizational processes. In this concluding chapter, we lay out some final thoughts about digital transformation, as well as how it will likely unfold in Norwegian organizations.

1 Closing Remarks on Digital Transformation in Norway

One of the key areas that will be subject to major changes in the upcoming years is that of the public sector in Norway. Norway is one of the countries with the highest percentage of people employed by the public, and a great number of services and organizations are publicly owned. This poses both a challenge and an opportunity for digital transformation in Norway [1]. On the one hand, the challenge is that the central government has to orchestrate funding initiatives and develop appropriate incentives for public bodies at different levels to initiate their digital transformation process while taking into account issues such as scalability, interoperability, and

P. Mikalef
Department of Computer Science, Norwegian University of Science and Technology, Trondheim, Norway

Department of Technology Management, SINTEF Digital, Trondheim, Norway
e-mail: patrick.mikalef@sintef.no

E. Parmiggiani (✉)
Department of Computer Science, Norwegian University of Science and Technology, Trondheim, Norway
e-mail: parmiggi@ntnu.no

© The Author(s) 2022
P. Mikalef, E. Parmiggiani (eds.), *Digital Transformation in Norwegian Enterprises*,
https://doi.org/10.1007/978-3-031-05276-7_12

agility in operations [2]. This poses a major issue since many public organizations are of a small size class and thus have limited human and other slack resources to engage in such future-oriented projects [3]. Furthermore, deploying digital technologies in public organizations usually is a lengthier process compared to those of private companies which do not have to deal with strict bureaucracy and tightly regulate processes on procuring digital solutions [4, 5]. On the other hand, Norway has a tradition of being one of the most advanced nations in using digital technologies in the public sector. The know-how and an advanced existing infrastructure make it possible to ride the wave of novel digital technologies. Furthermore, cases where digital transformation "went wrong" have served as important lessons for future deployments.

Looking at the private sector, although not primarily focused on high-tech exports, Norway has been at the forefront of digitally transforming operations in some of its key industries, including oil and gas, hydropower, seafood and fish farming, and the maritime sector [6, 7]. The capacity of Norwegian enterprises to leverage digital technologies can be attributed to several reasons, including an ability to attract highly skilled employees, a stable economical and political context, strong governmental incentives, and support, as well as the presence of some large enterprises which are industry leaders worldwide. Combined, these factors have contributed to making Norway a country where private organizations place a strong emphasis on digital transformation. Nevertheless, new emerging technologies also pose a risk of disruption for established organizations. Thus, it is important that Norwegian organizations engage in early prototype ventures leveraging new and emerging technologies that are likely to lead to a competitive edge in the future [8]. Doing so requires strong collaboration with leading research institutes and universities, as well as participation in collaborative projects that focus on high-risk high-gain digital transformation projects [9, 10]. In addition, private organization and university collaboration should take on the form of continuous education, as being regularly updated about new technologies, their applications, and how to develop them is key in remaining competitive in the long term [11].

A key dimension in considering digital transformation has to do with policy-making and how to plan at different levels of public administration. We know from extant literature that the decisions made by policy-makers have a very important impact on what happens in the private and public sector when it comes to digital transformation [12]. Norway has already issued a national strategy when it comes to emerging technologies, which was followed by an action plan of future funding at different levels of administration.[1] One of the challenges in implementing such policy-making is maintaining sufficient flexibility in the years to come in order to accommodate for shifts in technologies and formats of collaboration. For example, in recent years, there has been a growing interaction between citizens and governments through the use of digital technologies that enable such communication. Being able to create such channels and taking into account the content of such interaction

---

[1] https://www.regjeringen.no/en/dokumenter/digital-agenda-for-norway-in-brief/id2499897/?ch=8

will likely be an important part of the success of policy-making. Furthermore, changes in the global political landscape require from governments to adapt their funding approaches and steer toward different forms of collaboration patterns as conditions shift [13].

In closing this edited volume, we would like to encourage researchers, practitioners, and policy-makers to collaboratively tackle the issue of digital transformation. The perspective that each side can provide to the other is invaluable, and it is important that three key pillars complement each other harmoniously in moving forward. As digital technologies become increasingly embedded in everyday life, work, and in society, the need to forge channels of communication and collaboration between these three important pillars becomes increasingly important.

References

1. Joseph, S., & Avdic, A. (2016). Where do the Nordic nations strategies take e-government? *Electronic Journal of E-Government, 14*(1), 3–17.
2. Ngereja, B., Hussein, B., Hafseld, K. H. J., & Wolff, C. (2020). A retrospective analysis of the role of soft factors in digitalization projects: Based on a case study in a public health organization in Trondheim-Norway. In *2020 IEEE European Technology and Engineering Management Summit (E-TEMS)* (pp. 1–7). IEEE.
3. Mikalef, P., et al. (2021). Enabling AI capabilities in government agencies: A study of determinants for European municipalities. *Government Information Quarterly*, 101596.
4. Mikalef, P., Fjørtoft, S. O., & Torvatn, H. Y. (2019). Artificial Intelligence in the public sector: A study of challenges and opportunities for Norwegian municipalities. In *Conference on e-Business, e-Services and e-Society* (pp. 267–277). Springer.
5. Mikalef, P., Kourouthanassis, P. E., & Pateli, A. (2017). Online information search behaviour of physicians. *Health Information & Libraries Journal, 34*(1), 58–73.
6. Saunavaara, J., Laine, A., & Salo, M. (2022). *The Nordic societies and the development of the data centre industry: Digital transformation meets infrastructural and industrial inheritance* (p. 101931). *Technology in Society*.
7. Mäkitie, T., et al. (2020). *Greener and smarter? Transformations in five Norwegian industrial sectors*. SINTEF AS (ISBN starter med 978-82-14-).
8. Claussen, T., Haga, T. S., & Ravn, J. E. (2021). Deliberative and material organizational becoming: Sociotechnical leadership of digital transformation. *Strategic Management in the Age of Digital Transformation*.
9. Stokkeland, R. (2019). *Encourage risk and optimise the competitiveness of the Norwegian petroleum industry through a government digitalisation platform*. University of Stavanger, Norway.
10. Mikalef, P., van de Wetering, R., & Krogstie, J. (2018). Big Data enabled organizational transformation: The effect of inertia in adoption and diffusion. In *Business Information Systems (BIS)*.
11. Brunetti, F., Matt, D. T., Bonfanti, A., De Longhi, A., Pedrini, G., & Orzes, G. (2020). Digital transformation challenges: Strategies emerging from a multi-stakeholder approach. *The TQM Journal*.
12. Nambisan, S., Wright, M., & Feldman, M. (2019). The digital transformation of innovation and entrepreneurship: Progress, challenges and key themes. *Research Policy, 48*(8), 103773.

13. He, Q., Meadows, M., Angwin, D., Gomes, E., & Child, J. (2020). Strategic alliance research in the era of digital transformation: Perspectives on future research. *British Journal of Management, 31*(3), 589–617.

Printed in the United States
by Baker & Taylor Publisher Services